Wounds of the Father

A True Story of Child Abuse, Betrayal, and
Redemption

Elizabeth Garrison

DEDICATION

To all those who didn't make it. May you rest in peace.

ONE

I choked on the smell of burning flesh. Flames engulfed dismembered hands, arms, legs. Black smoke covered blank faces. My eyes blistered.

He was coming for me. I couldn't see him, but I was next.

A scream rang out, snapping my eyes open. There was water between my legs. A blue alarm clock with red digits came out of the dark. My bedroom. I threw off my covers, jumped out of bed, and sprinted up the stairs, leaving the darkness of the basement behind.

I furtively looked over my shoulder as I walked through the living room and into my parents' bedroom. My dad's throat clicked with each breath as if something was caught there. My mom lay flat on her back with her mouth wide open. I tapped lightly on her shoulder, and then rushed back against the wall because one time when I woke her, I scared her and she split my lip. She didn't move. I stepped forward and nudged her harder. "Mom ... Mom ..."

She opened her eyes, blinked over and over again. She looked at my dad lying beside her before speaking. "What? Elizabeth ... Go back to bed."

I whispered, "I had a bad dream."

"It's just a dream," she sighed. "Go back to bed."

"But Mom, it was bad. Real bad. I dreamt I was in hell."

"You know you won't go to hell as long as you've asked for forgiveness from your sins. Do you want me to pray with you?"

"No," I said softly. I didn't need any help praying to God for my forgiveness. At the age of six, I'd already been praying earnestly for my soul for years.

Anyway, it wasn't the devil I was afraid of—it was God. God was the one who wanted to send people to hell. My parents described hell as a lake of fire where you suffered and burned forever. I was terrified of going there, which was why I'd gotten saved for the first time when I was three. I'd told my mom I didn't want to go to hell, and she led me through the prayer that would save my soul.

I started getting saved on a regular basis. They said you only needed to do it once, but I wasn't taking any chances with burning forever and begging to die with no mercy. Ever. Besides, I already suspected something was wrong with me— that I wasn't like other little girls.

The first time I told anyone there was something different about me was the summer of fourth grade. I was riding my purple Huffy to the local pool with the sun burning down on my shoulders already peeling from their latest sunburn. I'd left my body and was desperately trying to get back into it. It was as if there was a ladder in my head that I could crawl up to get out of myself and watch my body perform from somewhere above me. Once again, I'd crawled up my ladder and was watching myself ride my bike, looking down at my pink swimsuit with the hole in the middle wondering when my blond hair had gotten so long. I wanted to get back into my body, but couldn't get there. I hated when I couldn't get back.

Garrison

Sometimes I crawled up the ladder and was lost there for hours. Other times for days. I never knew where I went when I didn't watch. I disappeared into nothingness. The ability to leave my body scared me because I'd lose pieces of time in my life. I had no idea why I did it. It dawned on me that afternoon that maybe other people didn't have a ladder. Maybe it was only in my brain. I decided to ask my older brother, Daniel, about it when I got home. I hoped he'd assure me I was fine and that the same thing happened to him.

Sitting cross-legged on his bed, watching him sort through his baseball cards for what seemed like the hundredth time, I asked Daniel, "Do you ever forget where you are?"

He looked up at me, "What do you mean?"

"Like you watch yourself do things, but you're not there? You see yourself." It was so hard to explain, but I kept trying. "You know you're real, but you can't feel it? Like you float. Up above."

He cocked his head to the side, wrinkled his forehead, and frowned. "I have no idea what you're talking about." He went back to his cards.

Daniel was more than just my older brother. He was my best friend and wiser than I'd ever be. If he didn't know what I was talking about, then it meant nobody else did either and they'd think I was a freak if I told them. I decided to keep my ability a secret. I had lots of secrets so I figured one more wouldn't matter. But even if I kept my secrets from other people, there was no hiding from God because he was everywhere and saw everything. There was no escaping Him.

"He can read your thoughts. He knows what you're thinking," my mom liked to warn us kids.

I'd feel ashamed because my thoughts were anything but pure like they were supposed to be. They were filled with rage. As much as I loved my brother, I also hated him for the things he did when we were left alone while my dad worked at the hospital and my mom ran errands. He'd terrorize my younger sister, Sarah, and I. He'd lock me in closets and pummel me with his scrawny fists while he sat on my chest and spat in my face. He'd force Sarah into our dark unfinished basement and bury her inside the antique chest carried over by my ancestors from Sweden. He'd sit on top of it, listening to her screams and I could never do anything to save her.

I imagined ways to hurt him back. I wanted to

be able to destroy him with my fists the way he beat Sarah and me, but he was bigger and stronger. I wished there was a way to make him cry and spit in his face the way he spat in mine. We tried to get him to stop, but every time we told on him, our tales were met with laughter and rebuke.

"Quit being a tattletale," my dad would respond. "You kids need to learn to get along."

"Daniel's an abuser," Sarah, would say quietly, tears welling in her blue eyes while she stood hidden behind my legs. She was only five the first time she said it. I didn't know how she even knew the word. My dad found this hilarious as if she'd just performed a stand-up comedy routine.

"Oh, Sarah. You're exaggerating," he'd say through forced and purposeful laughter. His wasn't the kind of laughter that flows naturally from the belly and bursts through mouth. His version of laughing was making noises that sounded like dry coughs while he moved his mouth in an upward sneer.

The conversation always ended there. If my dad decided a matter was insignificant, then that was the end of the discussion and according to him, the way Daniel treated us wasn't important. I didn't dare force the issue because each time I pushed or pressured an issue my mom would remind me I wasn't supposed to question my dad in any way. It was our job to do as he told us. Period. Over the years, my mom repeatedly instructed me that men were above us in the order of things. She explained that there was a hierarchy with God at the top. Men were next in line, which meant that my dad was the closest thing to God.

My dad had a working partnership with God and he took his position seriously. God had rules about everything. If you broke the rules you were a sinner and God punished sinners. He'd make your life miserable until you repented. The same rules applied in my house, only my dad punished the sins that occurred there.

Every time I disobeyed, my dad threw me over his lap and held my legs down with one hand while his other hand gripped a wooden paddle. He'd carved the paddle himself and painted it white. It hung in the closet in the living room. Before every spanking he'd say, "God loves us so much that he has to punish us. I'm doing this because I love you." Then, he'd extend his arm up and slam the paddle down on my butt over and over again. The longer it took for me to cry, the harder the paddle got and the longer it took before it was over.

Nobody in the house was allowed to argue with him. If I argued with him about anything, he'd send me to my room with instructions that I couldn't come out until I quit being angry and was ready to obey. Sometimes in my room, when I was really mad, I'd twist the heads of my stuffed animals until I almost ripped them off. Other times I took my scissors and stabbed them in the stomach until white puffs came out and floated around my bedroom. I wasn't let out until I could apologize for whatever transgression I'd committed. I'd apologize through gritted teeth, knowing I wasn't really sorry, and God knew I was lying. There was no way to win. I was a sinner.

Church was the central part of our family life. We went to church faithfully and consistently, but never to the same church for any length of time. Inevitably, my parents would find fault with the church's beliefs or practices, and we'd move to a different one. But we always went to church—Sunday morning, Sunday evening, Wednesday night, and any other Bible studies or church functions held during the week. If we couldn't make it to church for some reason, we'd have a service at home where we'd sing songs and my dad would preach a sermon.

I liked church and believed everything they taught me. Daniel hated it, and Sarah always fell asleep whenever we had to sit through the adult sermon, but I never minded because I needed to be there. I sang so loud to the hymns that I hurt my throat. During prayer time, I squeezed my eyes shut so tightly that blue spots appeared as I begged God not to let me be scared of all the things I was afraid of and to make the faceless monster stop coming into my room at night. I strained my ears, trying to absorb every word the preacher spoke. I knew each time he talked about bad seeds that he was directing his sermon towards me. He used lots of big words that I didn't understand, but once I got home, I looked them up in my parents' Bible dictionary.

No matter how long we stayed at a church, my parents were seen as upstanding members. My dad led Bible studies, prayer groups, and served communion on Sundays. My mom taught Bible school and stood by my dad's side at all church functions. They had the pastor over, and people from the church regularly came to the house to pray with my dad in the living room. He was respected and revered. My mom was the picture of a perfect Christian wife, supportive of my dad without question and submissive to his every word. She bustled around taking care of people, always the perfect hostess at dinners.

"You have such a wonderful family," fellow church members said. "Your children are so well behaved."

I was the golden child of Christianity—well-mannered and behaved, knew all of my verses since I'd read my Bible through cover to cover, and gave the right answer to every question. But not everyone in our family was like us. My mom told us kids that her extended family weren't saved and we were to look at them as examples of what would happen if we didn't stay on the right path. They all drank and drinking was something people who weren't saved did. She'd point to her father and say with a warning, "Look at him. You don't want to end up that way."

I saw what alcohol did to the adults at family functions. Their first few drinks looked fun. They were giddy and laughed about silly things. They paid attention to my cousins and me, impressed with anything we did. Our somersaults and cartwheels that usually went unnoticed were suddenly applauded. Sometimes they acted like children—free and careless, playing games with us. But inevitably, there came a time when the silliness disappeared and was replaced by angry outbursts. My grandpa would start yelling at my grandma about something trivial she'd said or done like forgetting to get the mail from the end of the driveway. Uncles waged wars against the aunts for unknown reasons. My mom would run in and out of rooms, trying to quiet the storms. Us kids would head downstairs to the basement or outside to hide from the chaos.

Everyone called my grandpa an alcoholic. I didn't understand what it meant, so I studied him carefully. His big nose intrigued me. Sometimes it was purple and at other times, it had red squiggly lines running a tangled web through the skin. His eyes always watered. At times, the water was so thick it seemed almost solid, like snot that might start moving down his face if he blinked hard enough. The color of his skin turned, moving from a yellowish green to a swollen red. His words slurred like he had a mouthful of marbles he had to speak around. And even though my grandma was the smoker, he coughed and cleared his throat constantly.

When we went up to northern Minnesota to visit, he never met us in the driveway like grandma always did. We'd have to wait for his entrance sitting around the kitchen table. Eventually, we'd see him walking towards the porch door, crooked and hunched over. He'd walk across the porch and into the kitchen with his beer in his right hand, tucked inside a Bud Light coolie.

"Hi, Dad," my mom would pipe up as soon he was inside. She'd jump up from her seat to stand in front of him, announcing her presence so he'd know she was there.

"Oh, Robin," he'd say, stopping in his tracks, always surprised to see her. His body swayed back and forth as he fidgeted with things on the table.

Daniel, Sarah, and I would be waiting to be given our freedom to play on the farm, but first we had to give our customary greeting.

"Hi, Grandpa," we'd say in unison.

He'd respond with a hello, looking over our heads towards the window. He rarely spoke to me directly and never called me by my first name. He'd commence to talk to my mom and it was the same questions every time.

"How's the weather?"

My mom would describe what the weather was like in our town located five hours south. They were fascinated with the weather, especially during the winter when they could talk about all of the storms.

"How was traffic?"

My mom would relate in detail all the roads where traffic got thick and our progress had been slowed. Her report included any areas of construction along the way and she never forgot to mention Interstate 494, which grandpa had a keen interest in at all times. Finally, she'd comment on anything that was out of the ordinary like a deer or a car accident.

"How long are you staying?"

It never mattered how long we were staying. My grandpa's response was always the same. He was happy whether we were staying for two days or two weeks. Sometimes I wasn't sure he knew time had passed since our last visit. He seemed oblivious like he might not have noticed Christmas if it wasn't for the huge tree in the living room. "Where's

Mark?"

It was unusual for my mom to do anything without my dad, but most of the time when we stayed at my grandparents, he stayed with his sister who lived a town away. He stopped in occasionally to see us or eat dinner.

My mom never tired of trying to communicate with my grandpa. She got up every day at five to sit with him. She said it was the soberest you could ever get him. Every time we left, my mom warned us to stay away from the sin of alcohol.

Given all of her warnings, I was surprised that taking my first drink didn't feel like a sin. I didn't get the horrible pit in my stomach or the sticky palms that other sins gave me.

I was twelve and it was the summer of sixth grade. It happened at my neighbor's house, the Palmers. They lived behind us on our dead end street. A chain link fence separated our backyards. My parents disapproved of the Palmers, but this wasn't unusual since they disapproved of most people. Other people were of this world, and our family was not—we were born-again Christians. The Palmers attended St. John's Lutheran Church down the block faithfully, but according to my parents, they still weren't saved. My parents had an amazing ability to know the fate of people's souls and the majority of them were going straight to hell.

Not only were they Lutheran, but Mr. Palmer owned the only bar in town, a heinous crime against God. On the weekends, cars would cover the length of their driveway and extend into the street. My mom would roll her eyes and say, "Looks like the Palmers are having another wild party." My dad would nod his head and glare like they were committing murder behind us rather than having a good time.

Wendy Palmer was my age. My parents didn't like for us to play together but occasionally they allowed it. Every time they relented, my mom watched us carefully, sure that Wendy would steal one of my toys.

Late one afternoon, my mom let me go to Wendy's as long as I promised to be home for dinner at five. I was excited to play with the bad girl. Trying to be good all the time was exhausting. We jumped outside on her trampoline until we got bored and went inside to do something else.

As we walked into the kitchen, bottles of booze

were scattered all over the counter in preparation for the party that evening. I eyed a bowl of the forbidden parents' punch. Wendy's parents were nowhere in sight. We looked at the punch bowl and then back at each other. One of us chose to voice what we were both thinking and said, "Let's drink it."

Wendy grabbed two small punch glasses and filled them to the top. We giggled with the excitement born of the fear of getting caught as we carried them into Wendy's bedroom and locked the door behind us. After setting the glasses on the dresser, we collapsed on the bed laughing hysterically.

"Shh," I warned through my laughter. I eyed my glass, wondering about the magical potion inside that made adults act like silly children or get so mad they threw things.

I picked mine up, silent now. Feeling like Alice in Wonderland, I sipped slowly, scared of what might happen. I swished the punch around in my mouth, savoring the strange taste. It was different than anything my taste buds had been blessed with before, very sweet and thick. I swallowed with more force than was usually required and the liquid left a warm trail on the way to my stomach. Tingles coursed through my body. I shivered, looked at Wendy, and smiled.

I was surprised to see her pudgy face scrunched up and her lips turned up towards her nose. "Ick," she said, "this stuff is gross."

What was wrong with her? I took another drink and another until I emptied my glass and felt the thick sweetness coated inside my mouth. Now I knew why people drank. It was incredible.

I wanted more of the punch and to stay for the party, but I was almost late for dinner. If I wasn't on time, my mom would huff exaggerated sighs all through the meal with her lips pressed together in a straight line, holding back the words she wanted to say and refusing to look at me.

The world looked different when I stepped outside. I didn't remember the sun shining so brightly before, but now it was beaming down on me. My body felt like it was humming a tune all its own. I was wild with excitement.

I'd spent my life living in fear of doing bad things. I constantly worried about the paddle I'd get across my butt if I stepped out of line and the awful things God did to girls who were bad. But at that moment, none of it mattered. It was the first time I didn't care about being bad and wasn't scared of God. I could breathe without feeling as if I'd choke on the air.

I didn't know how much you had to drink before someone could smell it, but didn't want to take any chances, so I held my breath as I took my seat at the dinner table. I couldn't put food in my mouth until after my dad prayed, but as soon as the prayer ended, I stuffed my mouth full of my mom's fried chicken.

Dinner was always a troublesome time at our house because we had to be careful not to upset my dad. He sat at the head of the table, which was appropriate since his moods dictated the event. Things ran smoothly if he was in a good mood. We could talk and laugh about our day. But if he was in a bad mood, things were different. He seethed anger as he ate. The silent anger lurking beneath the surface was almost worse than his explosions. When he brooded, his appearance changed and his movements became robotic—each move made with force and precision. His face tightened and his forehead lined with stress. He looked like he was in physical pain. My dad's eyes, usually blue, turned dark and cold.

His overpowering silence and demeanor were our cue to be silent during the meal, but sometimes we'd miss the cue or we'd accidentally do something to anger him. Anything could set him off like giggling or talking too loudly, and then whoever had misbehaved would get yanked off their chair and pulled into my parents' bedroom for the wooden paddle.

We screamed and cried as he paddled us until our butts stung and burned, leaving red welts to remind us of our wrongdoing. When he was done he'd say, "You can come back to the dinner table as long as you can behave yourself."

It was hard to decide whether or not I could behave myself since most of the time I didn't know what I'd done wrong. Were my eyes haughty again? Had I been swinging my legs without knowing it? Or was it nothing? Sometimes I refused to go back to the table just to prove my point that I hadn't done anything wrong. But he'd always return to his spot at the head and the meal would resume as if nothing had happened. Whoever was left at the table would follow his lead.

"Hon, did you get enough to eat?" my mom

would ask as he sat back down. "Do you want anything else?"

But tonight was different. Dinner didn't bother me. I didn't care if I made him mad. Released from the looming control of his anger, I felt separated from the rest of the family. The usual heaviness hanging over the dinner table wasn't there. Light and free, I smiled at my secret.

The glass filled with the shimmering liquid had awakened a hunger inside me. I'd never fit in my world where everything looked good on the outside, but slowly killed me from the inside. Parts of my soul were missing, but I felt whole for the first time. The emptiness was gone and replaced with a warm glow that made my world look brighter and more bearable. I had to have more.

TWO

I fell in love with alcohol in the same way a young girl falls head over heels for a cute boy. I looked forward to the next time I could get drunk in the same way you'd look forward to the next date. Everything about alcohol, from the taste and smell of it to the way the bottle felt in my hand, excited me.

I was immersed in my honeymoon period with alcohol when Eric Graham moved to town in seventh grade. We called him by his last name, and he was never known as anything else. Graham was a short kid whose squinty eyes and shiny, black hair made him appear Asian even though he was as white as white boys come. He entered the small town school I attended and quickly found his place among my crowd even though he didn't follow the rules for being cool that were a requirement for my group.

My crowd was considered the popular ones. Every grade has the cool kids and we'd always been it. There were specific rules for being cool in a small Midwestern town.

The first and most important rule was that you had to dress well. You had to wear the best clothes, which at that time meant Girbaud jeans, strategically rolled at the ankles. I saved my babysitting money all year to afford my designer clothes since my mom refused to buy them. Graham wore the standard Girbaud jeans, but his were always two sizes too big, and he never tucked in his shirt.

Besides the clothes, being cool meant being attractive and competing for being the best looking. But it was important to pretend that you cared nothing about this competition. The key was always to be a player in the game but never to let anyone know you were playing. The game was hard for me because I never felt like I beat the competition. I wanted to be skinnier and replace my dirty blond hair with the beautiful, sun-blond hair of the girls I envied. Despite my misgivings, the kids at school thought I was attractive. No one considered Graham to be competition because he was barely over five feet tall and his feet pointed out to the sides, which made him waddle like a duck when he walked.

You had to be smart and get good grades. I had no problem in this area. I could ace a test without a second of preparation or study. I never had to bring work home and still ended up on the A honor roll. Graham, on the other hand, barely got Cs and spent his time in class cracking jokes.

The last rule was that you had to play sports well. I was athletic and sports were easy for me since they'd always been a part of my family life. I'd spent many hours in the driveway shooting hoops with my dad while he coached me on technique.

"Look up, don't look down. Look at me!" he'd say, trying to tip the ball out of my hands as I dribbled past him.

"Practice your free throws. You've gotta make your free throws. So many games come down to the line." One summer, I shot a hundred free throws a day to make sure I never lost a game at the line.

I'd grown up tagging along with Daniel and the other boys on my block who played sports in the vacant field at the end of our street. I constantly fought to disprove the remark, "She can't play. She's a girl," which only made me work harder to make sure I could do everything just as good or even better than the boys.

I was also a runner and my mom would map out distances for me to run and then show me where I needed to go to achieve the desired miles. When I had a race coming up, she'd take me to the golf course where the meets were held and time me with her watch.

"Run! Go faster!" She'd jump up and down like she did at the real meets. "You can do it! You're almost there!"

All the practice and hard work paid off. In a school as small as mine, if you were a good enough athlete, the coaches moved you up to play on the high school varsity teams. I was one of the only two seventh graders on the cross country team. I played basketball for my school and a traveling team made up of the elite players. I started every game and led the team in scoring the most points. I ran varsity track in the spring. No matter which sport I played, my parents rarely missed a meet or a game. They were my biggest fans as well as my harshest critics.

An entire wall of my bedroom was devoted to my athletic accomplishments. A collection of medals, trophies, and ribbons hung on the shelves. I had trophies and plaques from basketball tournaments where I was named to the All-Tournament Team, a team made up of the best ten players in the area. My gold and silver medals from cross country meets hung on the wall, waiting for the day they'd be pinned on a letterman's jacket. Wooden pegs held the blue ribbons I'd achieved in freestyle swimming races.

What I lacked in looks, I made up for in athletics. I never knew if I was going to hold the coveted position of the most beautiful girl at school, but if there was a sport to be played, I'd be the one to take home the prize.

It became a standard joke that the only sports Graham played were the ones on his computer. Despite his sloppy clothes, mediocre grades, and lack of athletic skills, Graham quickly found his place in our crowd because he had a huge house where adults were rarely around—a teenage paradise.

We spent our time in the living room on the main floor. There was a huge TV against the center wall with surround sound, a comfortable black sofa against the wall in front of the TV, and reclining chairs placed in both of the corners by the stone fireplace. The stereo set up in the living room had speakers strategically placed all over the house, carrying the latest music throughout.

Two stairs led down to the kitchen from the living room. It was an ordinary kitchen with a white tiled floor, white cupboards, and standard appliances. My favorite part of the kitchen was the corner with the fully stocked liquor cabinet. It was never locked.

Graham introduced us to the liquor cabinet the first time he had a party and the format was the same every time. He'd grab tall glasses from the cupboard and set them on the counter. Then, he'd take a bottle of Malibu and pour a small portion into the glass. Next, he'd grab the Windsor Canadian, Absolute Vodka, Blue 100, and Captain Morgan's Spiced Rum, pouring parts of each into the glasses until they were full.

"We've got to switch which bottles we drink out of," he'd say.

I always made sure I got the first glass. Taking a huge drink, my body would shake and twitch as my stomach threatened to reject it. I'd close my eyes and take a deep breath before the next swallow. It was easy to drink the rest after I choked down the first few gulps.

Inevitably, Wendy or one of my other girlfriends would come up behind me and sniff my glass. "That is so gross. I can't believe you drink it."

I'd throw my head back, finish off the glass, and smile. "I don't care. I wanna get drunk."

Whichever girl it was would roll her eyes at me and return to sit in the living room with the rest of the girls, watching as I got drunk with the boys. None of the girls drank, except for me, but I didn't care. We quit hanging out anywhere but Graham's on the weekends.

We went to Graham's after the Friday night football games. He had two older brothers who were always hanging around even though they didn't live there. After the last game of the season, Graham and I stumbled through the door to find his brothers sprawled on the couches with glasses in their hands and drunken smiles on their faces.

Mike, the second oldest, yelled, "Eric, c'mon in!"

"I'm the one that lives here. Ya don't have to

invite me in." Graham laughed. "Did you guys buy booze?"

"Yep, no drinking mom and pops' tonight," Nick said, getting up from his spot on the couch and stepping down the stairs into the kitchen. He grabbed an unopened bottle of vodka from the table and handed it to us. "Here, little man. You and your girl can drink this." He thumped Graham on the back before going back into the living room.

The front door opened. Laughter and voices drifted in as people took off their shoes and hung their coats on the rack.

"Graham," I whispered in his ear, "let's go in your room to drink this."

Neither of us wanted to share our treasure so we ran upstairs and locked ourselves in his bedroom. We plopped down on the bed, pushing all his comic books onto the floor. We opened the bottle and passed it back and forth.

"Did you see Derick looking at you?" Graham asked, handing the bottle to me after he'd taken his turn. "I think he wants you."

"Was he the guy standing against the wall staring?" I asked.

"It's Mike's fr-shit!" He knocked over the

ashtray, spilling butts onto the comforter. "Anyways, he's Mike's friend. Mike's been bringing him over to the house lately. I guess he just got divorced or something like that."

It was odd that Derick was interested in me. I was in seventh grade and he'd graduated years ago, but I didn't pay it any attention.

"I love you, Graham," I said, as my head started to swim and my thoughts grew fuzzy. "I need a smoke. Gimme one."

"I'm out," he said, picking up the spilled butts and placing them back in the ashtray.

I yanked the bottle back and took another pull. "I'm gonna go see if I can talk Nick or Mike into taking me uptown. I'll be back in a minute."

I headed downstairs to where everyone else was hanging out. I started asking all the older guys for a ride to the gas stations and someone to buy cigarettes for me. Derick stood up from his spot on the couch.

"I'll give ya a ride, sweetie," he said. "Let's go."

I followed him outside to his green truck and climbed in on the passenger side. It had gotten dark and a wave of anxiety passed through me as I shut the door behind me. I tried to act like I wasn't nervous and played with the loose threads of the fraying mesh seat cover as my stomach did little flip-flops.

When we were a few blocks from Graham's, Derick murmured in a husky voice, "Don't sit so far away." I moved closer, within his hand's reach. The space between us was too close. My chest tightened.

He was talking about something. I heard his voice, but not his words. One minute his hands were on the wheel and the next minute one of his hands was underneath my shirt. I'd had a couple of boys' hands underneath my shirt, but this was different. This was a grown-up man's hand. It was big and strong, rough and calloused. He pulled my bra up over my breasts. My face felt hot and my head pounded like there was a bomb inside.

I started chatting and laughing. I couldn't talk fast enough. I talked about football and school. I acted as if nothing was happening like he wasn't really pinching and pulling at my nipples until they hurt or sliding his hand over the breasts that were barely more than two small lumps on my chest.

After what seemed like hours, we reached the gas station. He gave me a huge smile like he was proud of himself as he got out of the truck. I moved as fast as I could to the other side of the truck, kicking the empty beer bottles and papers out of the way. I pulled my bra down and tried to breathe. I kept telling myself that it wasn't a big deal, like what just happened didn't really happen.

He returned all too quickly with my Marlboro Reds and the journey back to Graham's began. I rhythmically tapped the pack of cigarettes on my hand in a long drawn-out staccato beat. My cigarettes would keep him away. He wouldn't intrude on my sacred act of smoking. I made an exaggerated production of carefully unwrapping the cellophane from the pack and removing a cigarette. I searched for my lighter, even though I knew it was in my pocket. Finally, my cigarette was lit and in my mouth. I was sure I was almost back to safety.

Then, without a word, he turned away from Graham's, and headed towards the only motel in town, pulling into the empty parking lot.

"What are we doing?" I asked.

"I just want to talk to you." He turned off the engine and the headlights. "I really like you."

How did he know he liked me? I'd never met him until tonight and we'd only exchanged a few sentences before getting into his truck. I didn't have any idea what to say or how to respond.

He crawled next to me and pushed me back against the seat. His calloused hands were all over my body, pulling and poking, as I stared at the pieces of green paint chipping off the ceiling of the cab. He started kissing my neck and covering my face with slobber. I kept moving my head, looking out the stained windows at the shadows moving around in the darkness so that he'd miss my lips. His breathing was heavy against me. My mind told my body to move, to open the door and run like hell, but I was frozen to the seat. My mind told my mouth to scream, to yell, to tell him to get away from me, but I was mute.

He unzipped his pants and pulled out his penis. It was huge. I closed my eyes. He grabbed my hand and put it on his penis. I didn't know what to do with it. It was the most repulsive thing I'd ever touched.

Swallowing back the taste of bile in my throat that threatened to escape from my mouth, I opened my eyes and looked at his face. His eyes were angry and cold. They'd turned from blue to black stones. I'd seen his look before, but couldn't remember where or when. I quickly looked back up to the ceiling, concentrating on the design that remained from the missing paint. He took my hand off himself and spit into the palm. Then, he put his hand on top of mine and began moving it up and down on his penis. My head felt like it was about to explode and spray pieces of my brain on the windshield. My thoughts raced so fast I couldn't discern any particular one. The puke rose in my throat and fell back down, over and over again, with the motions he made with my hand. Finally, with a groan that sounded like an animal, he sprayed his putrid white onto my stomach. I breathed a sigh of relief that it was over.

He grabbed a towel from the floor that was crusted with an oily substance. He wiped himself off and tucked himself back inside his pants.

"Here," he said, throwing me the towel with a look of disgust, "clean yourself up."

I wiped off my stomach as best I could and he started the truck back up. On the way back to Graham's, he looked straight ahead at the road and didn't utter a word. I lit up another cigarette and inhaled deeply, focusing only on the booze in the liquor cabinet that would be waiting for me when I got there.

I was mortified by what happened and didn't tell anyone about it when we got back to Graham's. After all, I'd asked him to take me to get cigarettes and should've known better. I moved through the house in a daze until the alcohol took control and blotted out the memory of the night—the sweet relief of a blackout.

My crush on alcohol grew into an obsession. Thoughts of wanting to get drunk reverberated in my head throughout the day. I couldn't drink during the week because Graham was my drinking partner and he looked at me like I was crazy when I asked him to drink on a Monday night. I had no choice but to wait for the weekend, which became harder and harder to do.

It grew more difficult to do anything without alcohol. My struggle to appear normal without drinking became obvious to those around me at a school dance in eighth grade when my boyfriend, Sean, broke up with me. It was the first time I'd been dumped and even though I hadn't been in love with him, I'd liked him and the status of having a boyfriend. I sat on the bleachers waiting for him when his friend appeared.

"Sean doesn't want to go out with you

anymore," he said. I stared at him, expecting him to say more, but his eyes were busy darting around the room checking out the girls wearing tight shirts. He tapped his white tennis shoes together. "Well, um ... see ya." He stepped down the bleachers and on to the gym floor filled with teenage bodies.

I sat on the bleachers, watching bodies move to the music. Sean walked in with his arm around a skinny girl whose dark hair cascaded down her back in waves. I wanted to run down the bleachers and slap his face, but my pride held me in place. A lump lodged in my throat, but I refused to cry, especially in front of people. It was a badge I wore proudly that nobody besides my family had ever seen me cry. If you cried, people knew they'd hurt you and I'd vowed a long time ago never to let anyone know they'd hurt me.

But I had to do something because I was afraid I'd start crying if I didn't and be more humiliated than I already was. Graham hadn't brought booze and I was empty-handed too. I got up from the bleachers and walked outside through the parking lot, hoping to run into somebody who had a bottle to share. I heard footsteps behind me and turned to see Wendy running to catch up.

"What's wrong?" she asked, matching my stride.

"Nothin'." She knew by the absence of expression on my face that she shouldn't ask any more questions.

She walked silently by my side down the gravel road in front of the school. No cars drove by and we didn't see anybody. Suddenly, a brilliant idea came to me. "Hey, let's go back to the dance and pretend we're drunk!"

She looked at me strangely but refrained from stating the obvious. I grabbed her arm and turned her back toward the school.

"C'mon, it'll be fun."

I walked back into the gym with a smile on my face and a bounce in my step. I skipped over to Sam, an older guy on my cross country team, and grabbed his arm.

"Dance with me," I said, pulling him onto the floor, making sure I was close enough for Sean to see. The music throbbed, and I moved up on Sam, grinding my pelvis against him seductively. He grabbed my butt and smiled at my aggression.

"Are you drunk? Do you ever come to these things sober?"

I giggled. "Yep, I'm drunk."

I finished with him and moved on to the next guy. I threw myself on him and did my best dirty dancing routine. I was dancing with my third guy when Wendy grabbed my arm.

"I've gotta talk to you," she said, pulling me off to the side. I stumbled along, letting her drag me.

She put her hands on her hips. "What are you doing?"

"Nothin'. Havin' a good time. I'm drunk."

She rolled her eyes and let go of my arm. "Whatever." She huffed and turned to walk way, but I caught what she muttered under her breath— "Something's wrong with you."

After that night, Wendy started to look at me differently, and it wasn't long before the other girls in my crowd changed the way they looked at me too. They started giving each other concerned looks when I'd disappear with Graham and return drunk or rolled their eyes when they caught me sneaking shots. They looked at me like I was a stranger they were meeting for the first time. I started to look at them differently, too. They didn't seem as fun anymore. Even Wendy seemed boring. I was insulted by their looks, but we had to put up with each other since I spent all of my time hanging out with the boys they liked.

One day in English, while we sat doing our homework together, my friend Melissa asked, "Don't you get nervous around Graham and those guys?"

"Not at all. I'm one of them."

I never told my girlfriends about the night with Derick because I took pride in being one of the guys. I convinced myself it wasn't going to happen again and that it was an isolated incident, but it wasn't long before it did. It happened the night Wendy decided to throw a small party while her parents were out of town.

She invited her older cousin, Dan, and he brought his friend Rich, a twenty-year-old former high school football star who hadn't done anything since his high school days except live in his parents' basement. Wendy and I were the only girls. Graham came and brought a few guys with him, including Wendy's latest crush, Peter. She'd spent months trying to get him to notice her, so she was thrilled when he wanted to spend the night making out in the camping trailer stored in her back yard. I didn't mind being the only girl in the house. I was happy to sit in the living room with the guys and drink.

I sat on the couch with Rich next to me. He smelled like a mixture of body odor and Old Spice, which made me want to laugh because the only person I knew who wore Old Spice was my grandfather. He kept looking at me with a lopsided grin, exposing teeth that looked like they'd been randomly stuck in his gums at all sorts of odd angles.

"So, I hear you used to go out with Rodriguez?" he asked, leaning so close to me I could smell his rancid breath.

"Yeah."

"What's it like being with a Mexican?" He put his arm around my shoulder. "Is it true they have small dicks?"

I knocked his arm off my shoulder. "Shut up. It's none of your business."

I got up from the couch and moved to the floor next to Graham, who was playing solitaire. But Rich followed me, so I moved again next to the TV. He continued his relentless pursuit.

"Look at your small boobies—can I touch them?"

The room exploded in laughter. He wasn't

going to quit harassing me and since nobody was saying anything to stop him, I decided to pretend to sleep. I could never fall asleep unless everyone around me was already sleeping, but the guys didn't know that. I curled up on the couch, tucked myself into a ball, and closed my eyes. I listened to them laughing and carrying on outside of my eyelids.

I was lying with my eyes closed when I felt someone invade my space. A hand rubbed my thigh and I shook it off.

"Mm mph ..." I mumbled, trying to sound convincingly sleepy. I rolled over so my head faced the back of the couch, pulling myself into an even tighter ball.

The hand returned to my leg and caressed it. I lay perfectly still. The hand moved up and tried to get between my thighs. I cringed and locked my knees. It was Rich. It had to be. The sounds of the small party carried on. I listened to the guys' voices talking and laughing.

One of the guys said, "Rich!"

"What?" he said, feigning innocence.

They all laughed again.

"You're a dog," Graham said sloppily, which brought more shrieks of laughter.

Unable to speak the words out loud, I screamed in my head—*tell him to stop. Do something! Don't just sit there. Tell him to leave me alone!*

I fumed inside. I was trapped. If I jumped up and got mad about Rich touching me, then they'd know I'd only been pretending to sleep. They'd think I wanted him to touch me and if I said I didn't, they wouldn't believe me. They'd make fun of me like they made fun of all the other girls who acted like girls. I could no longer be one of the guys if I acted like a girl. I had no choice but to lie there silently and wait for it to be over.

"God, I'm so sorry I've been screwing up so much, but please don't punish me like this. I can't go through this again. Make him stop. If you make him stop, I promise I'll start being good again."

Rich reached under my shirt to play with my breasts. I told myself he wasn't doing it. I focused on not feeling his hand and concentrated so hard that eventually I didn't feel it. I couldn't feel any parts of my body. I listened to the music and let the voice of Steven Tyler carry me away.

"I have to pee." Rich's voice startled me, jolting me back to reality. I heard his footsteps going down the hallway. The bathroom door clicked shut behind him.

I sat up and rubbed my eyes. I made a production of stretching and yawning. Graham and Dan were the only two guys left in the room. Graham was passing in and out of consciousness on the floor in front of the TV. Dan was lounging on the blue recliner across from the couch.

"Christ, I guess I was tired." I faked another yawn.

"What happened to partying all night?" Graham slurred from his position on the brown carpet.

"I guess I had more to drink than I thought I did." Really, I hadn't had enough and needed more.

"Hey Elizabeth, I bet I can pee through the whole national anthem," Dan said, holding up an empty milk carton. "I drank all this."

Rich appeared from the bathroom. I jumped up quickly and ran to stand outside the bathroom door in the hallway.

"Let's hear you do it. I'm ready to sing. You gotta leave the door open so I know you don't cheat," I said.

The next morning, I told Wendy I'd sung the entire national anthem while Dan peed and had finished the entire song, and gotten halfway through it a second time before he finished. We laughed and laughed. I never mentioned what happened with Rich. Graham and Dan didn't say anything to me about it and I assured myself it wasn't a big deal. I'd just have to add Rich to my list of guys to stay away from. After a while, I erased the incident from my mind. When I told the story of the night it went like this: I was just one of the guys who stayed up all night partying at Wendy's house while her parents were gone. I watched Dan take the longest pee ever while I sang the national anthem off-key, with my own lyrics added when I forgot the real words.

Garrison

THREE

"Margarita ... Margarita ..." my teacher called my Spanish name. I'd picked the name because it was the only one on the list that referred to alcohol. It still made me laugh every time she used it.

I shook my head and looked up at her through stoned eyes. "Uh, I don't know."

She frowned and called on someone else. I looked at the clock. Class was almost over and I'd missed all of it because I was high. I'd been in my seat, but I'd checked out as soon as I sat down. I wasn't in my chair or surrounded by the kids who'd given me dirty looks when I walked in late. I wasn't me. I was somebody else. Somebody who didn't care. Someone unaffected by others, who couldn't be touched.

Whenever I smoked pot, I experienced the

same transcendence as when I'd climb the ladder in my head and disappear. I had other tricks I played with my mind besides climbing my ladder. One of my favorites was to create a character for myself, usually an orphan girl, and transport myself to live in her world for a few hours. Whenever I wanted to, I could look down at my body and watch myself perform. I'd stare at myself and wonder why I was that girl, wishing I never had to go back inside the body. The body housed me, but my mind was the real me. Anything could happen to the body, but no one could touch my mind. Pot allowed me to be the mind anytime I wanted to. I could disconnect from the world and retreat to my special places, but it didn't take any mental effort.

I was in the grip of a downward spiral that felt so much better than any God I'd ever known. Since I was already doomed and going to hell, it was easy to destroy myself. I broke all the rules I'd been instructed to adhere to since I was a toddler. I lied to my parents about everything—where I was, what I was doing, and who I was with. I gave my virginity to the first guy who asked for it as if it meant nothing even though I was giving up my purity, the most important thing to God. I started shoplifting and stealing from kid's lockers to get money to buy pot.

By ninth grade, I'd become a poster child for what happens to kids on drugs. I rarely wore makeup anymore, which just made the dark circles under my eyes more obvious. My long hair hung in my face and I went days without washing it. I traded in my designer labels for baggy jeans and big T-shirts that hid the weight I was losing.

I was moved from the gifted and talented classes, but even in the regular classes, my grades continued to plummet. I skipped my classes most of the time and if I happened to be in one, I either fell asleep at my desk or created a disturbance to get kicked out. One minute I'd cuss and yell at anyone near me, but the next minute I'd be sullen and depressed, withdrawing from any contact with people.

The only part of my old identity I still cared about was basketball. I tried to make it to practice even though I missed most of my classes. My athletic photo from ninth grade was distinctively different from the pictures taken in previous years. My picture from the year before showed me kneeling next to three other players with a wide grin on my face and a ball in my hands. My face was fresh and clear, my hair pulled into a tight ponytail. My body was muscular and strong.

In my ninth grade picture, I was alone, leaning against a wall with my shoulders hunched over, holding a basketball. My body no longer had the strong confident muscles of an athlete. Instead, I looked pale and skinny. My eyes were red and the lids heavy. My head was cocked to the side and the marks of a fading hickey bruised my neck. The left side of my lip rose in a halfhearted attempt at a smile.

"You look high in this picture," my mom said when she saw the pictures.

I shrugged. "Tomorrow I find out if I get moved up."

A few days earlier, the ninth grade coach had gathered our team together and informed us that the varsity coach would be choosing players to play on his team. I had a sinking suspicion I wasn't going to be one of the chosen few.

"I don't think I'm gonna make it," I said. "I'm pretty sure the coach hates me."

"Let's say a prayer about it." She put her knitting down and kneeled next to the couch. I got beside her like I'd done so many times in the past, folding my hands together. She was on much better terms with God than I was so there was a chance her prayers would be heard.

"Dear Heavenly father, we come to you today to ask that you would be with Elizabeth. Help her to be able to play varsity. You know how much this means to her. We ask these things in Jesus' name. Amen."

She waited a few minutes with her head bowed to see if I wanted to pray out loud. When I kept my mouth shut, she stood up. I turned to look at her. "If I don't make the team, I'm giving up on God forever."

"Oh Elizabeth, don't say that. You know he loves you." She laughed nervously.

But I didn't. He didn't answer my prayers. Never had.

The next day at practice, I stood in line next to the rest of the players. I listened as the names of the girls I'd always played with were called and mine wasn't. I was left standing with the girls who'd been substitutes for me. They'd sat on the bench, only playing when one of us needed a break. Now, I'd be playing with them. I stormed into the varsity coach's office.

"How come I didn't get moved up?" I asked with my hands on my hips and chin jutted out.

"It's simple," he said, putting basketballs back into the wire container. "I can't have someone who skips school and uses drugs on my varsity team."

"That's bullshit! I still play ball just as good as I ever did. I've played with Paige and those guys since third grade. We've always been a team. They can't play without me."

He set the balls down and looked me in the eyes. "I think they'll do just fine without you. But I'll tell you what. You start going to school, get your grades up, quit messin' around with drugs, and we'll see if you can play on my team. How's that?"

"How's this?" I asked, kicking a ball in his direction. "You can take your basketball and shove it up your ass! I ain't playin' fuckin' ball anymore."

I turned and walked away, slamming the door behind me.

I slowed down, listening for his voice to call out to me, to tell me it was all a mistake and misunderstanding, but it didn't come. God had just taken away the last thing I cared about. I headed for the locker room to clean mine out.

Everyone had turned against me and were part of a big conspiracy to get me to change back into the compliant, good girl they wanted me to be. Everyone was in on it—my parents, my teachers, my friends, and the school principal. God sat at the top, orchestrating it all, but there was no way I was going back to who I used to be.

I'd spent my childhood years in a prison of thou-shalt-nots, and for the first time, I was free. Drugs had opened my eyes and mind to a freedom I didn't know could be mine. There was no way I was going to let anyone take it away. I was determined to defend my newfound freedom at all costs.

After I didn't make the team and dropped out of basketball, I was sent to see the school guidance counselor, Mrs. Rush, whose job usually consisted of helping people plan their careers. I slouched in the chair in her office with my arms folded across my chest and glared at her. Her blue glasses were too big for her narrow face. She nervously pushed them up her nose and then clasped her hands on top of her desk.

"Elizabeth, do you know why you're here?"

"Nope."

"People are concerned about you-"

"Yeah, right. Nobody gives a shit."

"Now Elizabeth, you can't use language like that." She pushed her glasses up her nose again and moved back in her chair.

"Whatever." I unfolded my arms and began tapping my fingers on the wooden armrest.

In the voice a kindergarten teacher uses when she tells her students not to run in the hallway, Mrs. Rush said, "Let's try to use nice language."

I laughed out loud.

She cleared her throat. "This isn't funny."

I folded my arms again and crossed my legs, watching the tips of her ears get red. "I think it is."

"You're a very different student this year. You've always gotten good grades, but now you're in danger of failing ninth grade. Do you know why?" She sat straight up, trying to gain control of the situation.

"Because I don't go to class and I really don't care."

"We've also noticed that you've changed your group of friends. Did something happen between you and your friends? Did you get into a fight?"

What had happened with my friends wasn't fixable and much too complicated to explain to her.

I retreated into silence, staring at her with angry eyes as she rearranged papers on her desk.

She returned to her kindergarten teacher voice. "I'm just going to ask you—are you on drugs?"

I laughed.

"We just want to help you."

I leaned forward, resting my elbows on her desk. "You know, you keep saying 'we' and I don't get it. Who the hell is 'we'?"

"Your parents. Your teachers. Your old friends. Mr. McKinnsey."

"Oh, yeah. I bet Mr. McKinnsey really wants to help me." I snorted. Mr. McKinnsey was the principal and I'd spent lots of time sitting in his office. "He just wants me to quit making my teachers cry-"

This time, she interrupted me. "This is getting us nowhere. I just want to let you know that I'm here for you if you need me."

I rolled my eyes. "Whatever. Can I go now?"

She nodded and I jumped up from my chair.

As an afterthought, she instructed, "Go back to class."

I stepped out in the hallway and saw my friend, Erin, walking towards the gym. I hurried to catch with her.

"How'd that go?" she asked, turning around at the sound of my footsteps.

"It was incredibly stupid. I've got a sack. Do you wanna get outta here?"

Erin followed me through the parking lot and to the storage sheds on the far side of the football field where no one would see us getting high. She lived on the same block as Graham and even though I'd known her since elementary school, we'd never been friends. Our friendship started the night she'd spotted me smoking a joint behind Graham's garage while she was walking through the neighbor's yard to get to her house.

"Hey," she called, walking over to where I stood.

"Hey," I said, cupping the joint in my hand.

She sniffed the air. "It smells like weed." I expected her to react like my girlfriends by rolling her eyes and walking away. Instead, she surprised me. "Do you get high? I was with Bobby and Nate earlier. They're these guys from Albertville. Bobby is so hot. Anyways, I'm like so baked right now, I can't think straight."

I grinned and opened my hand to reveal the

joint.

"Cool." She took it and brought it to her lips.

I watched her take a hit and smiled again. It was the first time I'd smoked pot with a girl. I'd been worried about finding new girlfriends since my old crowd had turned their backs on me. They'd tolerated my drinking, but smoking pot crossed an invisible line with them. They looked at me with contempt. Melissa had tried talking to me about her concerns a few weeks earlier when we were walking home from Graham's.

"You don't seem like the same person anymore. It's kinda starting to freak me out," she said.

I stopped in my tracks. "Whatever. Don't say anything to James about me."

"I'm not even talking about James. This has absolutely nothing to do with your boyfriend. I'm just saying-"

"I saw you talking to him tonight. You probably told him all kinds of shit about me." Wendy and Paige moved to stand behind Melissa. "I know you want him. You've always wanted him. Sorry to burst your little bubble, but he's never liked you."

"Ya know what? Forget it, Elizabeth. This is

exactly what I'm trying to say. You don't make any sense. I say something about you and suddenly you're yelling at me about James." She shook her head. "Not only that, you're being mean-"

"Mean? You think I'm mean? Whatever. First, I'm nuts, then I'm fuckin' mean. What else do you have to say about me? Huh?" I stepped closer to her.

"Nothing. I'm done. This is pointless." She stepped back and moved forward again.

"No, really. Go ahead," I said. "You might as well get it all out. I mean, Christ, all you do is talk about me behind my back. You might as well tell me to my face. Or maybe you don't have the balls, do you?"

She didn't say anything and tried to move away from me. Her silence angered me further. I pushed up against her, my face within inches of her nose. "C'mon, let's hear it. Get it all out. I knew you didn't have any balls."

"Knock it off!" Wendy yelled from behind her.

"Shut up, Wendy. This isn't any of your business." I maintained my position in front of Melissa. Before I even knew what I was doing, I grabbed her purple windbreaker and pulled it around her neck. "Listen, I don't care what you have to say about me. Stay the fuck out of my business and my life. You don't know anything. You ever mess with me again and I'll kick your ass!"

I let go of her jacket and shoved her backward into Wendy and Paige. I turned and walked away, wishing I'd punched her in the face. Who did she think she was?

No one dared confront me after that. My friends avoided me at all costs. When I caught their eyes, they looked away and turned their backs when I approached them in the halls. I told myself I didn't care and we'd simply grown apart. That way, I could remain unaffected by the gap that continued to widen between us until we were completely separate.

Erin was one of the people I turned to for friendship who I'd barely spoken to in the past, and there were others like her. They were people I'd always considered losers, but suddenly, I was attracted to the greasy-haired guys who wore leather jackets or Grateful Dead T-shirts. They talked about having wild parties. Most of them had gotten kicked out of regular school and went to alternative school. They stood in the hallway outside of their special classroom, arms crossed, and intimidating us with their presence. I wanted what they had.

Keith Bennett was the worst of the bad boys. He stood in the hall most of the time, making lewd comments to the girls passing by. He called me sweet cheeks whenever I passed and I blushed every time. He was seventeen, almost three years older than me, with long, blond hair that rolled down the back of his leather jacket. He'd been in trouble with the law and I'd heard rumors he sold pot. He got into fights and bragged about his conquests with older women. I set my eyes on him, determined to make him mine.

Our first date was simple—we planned to get drunk together. I told my parents I was staying overnight at a friend's house so I could stay out all night with him. He picked me up at the park a block from my house. His hair was bright and shiny, flowing down his back, and he smelled like Cool Water cologne. He held up an unopened bottle of vodka.

"Where'd you get that?" I asked, lighting up a cigarette.

"My mom," he said, bringing his cigarette to

his lips.

"Your mom?"

"Yep, she's a drunk. She's so wasted, she don't care. Now, are ya ready to get wasted or what?"

My answer was to grab the bottle and take the first drink. I wanted to impress him with my capacity to drink and show him I wasn't one of those girls who got drunk and stupid after one beer. I emptied out a bottle of 7-up and refilled it with vodka like he did and we headed out of town.

Keith belonged to the subculture of people who spent hours drinking and driving on the back roads outside of town. He and his buddies raced their cars, side by side, spewing gravel down the roads. Sometimes they crashed into each other. It was a dangerous game. Keith took me on my first ride.

"Hold on!" He pressed his foot hard on the gas pedal. I gripped the strap above the window and watched the speedometer jerk back and forth.

Trees and cornfields flew by. He raced towards a four-way stop.

"Watch this, woohoo!" He blew through the stop sign in front of us. The truck sailed into the air as if we'd gone off a jump. We landed with a scrape and a thud. He pulled the emergency brake, whipping us sideways before coming to a stop.

"Shit! We caught some serious air." I threw my head back and laughed. I grabbed my bottle and took a huge gulp. "Let's do it again."

"Whoa girl, you're crazy," he said, turning the truck around.

I laughed giddily, feeling the effects of what I'd drank, mixed with the adrenaline of driving fast. I'd show him just how crazy I was. I filled my bottle up again and drank it just as fast as I'd drunk the other bottle.

"We're gonna have to find more booze," he said, holding up the empty bottle. We hadn't even been driving for an hour. It was the last thing I remembered before coming to, lying on Keith's lap in the backseat of a strange car.

Keith was talking about something and there was someone else crammed next to us in the back seat. Keith's best friend, Josh, was driving and someone occupied the passenger seat. The car had an incredible stereo system that bounced and shook the car with its power. I could feel the bump of the bass and each time it thumped, my stomach heaved and my head swam. I couldn't move my body or lift my head. I was going to be sick and wanted to tell

Josh to pull over, but when I opened my mouth, vomit spewed out instead of words. My mashed potatoes from supper splattered on Keith's lap.

"Fuck! Pull over—he's puking!" Keith said.

Josh pulled the car over to the side of the road. Keith jumped out before it was completely stopped and pulled me out behind him. I hunched over on the road, puking until my stomach was empty. He held my hair away from my face while I heaved.

I stood up after I finished. I felt better like I always did after I puked. My head quit spinning and my stomach calmed. Keith was next to me using snow to wipe the puke off his pants.

"Ohmigod, I'm so sorry," I said.

"Don't worry about it. It's nothin'." He smiled. "It happens to the best of us. C'mon, let's get outta here before someone calls the cops."

He grabbed my hand and helped me back into the car. He put his arm around me and I snuggled close to him, inhaling his scent. I felt warm and safe.

Keith leaned forward to talk to Josh. "Drive to Kwik Trip so we can clean up."

"Man, that was so fuckin' nasty," Josh said, laughing. "I've never seen you move so fast in my life."

"I knew she'd puke but man, you should see this chick drink," Keith said. I beamed proudly. "Remember that one time, when that one chick ... what was her name?"

"Shauna?"

"No, it was ... God, who the hell was it?"

I drifted off, oblivious to their conversation. I closed my eyes, feeling the warmth of Keith's body next to mine and smelling cologne mixed with the sweet scent of alcohol. He was someone I could fall in love with. He'd held my hair while I puked. It was a sign that he was my Prince Charming.

FOUR

It became more and more obvious to my parents that I was drinking and getting high. Any evidence of the child they once knew was gone. I was done hiding and pretending to be the girl they thought I should be. My mom was convinced Satan was attacking me and our family, trying to tear us apart.

"Satan is taking control of your mind. You have to fight him," she'd started pleading with me any chance she got.

What she didn't know was that I'd crossed over too many lines, broken too many rules and no amount of prayer or asking for forgiveness would remove my sins. I was doomed. Even when I'd been almost perfect and done everything right, God still hadn't loved me so there wasn't any point in fighting for my soul.

Unlike my mom who was concerned about me,

my dad was infuriated with who I'd become. But I'd lost the fear of his anger and without that fear, he'd lost the ability to control me which only made him angrier.

They grounded me whenever I got caught skipping school, staying out all night, or getting high, but it never worked. My bedroom was in the basement with a window at ground level. I became skilled at removing the screen and sneaking out. I placed my dresser underneath the window so all I had to do was climb on top of it and head through the window to my freedom. Keith would be waiting in the driveway in his red truck with the lights turned off.

It didn't take long before my parents figured out what I was doing and I came home to find them sitting on my bed waiting for me.

"Where have you been?" my dad said, peering into my eyes.

"Nowhere."

"She's drunk, hon," my mom said quietly, her eyes welling with tears. She blinked rapidly to keep them from falling down her cheeks. "I can smell it on her."

My dad pinned me against the wall, his

forearm pressed against my collarbone. "Have you been with Keith? Did he come get you?"

"Get away from me!" I pushed him and turned away. He grabbed my arm and jerked me back around to face him.

"Who do you think you are?" His eyes bulged and his nostrils flared with quick breaths.

"What are you gonna do? Spank me?" I laughed.

"You think you're so smart. I'll show you what I'm gonna do." He grabbed my arms and pinned me back against the wall.

"Hon, stop. Leave her alone. She's just drunk." My mom got up from her spot on the bed and stood beside him, tapping his arm. "Let's just go to bed. We can't do anything about it tonight."

My dad released his grip slowly. He narrowed his eyes to slits and glared at me before opening the door and leaving my bedroom. My mom remained behind. We stood in silence, listening to the sound of his footsteps on the stairs.

"Why do you do this?" Worry creased her face and there were bags underneath her eyes.

"I'm not doing anything. Just leave me alone," I said. She tried to hug me, but I pushed her away.

"Get out of here. You're on his side."

She brought her hand up to her face as if I'd slapped her and touched her cheek, searching for a physical mark. She moved away from me with her eyes wide open, still fighting back tears. She followed my father upstairs.

The following day, they nailed my screen shut and placed boards over my window. I switched to escaping out the back door because they couldn't nail the garage door shut. My nighttime routine of waiting for them to fall asleep, sneaking out of the house, and running off into the night to get drunk with Keith continued.

Their solution was to send me to a Christian psychologist, Dr. Hawkins, an old man in his sixties who looked more like a minister than a counselor. He wore black three-piece suits with red ties. He spoke slowly and purposefully as he asked me questions. I got high before every session and stared aimlessly out the window at the trees blowing in the wind as I sat on his leather sofa.

He never asked me about my life or how I was feeling. He focused his questions on saving my soul. "Do you pray any longer?" he'd ask, moving his chair closer to me.

"Nope."

"Jesus is the only person who is going to help you get through this difficult time. You've turned your back on him, but you can come back to him at any time. He wants you to come back. He doesn't want to lose you to Satan."

"Satan already has me. Nothing anyone can do about it."

"Have you been worshipping him?"

He acted as if it was that simple—choose God or Satan. I was acutely aware of the battle between God and the devil for souls on earth because I'd grown up in the war. What he didn't understand was that I'd committed my life to God when I was three-years-old and it wasn't me that had abandoned God. Rather, God had abandoned me.

I'd never had a problem believing what was in the Bible. I read it as if God was speaking to me directly just like I'd been instructed. My parents and church leaders said it was a textbook and I treated it as such. I memorized verses and rehearsed them in my head, especially at night when my thoughts raced out of control and I was terrified about things I couldn't name. I even tried to do similar experiments like the great men in the

Bible did with God except mine never turned out like theirs.

As a little girl, I'd gotten on my knees in my bedroom all of the time, sobbing and begging Jesus to come into my heart. But no matter what, I still felt the same, like I was continually being punished for sins I didn't commit. Nothing changed. There was still a faceless monster that came into my room at night and I disconnected from my body. Only bad girls had monsters in their rooms and did tricks with their bodies. There wasn't any salvation for me.

I couldn't explain it to him, so I started refusing to answer his questions. He thought it was because I was too high to talk so he told my parents he wouldn't see me anymore if I continued to come to our sessions high. My mom made the mistake of telling me what he'd said so I made sure I was so wasted for my next appointment I could barely walk.

He looked at my red, watery eyes as I shuffled through his door and said, "I can't see you anymore unless you're sober."

"I'm never gonna be sober," I slurred, heading back out the door.

He called my parents and told them our sessions were over. They punished me by grounding me again, but I refused to stay in the house. Trying to keep me from leaving, my dad resorted to standing in front of the door, with his arms stretched out, blocking my way. The same scene replayed itself over and over again.

I would try to grab the doorknob and as I did, he'd grab me.

"You are not going anywhere, young lady," he'd say.

I'd reach for the doorknob again, quickly opening the door. He'd push back against it with his body as I struggled to keep it open. I'd plant my feet, pulling on the door, as he remained braced in front of it. I struggled against him, knowing I only had to get it open six inches and I could slide my body through.

He'd grab me, pulling me back into the house, and slam the door behind us. A wrestling match followed. He'd throw me down to the ground, pinning me underneath him. Once I was on the ground, he'd sit on me with his legs on top of my legs and my wrists held back with his hands.

"Get off me!"

Sarah watched our fights and would begin to cry in the doorway of the kitchen.

"Go to your room," my mom would say from her spot at the kitchen table, where she tried to stay out of the way. Sarah would run into her bedroom, slamming the door.

I'd quit fighting so he'd release his hold. As soon as he stood up, I made a frantic dash for the door again. I'd fling it open and take off at a dead sprint like I'd just heard the gun being fired at the starting line of one of my cross country meets. Sometimes he ran after me. He was a former cross country star too and could catch up quickly. He'd tackle me to the ground, throw me over his shoulder, and carry me back into the house as I kicked and screamed, pounding on his back with my fists. We'd return to the house, where the battle would continue until he finally gave up and let me go.

As soon as I was freed, I'd run the four blocks to Keith's house, looking frantically over my shoulder to see if my dad was chasing me. I didn't stop running until I was sure he wasn't. I did my best to calm myself down before I got to Keith's.

We'd been together for a few months now, and

he was officially my boyfriend. In the beginning, I'd spent all of my time with him because I loved him and I'd never been in love before. He wanted to be with me at all times, and if he wasn't, he wanted to know where I was and who I'd been with. He cared about and understood me in a way that nobody else did. At first, it was flattering but things were changing and I didn't like it anymore.

"Are you high?" Keith asked one night, opening the screen door before I even knocked. His muscular arms stretched out, bracing both sides of the doorframe.

"No," I lied, looking at my feet and trying to get my gums unstuck from my front teeth.

"Look at me!"

I looked up to meet his brown eyes, rimmed with thick black lashes that any girl would kill for. They could look so doll-like when they weren't filled with anger.

Open your eyes. Look at him. Don't look stoned. Look sober.

He grabbed my chin with his hand, lifted it up, and leaned forward within inches of my face. "You're wasted," he said, raising his upper lip in a disgusted smirk. He grabbed my arm and jerked me through the doorway. "Get in here."

I followed him through the small patio filled with miscellaneous tools and empty cardboard cases of beer and liquor. In the kitchen, the radio was tuned to classic rock, Lightning 107.1, as always. Leftover dishes from supper stank in the sink. Rocky, the small poodle, lay in her designated spot next to the stove. Keith's mom, Donna, sat at the table by the window in her gray sweatpants, with a cigarette burning in the ashtray and a can of Old Milwaukee in her hand.

"Hi, Elizabeth." The weary frown lines in her face straightened into a smile that showed her decaying, yellow teeth from years of drinking and chain-smoking. "How was your night?"

"Shut up, Mom. Don't talk to her," Keith said, walking through the doorway on the right to the pantry.

"Oh, Keith, I'm sorry," she slurred, making Keith sound more like "Keef." I heard the sound of aluminum being moved around in the fridge.

"I told you to get me more beer," he said as he walked back into the kitchen with one of her beers in his hand. He cracked it open.

Donna looked at the orange-carpeted floor left

over from the 70s. "I'm sorry. Gee, Keef. Big Keef didn't get home till late. I couldn't go to the liquor store."

Keith rolled his eyes and took another drink. "You're so fuckin' lazy. Can't you ever get off your drunk ass and do anything? Oh yeah, I forgot. You're too drunk."

"I'm sorry." She kept her gaze on the same imaginary spot on the carpet. Her shoulders tightened and her head hung low. She pulled her arms forward as if she wanted to disappear into her body.

"Get out of here!" He pointed to the doorway leading to the living room.

"Oh, oh, oh ..." She picked up her cigarettes and then dropped them on the floor. She bent over to pick them up, her hand shaking and her body swaying. I wanted to tell Keith to leave her alone but I was already in enough trouble. She shuffled through the door and clicked it shut behind her without looking back.

"Sit down."

I sat. I hung my head and copied Donna's gaze on the carpet. He sat across the kitchen table from me, setting his beer down. "I told you to stay home tonight."

He'd worked tonight in the kitchen at Stub's Pub, the only bar in town. He usually didn't get off work until the early hours of the morning. Lately, he wanted me to sit at my house from the time he dropped me off from school until he got home from work.

"I know you did and I was going to, but-"

He cut me off. "There are no butts! You never listen to me." His fist slammed down on the table, knocking over his beer and spilling it into his lap. "Dammit, look what you made me do!"

I jumped up and grabbed the towel from the rack. "I'm sorry," I said, setting his beer upright. I wiped off the table and his lap. I threw the towel in the sink and sat back down. He was silent, looking out the window and tapping his fingers on the table. The beat was deliberate: tap, tap, tap. The silence made a buzz start in my head that sounded like radio station static. I hated his silences.

"I hate sitting at home," I blurted out. "I go crazy."

"All you had to do was wait for me to get off work," he said, turning to look at me. "I would've come got you."

"But I didn't want to sit there till two," I said in a voice whinier than I'd ever used in childhood.

"I don't care. I know you're out there getting high and whoring around with guys when I'm at work."

"I'm not!" I wouldn't dare. He found out everything I did. If a guy even looked at me for too long, Keith punched him in the face. I'd seen him do it more than one once. "I just sat in Erin's basement all night getting high with her. It was no big deal."

He snorted and ground his teeth back and forth. "She's a fuckin' loser. I don't know why you hang out with her."

He hated everyone I hung out with. It never mattered who they were. Even though he'd introduced me to lots of his friends, he hated me hanging out with them. There was no way for me to win unless I gave in and only hung out with him. I used to want to spend every minute with him during our first few months together, but lately, it was getting harder to do and I missed hanging out with other people. Whenever we were together, he was angry and I could never do anything right. I was beginning to feel like I was suffocating.

"I've gotta go home. It's two-thirty and I was supposed to be home at midnight."

"See what I mean?" Now his voice sounded whiny. "If you just would've waited, your parents would've been in bed by the time I was done. We could've had you back by the time they got up. Now your mom is probably all freaked out again. God, you piss me off."

"But my parents-"

"Fuck your parents!" he snorted, raising his beer to his lips. It was his favorite thing to say whenever I mentioned doing anything they wanted me to do. It was easy for him to say. He'd never had a curfew or parents like mine. His mom was an alcoholic and one of his closest drinking buddies. His dad was in the army and gone for months at a time. When he was home, he was as drunk as Keith's mom.

I rubbed my hands on my face, trying to clear my head. I was tired of arguing and defending myself. He got up and walked over to stand behind me. My body tightened. I'd learned to prepare for the blows. It had only been a month, but it felt like forever since he'd pushed me down the stairs after I'd threatened to leave him if he didn't start treating me better. He put his arms around me and I cringed, gripping my chair with my hands. His arms were loose and he began to kiss my neck. I relaxed my muscles and hold on the chair.

I turned my head and brought my mouth to meet his. He stuck his tongue in my mouth and kissed me hungrily. I tasted the Old Milwaukee. He pulled me back and cupped my head in his hands.

"I just get so pissed off 'cause I love you so much," he said, his eyes finally soft.

"I love you too," I said and gave him another kiss. He pulled my chair back and moved in front of me. I heard the sound of his zipper going down. I automatically reached down to begin stroking him. He groaned and responded by unzipping my pants. I lifted my butt off the chair so he could pull my pants down to my ankles, panties and all.

His voice was muffled as he licked my neck with his tongue. "You drive me crazy."

I turned my head to look at the numbers on the microwave: 2:42. *Christ, I have to get home.* He grabbed my shoulders and pushed me back in my chair as I spread my legs. He entered me and began his frantic thrusting. I counted his strokes: one, two, three, four, five, and then he finished inside of me. From the time he entered me, he could never last more than five strokes so I counted each one to make the task easier. He went limp on top of me. The smell of fried food wafted up. Looking out the window, I noticed Donna had put up a new bird feeder. My eyes returned to the microwave clock: 2:45.

"I've gotta go, for real," I said, moving my legs underneath him.

He grunted. "I'm so tired. Can't you just sleep here with me?"

"Not tonight. My parents are still pissed about the last time I stayed out all night. Technically, I'm still grounded."

He laughed. "Yeah, that works real well."

"Maybe this weekend I'll stay here. Now, c'mon, seriously, I've got to go."

"Oh all right, fine." He stood and pulled his jeans up. I did the same. He grabbed his beer and finished it off. "Call me when you get home. Don't forget, I'm picking you up at eleven tomorrow. Don't bother going to school."

"I'll be ready." I leaned over and gave him a peck on his cheek. "I love you. I'll let myself out." I walked away without waiting for a response. I didn't want him to change his mind and become adamant that I stay. I didn't want to sleep next to him. Not tonight.

"Elizabeth?" He called out, just as my hand was on the door.

"What?" I braced myself.

"I love you, too. Don't ever forget that."

"I won't." I opened the door and walked into the crisp air. Snow fell around me.

What am I doing? How did I get myself into this?

I was running away from a dad who'd lost control over me into the arms of a guy who wanted to gain control over me. I lit a cigarette and continued walking. Maybe it wasn't as bad as I was making it out to be. Sure, my dad was a control freak, but Keith wasn't like my dad. Keith loved me. Our love was so powerful that it made him lose control. But a soft voice from inside me spoke up, *Look how he treats his mom. He hits her and he's started to hit you. He'll do it again. It's only gonna get worse.*

I shook my head, trying to erase the thoughts. I threw my cigarette onto the ground and grabbed my pipe from my pocket, bringing it to my lips, lighting it, and inhaling the sweetness. I held the smoke in my lungs as long as I could before releasing it back into the air. I sat down on the cold curb on the side of the road, smoking, and instructing myself to quit thinking until the familiar peace came over my mind.

It was going to be okay. I wasn't going to deny that Keith could be mean, but it wasn't that bad. Our situation was nothing I couldn't handle. Besides, there were lots of benefits to being his girlfriend. He was introducing me to all sorts of new connections and people. Just a few days ago, he'd even brought me to the place where he bought the pot he sold.

It was a beat-up trailer off a gravel road with a cornfield on each side. The woman who answered the door weighed about three hundred pounds and didn't have any teeth in her mouth. She smiled at us, all gums. As she welcomed us into the trailer, a black Rottweiler ran up to sniff my crotch. We walked into the kitchen and Keith motioned for me to sit down. He followed the fat woman to a room in the back of the trailer and shut the door.

The kitchen was a mess and smelled like rotten food. My feet stuck to the floor. Dirty dishes piled in the sink and lined the counters. Empty beer cans and bottles overflowed the garbage can and spilled onto the floor. A pudgy, brown-haired boy playing solitaire was at the table next to me. Across from him was a big man with a belly and muscular arms who eyed me quizzically. His intimidating presence filled the room.

He struck his hand out. "I'm Ryan Hedstrom. They call me Strom."

"Hey, I'm Elizabeth." I said, shaking his hand.

"Do ya wanna drink?"

"Sure." I reached down to pet the dog.

"That's Sasha," the little boy said. "I'm Zeke."

"Hi, Zeke."

"I'm six," he said proudly.

"Wow, that's pretty old," I said.

Strom grabbed the bottle of Windsor Canadian and mixed me a drink at the counter. He kept looking at me with a sideways smirk on his face. "Don't you go to school?"

"Not today."

He laughed. "I've heard about you."

I didn't know what to say. What had he heard and who told him? Was it good? I was a new person in this circle and it was important to be trusted.

He pulled out a bag of pot and loaded a one-hitter. I watched him smoke it as he joked with Zeke. I wanted to get high because I hadn't been all day, but I said nothing. When we walked up to the door Keith had given me very specific instructions, "Be quiet and don't ask for anything."

I didn't have to ask, though, because as soon as he finished smoking, Strom packed it again and handed it to me. I took it gladly. He watched me carefully as I smoked it and then gave me another. It was a test to see if I'd start laughing uncontrollably like beginning pot smokers do, but I'd passed that stage long ago. We didn't talk much. Keith was taking a long time. Right as I started to get paranoid, he returned and I followed him out the door.

Sitting on the curb in the cold at nearly three in the morning, remembering this, I realized Keith trusted me or he never would've taken me to Strom's. I was blowing his anger out of proportion. It wasn't like our troubles were only his fault. I was always doing things to make him mad. I would try harder to do what he asked me to do. He loved me and I loved him. None of the other stuff mattered as long as we loved each other. Besides, I needed him as much as he needed me. I got up from the curb with a renewed determination to make our relationship work.

Garrison

FIVE

I got kicked out of school in the middle of ninth grade, after a long, drawn-out game of being given chances to behave. I skipped my classes almost every day and had quit making up stories or pretending to be ill. When I was at school my time was spent in the principal's office, waiting to be given punishment for being wasted on school grounds, getting into fights, stealing money and cigarettes from lockers, or for whatever else I'd done the last time I'd been in school. The principal, Mr. McKinnsey, was running out of ways to punish me. I didn't show up for detention and suspending me only gave me a legitimate reason not to go to school.

Mr. McKinnsey led me into his office and ordered me to sit down. I sat in front of his long metal desk covered with papers and yellow Post-it notes. I crossed my arms and rested my head on the back of the chair, sprawling my legs out in front of me.

"Elizabeth, this is it. We've done everything we can think of to try to keep you in school. Nothing works. You don't seem to care." He paused, locking his eyes with mine "I've decided, along with the school board and your parents, to give you one final chance to stay in school."

"What if I don't wanna stay?" I cocked my head to the side.

"Then, I guess that's a choice you'll make because frankly, we don't care anymore. This is a sad situation. See, there are some kids that you know are going to struggle to get through school and probably won't make it. They struggle their way from kindergarten on. You've never been one of those kids, Elizabeth. You're smart, creative, a natural athlete, and you excel at everything you try. The only reason you're still here is because we all crossed our fingers and hoped one day you'd snap out of this and realize how badly you're screwing up your life. But I'm going to be real straight with you—no one believes that's going to happen."

He paused again, letting his words sink in. I

shifted my gaze to a brown stain on the padded chair next to me as a lump lodged itself in my throat. I refused to meet his eyes.

"Here's the deal, it's real simple. You're on a zero tolerance policy, which means you screw up once and you're out. No questions asked." He picked up a piece of paper from his desk and handed it to me. "This is your list of rules. All of your teachers have the same list. You break one of these rules and you're gone. For good."

I took the paper and skimmed the words without reading what they said. Why did I feel like crying?

He leaned back in his chair. "Got any questions?"

I shook my head. I couldn't speak around the lump in my throat. I just wanted to get out of there.

"All right, then. You can go." He picked up his phone and punched in a number.

The policy rules stated I had to be in class on time every day. Once I was in class, I couldn't leave for any reason not even to go to the bathroom. I wasn't to cause any disruptions. I couldn't get caught smoking on school grounds, be under the influence of any drugs, or have any drugs on me.

Last, I couldn't talk to any of my teachers outside of the classroom without Mr. McKinnsey being present.

It dawned on me as I walked into school the following Monday that I didn't know what I'd do if I got kicked out of school. I was only fourteen. I was supposed to be playing varsity basketball, going to school dances and football games, writing papers, taking tests, and making my girlfriends laugh at lunch. Instead, I was failing all of my classes, not playing any sports, not involved with any school activities, and none of my girlfriends from my childhood even spoke to me. How had I gotten here?

I shook my head, trying to clear it of serious thoughts. I told myself to relax and that I only had to follow their rules for a little bit. Once they thought I was doing better, they'd relax their hold and I could go back to doing what I wanted to do again.

The first day of the policy, I made it to all of my classes on time and didn't leave. I got through by laying my head on the desk and going to sleep. By the time my last period came, I was rested and proud of myself for having made it through the day.

My last class of the day was English. The teacher, Mr. Cameron, was my favorite teacher to harass. He was an easy target, a first-year teacher who wore brown polyester pants that hung on his hips and dragged on the floor. His pants were coupled with brown, striped shirts tucked into them. His short, squatty body carried a small neck and a big head. He wore thick glasses that made his large eyes appear even bigger. He looked like a turtle that was in the process of evolving into a human but hadn't quite made it there.

I started to get bored halfway through class. I ripped pieces of paper out of my notebook and folded them into tight triangles. I had a small pile on my lap. I waited until Mr. Cameron turned around to write on the blackboard and then threw one at his back. It connected. His hand stopped writing, and then he continued. "When you conjugate a-" Another one of my triangles hit his leg. The class started to snicker as he turned around.

"Who did that?" he asked. This only brought more laughter. "Quit it. Stop laughing." He sounded like a whiny, young boy begging his older brother to leave him alone. He waited until the laughter subsided. I decided not to push my luck.

At the end of class, he wrote the homework assignment on the board and turned to me. "Elizabeth, I need to see you after class."

"Is Mr. McKinnsey gonna be here?"

"No."

The bell rang and everyone grabbed their books, jumped up, and headed out the door. He walked over to my desk, crossed his arms on his chest, and peered down at me through his thick glasses. I stood up and stepped around him.

He grabbed my arm. "Where are you going? I said I wanted to talk to you."

"Look, Shit Pants, Mr. McKinnsey isn't here. You know the rules." I walked toward the door.

"I don't care," he said, keeping his hold on my arm and matching my stride.

"You're just gonna have to wait." I pulled my arm away and walked faster.

He moved in front of me again. "No." The tips of his ears turned red. "You sit down now!"

I stepped around him. "Why don't you sit down, Shit Pants? I'm leaving!"

He hurried to block the doorway with his body. "You insubordinate little brat!"

I pushed him aside and stepped into the hallway filled with students slamming their lockers and hurrying out of school.

"See ya." I smiled, looking over my shoulder. I started pushing my way through the other students. He came up behind me and grabbed my arm. I jerked away and continued walking. He grabbed me again and pulled me backward.

My head started to pressurize as if it was a balloon being stretched to the limits. It was my signal to fight or run. I turned around to face him. Through gritted teeth, I spat, "Get your fuckin' hands off me!"

I started walking, moving faster, the sound of his footsteps behind me. He shoved me up against a row of lockers.

"Get Mr. McKinnsey!" A female voice yelled.

Mr. Cameron pinned me against the locker, the red from his ears moving into his face. I shoved him and he flew backward into a student. He lunged back at me and wrestled me to the other side of the hallway, throwing me into the science lab, and shutting the door behind us. I broke free and ran to the teacher's desk at the front door of the room, grabbed the electric pencil sharpener, and threw it at his head. He ducked and it smashed into the wall. The air in my head threatened to explode.

"Fuck you!"

He moved towards me through the rows of desks. "No, fuck you!"

I stood at the front of the room, by the first row of chairs. Picking one up by the legs, I brought it over my head and threw it in his direction. I picked another one up and did the same. The chairs landed on their sides and upside down. He shoved the chairs out of the way and kept strutting towards me. Suddenly, Mr. Dixon, the three hundred pound science teacher burst through the door, ran up behind Mr. Cameron, and held him in a tight bear hug.

"Knock it off!" he said. "You need to settle down!" Mr. Cameron jerked forward and shook his head back and forth before going limp in Mr. Dixon's arms. He breathed in and out rapidly as if he'd just finished running a marathon.

"Looks like you're not so tough now." I laughed, giving him the finger and holding back the urge to spit in his face. He sprang back to life, kicking and wiggling to free himself from Dr. Dixon's hold.

"Elizabeth, get out of here," Mr. Dixon said without releasing his hold. "Go!"

I turned and stormed back into the hallway filled with students and teachers who'd gathered to watch. When I caught their eyes, they looked away. They moved to the side as I marched through the stony hallway. I looked down at the floor, a sinking feeling in the pit of my stomach. I was one of the kids that other kids were scared of, but it didn't feel like I'd always thought it would. I'd thought being the one who was angry and the one to inflict the pain meant being in control, but instead, I felt completely out of control. People's eyes bored into my back, questioning what was wrong with me in the same way I questioned my dad's anger.

I shoved open the heavy doors and walked into the parking lot. Quickly spotting Keith waiting for me, I hurried over, opened the truck door and slid in.

"What took you so long?" he asked, giving me a quick peck on the cheek.

I tried to shut off the leftover anger pounding in my head. "You don't even want to know. I don't think I'll be going back to school."

A school board meeting was held at the end of

the week. I was expelled and Mr. Cameron lost his job. With my expulsion, any semblance of a normal teen life disappeared. My emergence into the adult world of drugs and desperation was complete.

Keith was happy I was done with school. He saw it as an opportunity to spend more time with me. But I was growing more and more tired of his possessive demands for my constant presence and attention. I no longer found his relentless questioning about my whereabouts flattering. All we did was argue about where I'd been when I wasn't with him, who I'd been with, and what I'd done. Our arguing always ended in fights that were growing increasingly more violent.

I started spending less and less time with Keith and more and more time with Strom, the drug dealer Keith had introduced me to a few months earlier. I became a frequent visitor at the trailer in the country between two cornfields. I didn't know who owned the trailer, but Strom spent a lot of time there along with the toothless fat lady who I learned was his sister.

Keith's connection for pot was slowly becoming my own. Strom was beginning to trust me. Before long, he started carefully schooling me in the mathematics of splitting up large quantities of pot into smaller amounts to sell. Pot was scattered all over the trailer. It was on every table, counter, and the bathroom sink. He even fed the dog green buds for doing tricks. I was in awe. He was a great teacher and I was an even better student, eager and willing to learn everything he had to teach me. His school replaced high school but now I showed up every day on time. The only reason Strom initially trusted me was because I was Keith's girlfriend, but the title only got me limited access into his world and I wanted complete access to everything that went on in the trailer.

Strom and I spent our time sitting on the plastic chairs around the white table in the kitchen, with pot and booze spread out around us. Throughout the day, people knocked at the door and Strom would peek through the faded yellow curtains before he hollered for whoever it was to come in. If the person was uninvited or unknown, we sat in silence until they were gone.

People walked in and pulled up a chair next to us. Strom would take their money and give them what they came for. If anyone ever questioned his dealing, they were cut off.

One afternoon after an exchange, a guy with a pair of khaki pants and a white shirt asked Strom, "Do you have a scale?"

Strom snorted and grabbed the bag he'd just handed the man. "It's a fuckin' half. Don't you trust me?" His eyes bulged and he worked his jaw.

"No, I mean, yes ... I just, it's just ya know, sometimes people ..."

"I'm not one of those people." Strom dug into the pocket of his jeans and pulled out the wad of bills the man had given him. He tossed them in his direction.

"Man, shit, I didn't mean nothing. I still want it. I trust ya." A bead of sweat formed on his forehead.

"Get the fuck outta here, dude." Strom's voice made grown men act like dogs tucking their tails between their legs. It was direct and cold, with every syllable enunciated perfectly in such a way that no one questioned his authority.

The man stood up, took his money from the table, and let himself out without saying another word. I watched how Strom treated people, noticed how they responded to him, and stored what I saw in my memory. I wanted to be one of the people he trusted and respected. I watched everything going on to determine how I needed to act and talk to be that person.

Other times when people came, Strom would stand up when they reached the kitchen before they had a chance to sit down. These people were different from the potheads. They were skinny men with mullets and eyes that darted around the room.

"Answer my phone if it rings," Strom would instruct as he turned to walk down the hallway with the others following. I'd hear the click of the door as they shut it behind them and strain my ears, but could only hear muffled whispers and occasional outbursts of laughter. I'd sit at the table, anxiously chewing my fingernails and chain smoking. They'd never stay in the back bedroom long. When they returned, they were animated and lively, talking so fast I couldn't follow their conversations. Their pupils were large black circles. I'd seen enough movies and been around drugs long enough to know they were on some kind of speed. They were so energized and full of life. I'd watch them through eyes covered in a blanket of stoned numbness and wanted to feel like they felt.

I never said anything, asked to come along, or

what they did behind the door. You needed an invitation and I knew better than to ask for one. I wanted to try something new. Pot and booze had become old and boring. There was no excitement in them any longer. Smoking and drinking had become habitual routines I performed over and over again, like brushing my teeth. But there was an entire world of drugs to use and Strom was my key to getting there.

Keith was holding me back from being able to try new drugs and gaining complete access to Strom's world because I wasn't seen as a separate individual. Since I was his girlfriend, I was associated with how he behaved and Keith was erratic and unpredictable. You never knew when he was going to get angry and just start destroying things for no reason. I didn't want to be known as Keith's girlfriend anymore. I wanted my own identity and place in Strom's world.

I started trying to breakup with Keith with the least amount of difficulty. I made it seem like the breakup was about me, focusing on the fact that I was young and stressing it had nothing to do with him. Each time I tried to end our relationship, he either cried like a baby, promising to change and begging me to stay, or got so mad that he hit me. I switched tactics and began trying to avoid him because I thought he would go away if I didn't give him any attention, but it was impossible. He refused to be ignored. He called constantly, followed me around town, hid outside my house until I got home, or showed up uninvited wherever I was.

Strom and I didn't talk about my relationship with Keith. He wasn't the type to delve into anyone's personal life. But one day he brought it up while we were parked on the street outside his parents' house in his beat-up Chrysler LeBaron. I was smoking my Marlboro Reds, blowing the smoke through the window crack. The drivers' seat was moved back as far as it would go, but even so his big belly still pushed against the steering wheel when he moved. I didn't understand how his stomach could be so big while his arms looked like the muscles I'd seen on bodybuilders on TV.

"Where are ya headed now?" he asked, giving me a bag of weed.

"I'm supposed to go to Tara's. She's having people over, but Keith doesn't want me to go." I'd met Tara at a party a few weeks before and we'd been spending a lot of time together since then.

"Keith doesn't want me to go," Strom mimicked in a little girl voice, rocking his head back and forth.

"Shut up!" I said, punching him on the arm as he laughed. He had the best belly laugh and I loved it.

"Christ, it's like he's your dad. Don't you ever get sick of it?"

"Hell, yes. You don't even know how tired of it I get. I'm gonna break up with him."

"Yeah, right. I've heard that one too many times before."

He was right. Everyone had. I was always announcing I was breaking up with Keith, but a few days later I'd admit we were still together.

"I mean it. This time it's for real. I don't care what he does to me." I took my pipe and loaded it with pot.

"What do you mean you don't care what he does to you?" Strom jerked his head up from the pot he'd started sorting on his belly.

"Never mind." I looked out the window at the empty baseball diamond across the street and started smoking.

"Listen kid, I kinda like you. I don't like too many people but I take care of the ones that I do. I'm gonna ask you a question and I want you to tell me the truth. Does he hit you?"

"Yes." As soon as the words were out of my mouth, I wanted to take them back. I looked at girls who let men hit them as being weak and pathetic. I didn't want to admit I was one of those girls and didn't want Strom to think of me as one of them.

"If that motherfucker ever lays a hand on you again, you come to me. I'll take care of his stupid ass. After I'm through with him, he'll be too scared to come near you again. Seriously. Fuck him!" He punched the steering wheel. "You got that?"

I nodded my head, startled by his reaction. I'd heard a rumor that Strom had killed a man and didn't doubt it was true. For the first time in a long while, I felt powerful. If I had Strom on my side then I could end my relationship with Keith. I didn't need or want him anymore because as long as I had Strom, I had power.

I opened the door. "I've gotta go."

"Are you gonna go to Tara's?"

"She's supposed to pick me up with Troy at the park at nine. I'm gonna stop at Keith's and dump his ass before I go out there," I said with determination and conviction.

"All right." He started up the car. "You know where to find me."

I got out and shut the door behind me, waving to Strom as he drove off. It was only a few blocks to Keith's, and I rehearsed what I'd say as I walked.

First, I'll tell him I only have a minute 'cause I'm supposed to be meeting Troy and Tara. I'll tell him I love him but I can't be with him right now. I'll tell him I'm too young to be in a serious relationship. It's not a lie. I'm telling the truth. I don't wanna feel like I'm married at fourteen. I need to be free. That's all I'll say. Then, I'll just say I've got to go. He'll probably think I don't mean it. But this time, I do.

As I strutted up Keith's driveway, I saw him sitting on the front steps with a bottle between his legs. I hoped he hadn't been drinking all day. My heart started to beat faster.

Just stick to the plan. Just stick to the plan.

I slowed at the sidewalk. His eyes bored into me, the pupils dilated with anger already. *Don't be scared. You can do this.*

"Hey," I said, looking down at my feet and

taking a deep breath.

"Where ya been?" he asked, swaying to the left as he stood up.

"I drove around for a while with Strom." I took my cigarettes from my pocket.

"God, I wish I'd never introduced you to him. He's nothing but trouble." Keith took a swig from his Captain Morgan.

I didn't say anything. I didn't want to get into the argument we'd already had many times before. I only wanted to say what I had to say and go meet Tara.

"I've got to tell you something."

"What? Are you cheatin' on me?" He stood up and put his hands on his hips.

"No, I-"

"You are, aren't you? You little slut, I knew it!" He ground his teeth together.

See, you're doing the right thing, Elizabeth.

"Keith, listen. Just sit down and mellow out." I chose my words carefully because of how easily he could be set off. "I'm not cheating on you. I just want to tell you something."

"What?" He stepped in front of me and peered into my eyes with his teeth clenched together.

You can do this. You can do this.

I lit my cigarette and took a long drag. I spoke the words as fast as I could without giving him a chance to interrupt. "Okay, this is it. I love you, Keith. I really do. Don't get me wrong. This has nothing to do with love. I'm young. And I wanna do lots with my life. I don't wanna be tied down. You're ready to be so serious. I'm not. Not that I never will be. But right now, I just can't. I don't wanna have to worry about hurting you all the time and I always seem to hurt you. I don't wanna do that anymore. Please, don't hate me, but I'm breaking up with you. I don't wanna be with you anymore."

I turned around and started down the sidewalk, holding back the urge to sprint. I didn't want to give him an opportunity to change my mind like he'd done so many times before. I needed to stay calm and focused.

He yanked my arm from behind. "Where do you think you're going?"

Without turning around to face him, I said, "I'm leaving. It's over and I don't wanna talk about it anymore. I'm going. I've gotta be somewhere."

"You don't get to just break up with me without me saying a word. You really think you can get away from me that easy?"

"Keith, please. Let go of me. I have to go. People are waiting for me. I don't want to talk about this. I'm done."

I took a step forward. He grabbed me again and jerked me around to face him.

"You're not going anywhere. Not until we talk." His nostrils flared in and out as if he were a bull waiting to be released from the pen. His breath smelled like rotten cheese, the way it often did after he'd been drinking for days. I held back the urge to gag.

"There's nothing to talk about. I've made up my mind." It wasn't until I tried to turn around to leave that I realized he was gripping both of my arms. I'd been so focused on saying what I needed to say and not being affected by his words that I'd forgotten he'd use his physical strength to control me when his words couldn't.

Here we go again. I tried to free my arms. *I can't believe I thought I could do this so easily. I can't go back on my words. I have to stay strong this time.*

"Don't. Fight. Me," he said.

My head filled with pressure and I forced

myself to look him in the eye. "Listen, if you let go of me, we can talk. Just let go of me so we can talk about this, okay?"

"Promise?" he said, cocking his head, his dirty blond bangs falling over his right eye.

"Yes."

"Okay." He slowly released my arms.

I stood there for a second, then turned on my heels and ran. I only made it a few strides before he tackled me and threw me onto the concrete.

He jumped on top of me. "You bitch!" He sat on my stomach, pinning me down. The faces of my dad and brother crossed his face, contorting into a three-headed monster as the pressure exploded in my head with a violent rush. I arched my back, brought my knees up and smashed them into his back.

He cried out, releasing his hold on my arms. I sat up and shoved him off me, scrambling to my feet, but not fast enough. He shoved me back to the ground. I fell on my hands and knees. He brought his foot up and slammed his steel boots onto my small hands. The pain shot through my body, making me feel like I had to puke.

"Get off me! Leave me alone!"

He reached down and grabbed a handful of my hair with his hands. His pull made my head snap back. I was afraid he'd tear the hair out of my head.

Like an army general, he ordered, "Get up."

I stood slowly, trying to keep my head steady. He dragged me by my hair to his steps, pinned me against the side of the house and looked into my eyes.

He's crazy. He's out of his mind. I closed my eyes, wishing he'd disappear.

"Nobody loves you like I do. Nobody will ever be able to put up with your shit like I do. You're worthless." He narrowed his eyes to slits.

"Fuck you! You're crazy!"

Suddenly, the door opened. Donna peeked her head outside. "What's going on?"

Without turning around, Keith said, "Mom, go back in the house. Don't come out again."

"Help me!" I cried, turning to look at Donna. She looked away, refusing to meet my eyes.

"Get in the house!" He raised his fist up toward my face.

"I'm sorry, Elizabeth," Donna said softly, turning back into the house. She began to cry as she shut the door.

"Please Keith, just let me go. I love you. I do. I'm sorry. I didn't mean it. Really, I didn't."

The tension in his face eased slightly. "If you're fuckin' with me this time, I swear to God, you'll regret it."

"I'm not."

"I'm warning you—you better not be." He searched my eyes.

"I love you. I don't know what I was thinking. Just let me go. You're hurting me. I'll stay. I will. I promise."

He eased his hold and moved back a step away from me. "I mean it, Elizabeth. You don't understand how much I love you. If you leave me, you won't have anyone to love you. I'm all you've got. Think about that."

"I know. I know, Keith." I kept my voice steady even as my heart pounded in short, quick spasms. "We can work this out."

He let go of my hair and took another step backward. I smashed his chest with both hands. I swung at him with my fists, connecting with his face. I heard the sound of my voice screaming but couldn't understand my words. I flailed my arms and legs against him in a fury.

He grabbed me by my hair again, jerked my head back, and slammed it against the stucco siding on his house. A loud crack resonated through my head. Blackness covered my eyes.

I came to sitting on the steps, holding my pounding head in my hands. I brought my fingers away from my head and saw they were covered with a sticky substance.

My head is bleeding. What is happening? What just happened?

I winced in pain as I turned my head to find Keith sitting next to me—his arm around my shoulders. Sobs wracked his body. He peered at me with tears streaming down his face and snot running from his nose into his mouth.

He whimpered like a small child in pain. "I'm sorry, baby. God, I'm so sorry. I didn't mean to hurt you. I just love you so much that I lose control. I can't help it. You don't know what you do to me. I can't live without you. I'm sorry."

"What ... Where ... my God ... I ..." My words wouldn't come together. *Leave. Just leave. Go.*

I stood up, swayed to the side and tried to regain my balance. I took a step forward as if I was in a trance. Keith grabbed me and pulled me back down to the steps. I cried out because the sudden movements made my head feel as if it was being split in half. He brought his fingers to my neck and wrapped them around it.

"I'm sorry, baby. I'm sorry, baby," he cried, beginning to squeeze my neck. "I don't want to hurt you. I love you."

His grip tightened, shutting off my air. It was like I'd been shoved underwater. I kicked my feet and waved my arms before my body went limp. My head swirled as I looked up at him from someplace warm and fluid in my mind, watching the vein on his forehead pulsing while he squeezed.

He's finally going to kill me.

Then darkness again.

When I came to for the second time, I was sitting on the front steps of Keith's house and heard yelling. The voices came from the yard and one of them was Keith's. I turned my aching head to see Keith pinned to the ground by a man who held him down in the same manner Keith had held me down so many times. Keith kicked and struggled to get up. I felt a hand on my shoulder and turned the other way to see Tara sitting beside me.

"Can you get up? Caleb is gonna take care of

Keith." Her blue eyes were filled with the concern of a mother.

"I think so." It hurt to talk. I barely knew Caleb, but he'd just saved my life. My head was filled with a thick blanket of fog. Tara stood and offered her hand. I grabbed it and she pulled me to my feet. She brought her arm around me and I took a few steps as I leaned against her. I felt disconnected like my head wasn't part of the body walking across the yard.

"C'mon. Troy is parked around the corner." She turned me towards the street on the side of the house.

I looked behind to see Caleb still sitting on top of Keith. We walked slowly and silently to the car where Troy waited in the driver's seat with the car running. Tara opened the front passenger door for me and I slid in, leaning my head back against the seat.

"You okay?" Troy asked, turning to look at me.

I felt like I was in the middle of a dream, trying to force myself to wake up. "Yeah. What the hell happened?"

Tara leaned forward in the back seat. "We waited and waited for you, but you didn't come. I knew you probably stopped at Keith's so I thought we'd come get you 'cause I know how hard it is for you to get away from him."

"Obviously." My laugh came out like a dry, raspy cough.

Caleb came running to the car and jumped in the back seat.

"Let's get the hell out of here," he said to Troy, who quickly put the car in drive and headed down the block.

"He won't bother you again, Elizabeth," Caleb said, patting my shoulder from behind.

"Thanks."

"Elizabeth, your head is bleeding," Tara said. "We should probably take you to the hospital."

"I'm fine." I snapped. "Did you guys get my bottle?"

"Are you serious?" Tara asked.

"Yeah, did you get it?" I grabbed Troy's cigarette burning in the ashtray and brought it to my lips.

Caleb reached into a bag and grabbed my bottle.

"Don't let her drink. That's like bad when your head is all fucked up." Tara stopped Caleb's arm.

"Don't worry about it, Tara." Caleb pushed her arm away and handed me my bottle. "She needs a drink."

"Hell, yes," Troy said.

I took the bottle from Caleb as Tara sat back in her seat and let out a huff. I unscrewed the top and brought it to my lips, taking a huge pull. I drank as if I hadn't had a drink in weeks. Nobody spoke. Keith had almost killed me and it was over. This time, it was really over. I was no longer his girlfriend.

I yelled out coarsely, breaking the awkward silence, "Let's party!"

Caleb raised his bottle into the air. "I'll drink to that."

Garrison

SIX

The first rule in the world of junkies was that there was no moral code. Anything was acceptable, and even if it wasn't, you kept your opinions to yourself. People who didn't follow the rules of the game didn't get to play. If you valued being a player, you kept your mouth shut. The only moral was the unspoken understanding of the need to get and stay high, no matter what. I understood unspoken rules because my family was filled with them. I wasn't surprised that no one spoke about the night Keith almost killed me. It was simply understood we'd broken up. No questions asked.

With Keith out of my life, I began to find the place I had longed for in Strom's life. I could spend all of my time with him without having to worry about upsetting Keith. Strom let me into his backroom world shortly after the breakup. The night he did was also the first time I got into trouble with the law.

The night began in Strom's brown LeBaron. Justin, a short, stocky kid with unruly black hair, was in the passenger seat next to Strom. I wanted to occupy that seat, but for the time being I was content just to be in the car. Justin snuck looks at me in the rearview mirror. I caught his glances and smiled back at him knowingly. Whenever Justin and I partied together, a weird chemistry ignited between us. We played a game of flirting that included sly smiles and suggestive glances—not leading to sex but instead to doing something wild. We both got excited and turned on by stealing cars, picking fights, trashing houses, destroying property, and anything else that was illegal. I could tell by the looks we'd already exchanged that tonight was going to be one of those nights.

I was stuck sitting next to Tim in the back. We called him Rocket Man because his girlfriend told us he wasn't circumcised, but he thought it was a reference to Elton John. Rocket Man thought he was tough, the worst sixteen-year-old around, because he'd spent six months in juvenile detention. But I didn't think he was tough and didn't mistake the fat rolls underneath his white T-shirt for muscles. He annoyed me by teasing me about being younger than him.

We were on our way to a party. The images of parties at Graham's were gone, replaced by dark basements and deplorable smells. Our parties consisted of cramming as many people as possible into the basement of a house or trailer somewhere in the country. Most of the time the party lacked furniture or effective plumbing. We'd squeeze in on the few pieces of ratty and torn furniture, which looked worse than any furniture at the Salvation Army. Once the furniture was occupied, the bodies of people lined the walls. A mixture of alcohol, pot, urine, body odor, and puke permeated the air. After a while, I didn't even notice the smell. There was always a radio tuned to the classic rock station. We drank and passed around drugs until the room exploded into meaningless conversation.

There was a strange excitement in the car. I could sense it in my stomach, a gnawing like I used to get before a big game. I chewed on my fingernails, anxiously watching up front as Justin grabbed a Fleetwood Mac CD from the glove compartment. He put it on his lap as Strom turned the car onto a gravel road, out of sight from the highway. The car stopped and Strom reached under his seat, pulling out a Ziploc freezer bag. The bag was filled with chunks of dirty white the size of miniature Snickers bars wrapped in cellophane. He took out a chunk and handed it to Justin. Justin took a razor from his pocket and began to chop it up, forming long trails of powder across the CD. My heart started to beat faster in anticipation and my palms started to sweat. I watched them snort the powder up their noses, holding my breath, hoping to get in on it.

As Justin handed me the CD covered with powder, Tim warned, "I don't think you should do this."

I ignored him and looked up at Strom in the rearview mirror. He winked at me, and I smiled back. I took the rolled-up dollar bill, brought my face down to the powder, stuck the bill at the beginning of a thick, long trail of white and plugged my left nostril. I started at the top of the line and snorted all the way to the bottom. My nose burned terribly, my eyes watered, and I gagged as I felt a putrid drip down the back of my throat. I kept sniffing over and over again as my nose tingled and burned all the way up to my head. I held back the urge to gag.

I passed the CD to Tim and waited for something to happen. It wasn't long before a powerful rush shot through my body and my heart started to beat faster while my mind became crystal clear. Thoughts flew through my head with a clarity that hadn't been there for so long. I could feel my hair growing. I was light and free, completely energized. My feet moved back and forth. I hadn't run in years, but I felt like I could run a marathon if I got out of the car. I wanted to jump up and down, to scream and laugh hysterically. I felt as if the excitement might burst through my chest at any moment.

I looked up front and caught Justin and Strom exchanging wide smiles with each other. Strom elbowed Justin, "Told ya she'd love it."

He was right. I'd been in a stoned numbness for so long that having clarity in my mind made me ecstatic. Ideas rushed through my head and I couldn't get my words out fast enough. We spent the night driving from basement to basement, dropping off meth and filling our noses with the magical powder. I could drink booze like it was water. Smoking pot was just like smoking a cigarette.

I followed Strom in and out of different rooms at strange houses. My nose started to bleed and he dropped chunks of powder into my Captain Morgan so I could drink it instead. It wasn't long before strangers sitting on a bed showed me how to lay a long line on tinfoil, hold my lighter underneath it until it smoked, and then bring my face down into the smoke. The smoke filled my brain with sweetness. I would've put the powder anywhere.

We dropped Tim off at his grandma's house at three in the morning. Cherries appeared behind us as we were driving to our next stop.

Strom looked into the rearview mirror, "Fuck."

Justin flipped open the glove compartment and began pulling out baggies and folds of powder. He frantically handed them to me.

"Crotch 'em," Strom said.

He slowed the car down while I shoved the meth down my pants and into my underwear. We came to a stop. Squeezing my knee, Strom said, "Be cool. Don't worry. They can't search your crotch 'cause you're a minor and a chick."

I didn't care if they searched my crotch and I

got in trouble. Strom and everyone he'd introduced me to had been arrested and I wanted him to know I'd get in trouble for him. He rolled down his window and the officer peered into the car. He shone his flashlight into Strom's eyes, my eyes, and finally Justin's. I squinted in revulsion.

"Where you guys been tonight?"

"At a friend's house," Strom said.

"Doing what?"

"Hangin' out."

"Been drinking?"

All three of us shook our heads in unison. I turned around to see another squad car pulling up behind us. I didn't think it was possible for my heart to beat any faster, but it did.

"I smell alcohol and I'm gonna ask you to get out of the car one by one." The cop pointed to Justin. "You first."

Justin stepped out and the cop walked over to meet him. He put Justin's arms on top of the car and started to pat him down. Strom quickly rolled up his window.

Looking straight ahead, he whispered, "Whatever you do, just don't let that shit fall out of your crotch. They're gonna know you've been drinking, but they can't prove anything else. Whatever he says he knows—he doesn't know shit. Just keep your mouth shut and you'll be cool."

I kept nodding my head. When my turn came to step out of the car, I looked over at Strom one last time to assure him not to worry. I followed the cop's instructions. I stuck my tongue out for him to feel, followed his light with my eyes, stood on one foot, said my ABCs, walked ten steps forward and took a breath test.

"You're drunk. What else are you on?"

"Nothin'."

"I'm going to ask you to empty your pockets." I pulled the inside of my pockets out, and my one-hitter clanked to the street. The officer picked it up. I shrugged my shoulders. "Turn around." I turned around and heard the sound of metal jingling. I felt the pressure of the cuffs on my wrists and heard the clicks. He turned me around and walked me back to the squad car.

The crisscross wire mesh was close to my face, and my knees smashed up against it, but I didn't care. I was proud because I'd kept the drugs safe. I smiled. I'd just earned a badge symbolizing I was officially a badass.

The cops brought me down to the station and called my parents to get me. I slid into their blue minivan, and neither of them uttered a word. The sun was coming up when we got home. I ran downstairs to my room and called Strom.

"I didn't expect you to answer," I said when he picked up. They'd taken Strom and Justin to jail.

"Hamilton bailed me out."

"There's no way I'm going to be able to sleep tonight."

Strom laughed. "Nope. You got that right. So, we took away your virginity tonight."

"What do ya mean?"

"Wait and see," he said.

I had no idea what he was talking about until a year later when I took away a twelve-year-old girl's virginity. By that time, I was fully immersed in the court system. I had a probation officer, a social worker, and a judge who made decisions for me and ruled my life. I'd just been put on a court-ordered curfew after being charged with my third minor consumption, possession of marijuana, possession of paraphernalia, and failing all of my drug tests.

The conditions of my curfew were clear. I was to be at my parents' house every night by ten and couldn't leave until eight the next morning. If I didn't make it home or left during the night, my parents were court-ordered to call the police. Every time I broke my curfew, it was a probation violation that moved me closer to spending nine months in a juvenile detention center.

I didn't want to get sent to a juvenile detention center so I did my best to comply with the curfew. I'd come home at my assigned time and hang out downstairs in my bedroom. My mom would get up periodically to check on me. By this time, I was hooked on meth, so sleeping was rarely an option. I'd lie in my bed with my eyes closed, wishing to sleep and knowing it was no use. I sipped on the vodka hidden in Mountain Dew bottles on the nightstand next to my bed. My CDs repeated themselves over and over again as candles burned down to nothing on my dresser. I'd stare at my blue alarm clock's red digits, counting every minute until I could leave again.

I alternated between lying in my bed and sitting in the bathroom with the door locked. My dad had remodeled the old storage room into a small bathroom. It was cramped with the necessary toilet, sink, and shower. There was a small space between the sink and the wall where I sat cross-legged on the white tiles. I snorted my lines off the toilet lid. The only sound was the overhead fan, constantly whirring in a vain attempt to clear the air of my endless pot smoke.

My only company for hours was my mind. The bathroom grew smaller and smaller as the voices running through my head grew louder and louder. I'd plot ways to burn the house down or fantasize about killing myself with the pink razors in the shower that I used to shave my legs. The small blue flowers on the wallpaper talked to me, encouraging my plans and harassing my weakness for being compliant to the rules.

On one of those nights, I stepped outside to smoke a joint. It wouldn't do any good for the madness in my mind but it was a comforting habit. My body ached for sleep, for some sort of a rest, but my mind ran on in circles. My thoughts were stuck on a treadmill that never slowed down.

The garage was attached to the left side of the house and I walked around the corner to stand beside it. I noticed a dark figure making its way through the field across from me. As it got closer, I saw it was Tom carrying a case of beer. All of my friends knew about my restrictions and now and then, when nothing else was going on, they'd show up. It was a welcome break from my solitude, but I wasn't happy to see Tom because he was really loud and would wake my parents.

The minute he got near enough to hear me, I said, "You gotta go."

"C'mon, girl. Just have a beer with me." He leaned next to me on the garage, hitting a garbage can and causing it to clang.

"Shh. I'm going inside," I said, finishing my joint. "You can leave me a couple beers, but I've gotta go in."

"Man!" he yelled. "This is fuckin' bullshit! You shouldn't have to put up with this shit! They can't trap you here. You've got rights! Mother-"

"Tom, shut up. You're gonna wake-"

"I don't give a fuck! I'll-"

"Shut up," I hissed through gritted teeth, stressing every syllable. "I mean it. Get outta here."

"I don't have to-"

My dad's voice broke into the night. "Elizabeth?"

"Shit. Get outta here."

Tom grabbed his case of beer from the ground

and took off running back through the field. I walked to the front of the garage. My dad marched towards me. He reached me quickly, took my chin in his hand, and peered into my eyes. "What are you doing out here?"

I kept my voice low, trying not to anger him further. I didn't want to fight. "Smoking before I go to bed."

"I'm so tired of your games," he hissed, flicking my chin with his other hand, making my teeth clank against each other. "You think you're so tough."

"Dad, I just want to go to bed."

He paid no attention. He kept flicking my chin with the top of his hand. "You aren't so tough. What? What? You wanna go a couple rounds?"

"Leave me alone. I'm not doing anything. I was just getting ready to go in the house." I didn't move from my spot. He pushed me backward and jumped in my face.

"Please, I don't wanna fight." I looked at the ground, avoiding his eyes.

"Oh yeah, let's see how tough you are. C'mon tough girl. Let's see what you've got." With both hands, he grabbed me by my shoulders and shoved me again. I tried to move around him. He jerked my shoulders from behind, snapping me back. My mom opened the front door and stood on the steps with her pink bathrobe tucked around her.

"Hon, leave her alone," she called out, her small body shivering from the cold.

He ignored her. His fingernails dug into my arms as he pulled me toward him. I pulled away and ran down the driveway, his footsteps pounding behind me.

"You leave this yard and I call the cops. You're not so in control now are ya little girl?"

"Leave me alone!" I stopped at the end of the driveway and turned to face him.

He stormed towards me, grabbed my head in both of his hands, and jerked me within inches of his nose.

"You're not tough. And you're not in control." His spit hit my face.

"Leave her alone. Come inside, please," my mom said. She hadn't moved from her spot on the steps.

He slapped me under my chin with the back of his hand. I bit my tongue as my jaw snapped closed. Hatred and rage seethed through my body as a rush of air exploded in my head.

"I hate you!" I punched him in the face.

"I'm calling the cops, you little brat." He turned around and strutted towards the house.

I wanted to leave, to run across the field and find Strom, but I was trapped. My heart thumped against my chest. I took out a cigarette, brought it to my lips, and lit it.

I hate him. I hate this house. I hate this bullshit.

I brought my cigarette in and out of my mouth, taking hurried drags and blowing the smoke out rapidly.

Calm down. Don't leave. He's gonna go to bed. You didn't do anything wrong. He's not gonna call the cops.

Slowly, my heart quit thumping, and my breathing returned to normal. I was filled with a mixture of surprise and anger when I spotted red lights making their way down my street. I tossed my cigarette and ground it out with the tip of my shoe.

Three squad cars arrived. One pulled into the driveway and the other two cars parked on the street. Two cops stepped out of the car in the driveway. I recognized the short fat one, Walt

Mitchell, because he'd arrested me before. I didn't know the tall bald guy.

"What's going on here, Elizabeth?" Walt asked, shining his flashlight into my squinting eyes.

"Nothin'."

My dad burst through the front door, running across the yard. My mom followed behind, still clad in her pink bathrobe. "Take her away. She's out of control." He pointed to the red mark underneath his eye. "She attacked me."

"I did not."

Walt moved behind me and took hold of my arms.

"What the fuck. You can't take me away. I didn't do anything wrong!"

The handcuffs jingled. I jerked away, but he held tight.

"See, told ya she's out of control. This is what we have to live with," my dad said in a calm voice that infuriated me.

"Fuck you!" I kicked at Walt's legs.

As I struggled to get free, Walt said firmly, "Calm down, don't make this hard."

"Ask my mom. She saw the whole thing. He started it. I was just defending myself." I heard the click of the cuffs behind me.

Walt turned me around with him to look at my mom. "Is she telling the truth?"

My mom looked at Walt and avoided looking at me. "I didn't see anything."

"Let's go," Walt said. He pushed me toward the squad car and the tall cop opened the back door for me. I slid in, staring straight ahead, refusing to watch my parents walk back into the house without me. The police scanner crackled in the background as Walt and the other cop took their places up front. The other two squad cars pulled away. I watched their red taillights disappear down the street.

"We've got the juvenile in custody," Walt spoke into the CB. "We're en route."

Walt looked over his shoulder at me as he backed out of the driveway. "Kid, you just keep digging a bigger hole for yourself."

Normally, I would've given him an angry comment, but I didn't have it in me. I stared out the window at the stars in the sky, shining brightly because the moon wasn't in sight, wishing my mom had told the truth. A wave of despair washed over me. When it came down to my mom choosing between my dad and me, she'd always choose him.

She'd told me since I was a little girl that he was the man of the house, and she would do whatever he instructed. She'd explained to me many times in the past, "The Bible tells wives to submit to their husbands and I have to do what the Bible says. Your dad has to come first."

I stared at the stars, wishing there was some way I could disappear. I wanted to vaporize into the empty black spaces between them. It seemed like we drove forever before pulling into a driveway leading up to a two-story house.

"Where are we?" I asked.

"Mrs. Morrison's house. She takes in foster kids. You'll be staying here tonight." Walt opened his door and stepped out. He unlatched mine, releasing me into the driveway.

"C'mon, let's go." He pointed to the house.

"Can't you take the cuffs off?" I asked.

"Nice try, kid. Move it." He held my arm and walked me up the steps. The door opened before he had a chance to knock.

Mrs. Morrison was an older woman wearing a red nightgown that trailed down to her knees and a face lined with stress and tension. Wrinkles formed at the corners of her mouth from years of frowning.

Her eyes were small and pointed, hidden by round glasses. She ushered us inside, telling Walt, "I'll call her probation officer in the morning."

"Okay." Walt turned me around, undid the cuffs and left. Mrs. Morrison shut the door behind him.

"Are you on birth control?" Her voice was high like she had to squeeze to get it out.

I stared at her. What did that have to do with anything?

"Not gonna talk to me, huh? You come into my house in the middle of the night and don't have the decency to answer my questions. You kids are all so ungrateful," she said.

She turned to punch in numbers on a pad next to the door. There were huge varicose veins wrapping themselves around her calves that peeked out from underneath her gown. I couldn't help but wonder what would happen if I poked one with a pin.

She turned around. "What are you smiling at?"

"Nothing," I mumbled, still grinning.

"The alarm is set. If you try to go out the door or any of the windows, it's wired directly to the police station. Don't even try it." I didn't understand how her voice could be so high and forced at the same time.

"Can I go to bed now?"

"You'll be sleeping with Molly, but I'm not going to disturb her just because you're here." She pointed to a couch in the living room. "Sleep there."

I walked over and sat on the couch, in front of a large window. It was hard and smelled like old people. Mrs. Morrison hovered over me. She had shoulders the width of football players. She dropped a folded blanket on me.

"Here." She sighed as if I'd just required her to run ten laps around the house. "Oh, and by the way, don't expect to be sleeping until noon. In my house, the kids get up early to work."

I heard the sound of her feet shuffling away and a door being latched. I rested my head on my arms and closed my eyes, hoping I'd be able to sleep. Birds were beginning to chirp. I dozed off and woke to someone shaking my shoulder.

"Get up," her high voice broke in. "Molly and Tony have been outside for half an hour. You're going to do your part."

I grunted and rolled over. She grabbed the blanket and tossed it aside.

"God," I moaned.

"I said get up. You will do as you're told. I don't have time for your games. Move."

I slid off the couch to get away from her voice. I walked out the front door, and the sun shone in my eyes, making me shrink in revulsion. I was in the middle of nowhere. A gravel road ran in front of the house and all I could see was a small white house miles down the road. Besides that, there were only lines of trees and cornfields surrounding Mrs. Morrison's house. I walked to the backyard, noticing the form of a boy by the side of a red shed. A pudgy girl bounced up to me.

"Hi, I'm Molly," she said. Her cheeks were chubby as if she hadn't lost all of her baby fat yet. Her short brown hair looked like pieces had been randomly hacked off. "Who are you? Mrs. Morrison told me this morning we got a new girl. I'm so happy. We never get girls, always boys. Boys are so stupid. I hate them. Don't you?"

"I'm Elizabeth and I'm not staying," I said.

"Oh." Her big brown eyes drooped. "I've been here for six months. Tony's been here for like a year or something. Mrs. Morrison loves him. He's like her pet. I guess his dad almost killed him. He doesn't talk about it, though. I've asked him. He just says never mind."

I grunted and walked a few steps over to a big oak tree. I recognized Molly because we rode the same bus in elementary school. She was twelve, the same age as Sarah. I plopped on the ground, sprawling out in the shade.

"We're supposed to pick up sticks in the yard," Molly said.

"Go ahead." I closed my eyes.

"She's gonna get pissed. You don't want to piss her off."

"I don't care."

Molly whispered, as if somehow Mrs. Morrison might hear her from the house. "Really? She doesn't scare you? She scares me. She totally freaks me out when she's mad. You should see her. Her eyes get all huge and her nose flares out. And she yells, which makes her face look so red. Oh my God, she could like yell forever."

"If you're so scared, then you better go pick up sticks."

"Okay." She grabbed her black garbage bag and skipped off. It wasn't long until I fell asleep in my spot underneath the tree.

"She's coming. Get up." Molly kicked my shoe.

I opened my eyes to see Mrs. Morrison stomping across the yard. She was yelling and waving her hands in the air. "Your probation officer is going to be here in five minutes. And don't think I haven't seen you doing nothing. I wish they'd warned me about you."

"Yeah, it's too bad," I said as I stood. "It's too bad I'm not some twelve-year-old kid you can just boss around."

I turned on my heels and walked to the front of the house to wait for Rubin, my probation officer. He arrived shortly in a navy blue car with an Aimes County sticker on the side. He wore his usual button-down dress shirt, tucked into black pants.

"Hello, Elizabeth," he said drawing out the syllables in hello like he always did.

"Hey. Are you taking me to my parents?"

"You're going to be here for a while."

"You've got to be kidding me! First of all, last night was not my fault and second of all, she's a nut job."

"Always so dramatic." He laughed.

"Don't patronize me. I'm serious. She's whacked." I tried to stay calm. "How long?"

"I don't know. We're not sure. You'll at least be here for the weekend-"

"That's three days. I don't have any of my stuff. Nothin'. Not even clothes. I'm not stayin'."

He crossed his arms. "You don't have a choice."

I didn't have any choices because the court system made them for me. I didn't care about not having clothes, but I didn't have any way to get high. Anxiety gripped my mind, the way it did every time I was faced with having to be without chemicals.

"Your mom is going to bring your clothes down to the courthouse and drop them off so that I can bring them to you."

"Why can't she just bring them here?" I asked, running my hands through my hair.

"She doesn't want to. She knows you're mad." He was so calm it made me want to tear the hair out of my head to get an emotional reaction from him. "I'll bring you your stuff some time tomorrow. While you're here—you follow her rules."

"Not a chance," I said.

Rubin shrugged his shoulders. "We'll be in touch."

He was on his way to the next number on his

list. I'd become a case number he filed away at the end of his workday. I stood frozen in my spot, wanting to run but I had nowhere to go.

The weekend dragged. I was exhausted, but couldn't sleep. I lay in the room I shared with Molly, gazing at the cracks in the ceiling, wanting to crawl out of my skin. I couldn't stop sweating and shaking. Nausea wracked my body and every time I moved, my head spun. My body yearned for drugs in the same way a new mother yearns to hold her newborn infant in her arms.

Finally, Monday came. I didn't care where I was going as long as I got to leave. It didn't matter if I was getting locked up because at least then I could stop by my house and get the drugs stashed underneath my mattress. I sat on the front steps and watched the few cars drive by, disappointed each time it wasn't Rubin. After a while, Mrs. Morrison opened the door and handed me the phone. I was shocked because she was the only one who got to use the phone. No one else could receive calls, and you couldn't dial out without using a code that only she had.

"Hello," I said.

Rubin's drawn-out greeting was on the other

line. "Hello, Elizabeth."

"What's going on?"

"It looks like you're going to be staying awhile longer. Your parents both agreed this was the best thing. I-"

"Fuck!" I threw the phone on the ground and stormed outside. This was my dad's way of letting me know he was still in control. He always gained the upper hand. I started punching and kicking the siding on the house until my knuckles bled and my toes ached.

I was allowed the privilege of going to my job at the Dairy Queen while I stayed with Mrs. Morrison. I'd worked part-time at the Dairy Queen since I'd gotten kicked out of school. The only reason I still held the job was because it was easy to steal money from the cash register and it wasn't hard to make ice cream cones when I was high. If I was too messed up to be at the counter, my manager just put me in the kitchen where I flipped burgers during my shift. I was never so happy to be able to go to work.

I got on the phone in the office and called Strom. By this time, he was my closest friend and the only person I trusted. He'd become like a big brother to me. I'd earned my treasured spot next to him, always riding in the passenger seat of his car and on the back of his motorcycle. It was a spot I held proudly.

I told him where I'd been for the past week and that I was without pot or cigarettes to get me through. As usual, he promised to come through for me. Within a few hours, I heard his familiar voice in the speaker at the drive-thru. He requested me to take his order, pulled up to the window, and we made our exchange. I gave him a vanilla cone, and he gave me two packs of cigarettes. One held Marlboro Reds and the other held tightly rolled joints.

"It sucks that you're there," Strom said. "Hopefully, you'll only be there for a few more days. Stay out of trouble and don't do anything stupid."

"I won't."

He smiled. "Let me know if you need anything. Hang in there, kid."

"I always do."

I ran outside afterward, telling my manager the trash needed to be taken out. I lit up a joint behind the dumpster, carefully watching for anyone. The sweetness tasted so good. My nerves relaxed as the familiar numbness crept into my body and filled my head. After work, I returned to the room that Molly and I shared with a smile on my face.

"What happened at work?" she asked. "I haven't seen you smile since you got here."

"I'll tell you tomorrow," I said. She looked at me with a glimmer of excitement in her eyes as we got ready for bed. I slept peacefully for the first time since I'd been brought to Mrs. Morrison's.

The next morning, Molly was anxious to discover what had put a smile on my face. We told Mrs. Morrison we were going for a walk, and headed a mile down the gravel road into a thick area of trees. I made sure we were far enough away from the ever-present eyes of Mrs. Morrison before I pulled out the box of Marlboro Reds holding my joints.

"Have you ever gotten high?" I asked, lighting the joint and bringing it to my lips.

"No, but my sister does. She's always smoking pot. You probably know her. Rachel? Anyways, she gets high. She lives with her boyfriend." Molly watched me inhale the smoke, hold it in, and then exhale. She cocked her head to the side, her gaze fixed on me and her eyes filled with curiosity. I didn't want to push her. It had to be her choice. I wanted her to get high, though. There was no way she'd tell on me if she got high. If she didn't, I didn't know what I'd do to keep her quiet. I didn't want to have to resort to threatening her because she was so sweet.

"What does it feel like?" she asked after I was halfway through the joint.

I chose my words carefully, fully aware of the manipulation that lay behind them. "It's kind of hard to explain. You don't really know until you've tried it."

"I wanna get high. I'm not scared. They say drugs are bad, but whatever. Who cares? I don't. God, you're so cool. My sister never lets me get high with her."

I had a sick feeling in the pit of my stomach, but it didn't stop me. I taught her how to smoke a joint in the same way someone had taught me. I showed her how to hold it, put her lips around it, and keep the smoke in her lungs for as long as possible before releasing it back into the air. Then, I handed it to her. She took it and focused on her performance. She brought it to her lips and began to inhale. She coughed and choked on the smoke as it escaped from her nose and mouth in thick clouds.

"Hold it in," I said, giggling.

She kept on smoking, eventually being able to hold the smoke in her lungs. We smoked another joint before she started to feel it since it was her first time. I watched the transformation take place. Her eyes grew bloodshot and her lids grew heavy. They drooped down as if she had a slight case of Down's syndrome. She had a goofy smile on her face and she started to laugh uncontrollably.

"I ... think ... " she giggled a bit. "I'm ... high..." She burst into laughter and clutched her stomach. "Ohmigod. Mrs. Morrison ... We are so in trouble." She burst into laughter again.

I watched her with a smile on my face, reliving the first time I got high. I missed the silly goofiness it used to bring. I wished I could still feel the way she was feeling. The closest I'd ever get to my first experience was to watch her have hers.

"Do you have any more?" she asked. "I'm thirsty."

She was just like me. She'd want more and eventually never be able to get enough. She'd chase this moment forever just like I chased mine. At that moment, I understood what Strom and Justin had felt the day they gave me my first line of meth. They'd taken away my virginity in the same way I'd just taken away Molly's. Doing a new drug was just like first-time sex because even though you have sex hundreds of times, you always remember your first. At times Molly would hate me, at other times she'd love me, but no matter what, she'd remember me. She'd remember, love, and hate me in the same way I remembered, loved, and hated those who'd taken away my virginity.

Garrison

SEVEN

I was fifteen the first time I got sent to treatment, and didn't remember the first three days there. The last thing I remembered before coming to was walking through my neighbor's field. I was going home to come down after being strung out on meth and tripping on acids for days. I'd just left Strom's house, where I'd been sitting on the brown couch underneath the window, grinding my teeth and trying to remember the last time I'd slept. Strom sat on the floor next to the couch, staring at the dirty white wall across from us. Neither of us talked because our brains were mush and we'd run out of things to say. Thoughts were difficult to formulate and speaking out loud was almost impossible.

According to my mom, I stumbled through the door Monday morning. She met me at the front door. She hadn't seen me since Thursday when I'd told her I was going up town to get a pack of cigarettes. Although she hadn't heard from me, she'd heard from others about me. A woman had called her earlier that morning refusing to give her name.

"Your daughter is going to die. I saw her last night. I don't know if you know this, but she hangs out with a 26-year-old guy, Ryan Hedstrom. He's the biggest drug dealer in Oxford. He's been in lots of trouble with the law. Your daughter is always with him, and she's hooked on meth."

"How do you know all this? Are you sure?"

"Positive. I can't tell you how I know, but I'm telling the truth. When was the last time you looked at her? Have you noticed her eyes? Look at her nose and the way it drips constantly. I bet she constantly grinds her teeth. She's so skinny she looks like she's about ready to fall through her own asshole. Those are all signs of using meth."

"I appreciate all of this, but I can take care of my daughter."

"I called her probation officer-"

"How do you know her probation officer?"

"I'm involved with the police department. I've

been dealing with Ryan Hedstrom for a while. Don't worry, he's going to jail. But I just think it's so sad to see a little girl running around with him. I felt compelled to call and tell you how much trouble your daughter is in. If you don't do something quick, you're gonna lose her."

As soon as my mom hung up the phone, it rang again. This time, it was Rubin. He informed my mom that the woman worked undercover for the police department and arrangements had been made to bust Strom and others involved in our drug dealing circle. They'd be going to jail but I wouldn't because I was a juvenile. He suggested my parents take me to treatment as soon as possible.

When I got home that Monday morning, my mom noticed my huge pupils, the outline of my bones underneath my clothes, my sunken face and yellow skin. She had no choice but to accept that the woman had been telling the truth, and I was doing a lot more than smoking pot. I stumbled past her and went downstairs to my bedroom and lay on the bed. She followed me and started throwing my clothes into a bag.

"What's going on?" I asked.

"We're taking you to get some help."

"I'll be fine. Seriously. I've been like this many times. You don't have to worry." I must've thought she was talking about taking me to see a doctor.

"We're taking you to treatment. The people there will help you get off drugs."

My mom said I went hysterical, twisting and turning on my bed as if I was having a seizure. I alternated between screaming hysterically and bawling like a small child. One minute I was screaming, "You can't take my drugs away! You can't! Stay the fuck away from me! I'm not going! Fuck! You can't do this!" The next minute I was crying, "Please, ohmigod, you can't do this to me. Please! I'm going to die."

My mom just kept throwing clothes into a bag and praying quietly.

"There is no God." I sat up and glared at her. "Don't you dare try to tell me to believe in God. He hates me and I hate him."

My next conscious memory was three days later, standing next to Lindsey, a girl I'd partied with before, in an unfamiliar bathroom. I didn't know where I was, how I'd gotten there, or what day it was. None of this was unusual. I was losing more and more chunks of time, coming to in the middle of conversations I was having happened more and more frequently.

My mind was a blur, overloaded with chemicals and booze, coupled with starvation because the thought of food made my stomach heave. I checked in and out of consciousness. I liked it. It was as close to death as I could get without physically dying.

I looked around at the toilet, sink, and tub made of shiny white porcelain. I stared at Lindsey, who was leaning over the sink and spitting out wet brown slime. I'd gotten good at not letting anyone know I didn't know where I was or what was going on. Sometimes I could put the pieces together and figure it out. But most of the time, I didn't even try because it was only a matter of time until I'd black out again.

"C'mon," she said. "You can't go to group with chew in your mouth, dumbass."

I realized I had a thick wad of chew in my mouth. I did what I was told and dug it out of my mouth, spitting my brown slime into the sink next to hers. Why was I chewing? What had I gotten myself into?

"What's group?" I asked.

She giggled. "Shut up, let's go."

I followed her out of the bathroom and walked through a small room with a bed and desk. She opened the door and we stepped into a long hallway. The hallway was lined with doors on both sides. There was a big desk at the front of the hall. Nurses dressed in white scurried around it, answering the phone and talking to each other.

I'm in a hospital. How did I get here? What's Lindsey doing here? Why am I in jeans if I'm in a hospital?

Lindsey opened a door on the left right before we reached the nurse's station. I followed her into a big room. Windows with thick black trim lined an entire wall. There were fifteen kids sitting on chairs arranged in a circle. Behind the chairs was a table covered with playing cards and a Scrabble game. An entertainment center with a TV stood at the front of the room.

Lindsey sat in one of the chairs in the circle and I took the empty one next to her. I eyed the girl across from me. She was curled into a ball with her legs tucked underneath her. Short, red hair haphazardly framed her face and freckles sprinkled her nose. She reminded me of a Strawberry

Shortcake doll with her pale skin and rosy lips. She clutched a big white teddy bear in her arms.

I didn't have time to finish my observations before the door opened. A woman walked in with brown hair neatly curled and sprayed in place. She wore a red sweater stretched tightly across her chest. Her upper body was slender but from the waist down she ballooned into wide hips and a huge bottom. She wore red lipstick and makeup that looked like it took hours to perfect. She smiled at everyone and stood next to me.

"Should we open?" she asked, cheerfully.

Everyone stood and grabbed hands with the person standing next to them, so I stood too. Lindsey and the woman each grabbed one of my hands. I jerked them away.

"Elizabeth," the woman said, frowning at me. "Let's not go through this again."

She knows my name. This is weird.

I took her hand. They recited a prayer together. I was surprised I'd never heard it before. I didn't think there were any prayers I didn't know. I looked at Lindsey. She had her eyes closed and a smile pulled at the corners of her mouth. What was she doing? Where was I? As soon as the prayer ended, they dropped hands and sat down. Everyone seemed to know what was going on and acted like they were doing a perfectly normal activity.

"Let's do introductions," the woman said. Her voice was one of those fake ones where you could hear the forced happiness behind it.

"I'm Jeremy. I'm an alcoholic and a drug addict," The boy with the long hair, dressed in black, announced from the right-hand part of the circle.

"I'm Jay. I'm an alcoholic," the Latino-looking kid next to him said.

I listened and watched as each kid in the circle took a turn saying their name and announcing that they were a drug addict or an alcoholic.

Oh my God. I'm in treatment. Jesus Christ. How did I get here?

My friend Bobby had gone to treatment a few months before and he'd told me about it. He'd shared stories about everyone sitting around in circles just like we were doing now. He said the counselors tried to brainwash you into getting sober by getting you to cry about your life and then tricked you into believing getting sober would make you feel better. They'd almost succeeded in brainwashing Bobby. He'd sworn he was done doing drugs after he got out. But, drugs weren't his biggest problem. He'd just had a nervous breakdown after Nate died.

Nate had been Bobby's best friend and one of my close friends, too. Strom had introduced us. We were the only high school kids in the group and soon became a threesome. We spent lots of our time selling drugs at the high schools in our area. Six months ago, Nate had died from an overdose that the papers reported as undiagnosed heart failure. I did my best not to think about his death but the memories flooded back as I sat in the circle of chairs surrounded by strangers.

On the night he died, the phone rang outside my bedroom door. It stopped and then started again, waking me. I was annoyed to be awake because I only went home to sleep when I needed to come down and didn't like to be disturbed during it. I rolled out of bed and walked to the phone.

"Hello," I said groggily.

"Elizabeth! Elizabeth! I'm comin' to get ya. I'm coming to get ya."

"Huh? Bobby, no. Not tonight. I'm tired."

"But Nate, Nate. He's on the driveway-"

"My driveway?"

"Nonono. The driveway. His driveway. I'm coming. There's lights, everywhere. I'm telling ya. Lights! Red! Nate, ohmigod!" Bobby was crying.

"What are you talking about?" I asked. "Did you drop again tonight?"

"Yes. No. The cops. All the cherries. My brother saw. He's dead. They say he is. I'm coming."

"Whoa, hon, slow the fuck down. You need to chill out. Are you tripping?"

"I don't know. Acid. Yes. Nate."

"Okay, you listen to me, are you listening?"

"Yes, but Elizabeth ... I ..."

"Just listen to me. You're gonna take a few deep breaths. You're havin' a bad trip. You just need to settle down." Bobby had bad trips a lot but it was usually pretty easy to talk him down. "Nate is fine. I just talked to him last night. He's not in anyone's driveway. He's okay. You're okay. Do you hear me?"

"Yes." He sounded like a little boy.

"You're gonna be fine. It's just the drugs messing with your mind. You can't let them take over. You control the trip. The trip doesn't control you. Okay, are ya with me?"

He took huge gulping breaths. "Yes, yes, I am. Are you sure?"

"Positive. Everything is fine. Listen, you've been up for too long and are starting to lose it. You've just gotta come down for a while."

"I do. Can I come sleep with you?"

"Now you sound like yourself." I giggled.

He laughed. "I guess. Still, can I?"

"Darlin', you're never gonna get in my bed. Are you gonna be okay? 'Cause I really wanna go back to bed."

"Yeah." The hysteria in his voice was gone.

"Okay, I'll call ya tomorrow."

"Promise?"

"Promise."

"I love you, Elizabeth. Thanks."

"You, too. Talk to ya tomorrow." I curled back up in bed.

The next day I discovered Bobby wasn't having a bad trip and Nate had died on his driveway. His heart had stopped and the paramedics weren't able to revive him. My mom drove me to the funeral. I expected her to comfort me because I'd lost a friend and I'd never lost anyone close to me before, but she only spoke once during the ride.

"Was he saved?" she asked. I shrugged my shoulders. She let out a deep sigh. "Well, I hope he was." What she really meant was that she hoped he wasn't burning in hell.

Bobby started to go nuts shortly after the funeral. He'd burst into tears for no reason and not be able to stop. He'd always gotten into fights, but now he started to freak out and get violent without being provoked. At parties, he'd suddenly jump up and grab someone's head, smashing his head against theirs. He punched walls and crashed his car into stop signs. He started to call me up in the middle of the night, talking about Nate and how he wished it'd been him. I didn't want to think about Nate and talking to Bobby made me do that. I always tried to get him to talk about something else, but it was no use. Shortly after one of our late night conversations, I didn't hear from him or see him for three days. I kept calling his house.

Finally, his mom answered the phone.

"Is Bobby there?" I asked.

"No. Is this Elizabeth?"

"Yes."

"Listen to me. Bobby is in treatment. He's getting off drugs. You stay away from him. He doesn't want to talk to you and I don't want you anywhere near him. You tell that friend of yours, that unemployed loser Strom who sells drugs to little kids, to stay the hell away from my son, too. You people are evil." She hung up.

I blew her off. I was used to parents not wanting their kids to hang around me. I ran into Bobby at a gas station about a month later.

"Hey!" I ran through the parking lot to his car.

He turned around. "Hey."

He looked different. His eyes were bright and shining. His skin glowed and he'd gained weight. He looked like an actual high school student in his clean blue jeans and black hooded sweatshirt.

"What's up? I didn't even know you got out. What are you doin' tonight?" I asked.

"Goin' to a meeting," he said.

"A meeting? For what?"

"It's for treatment. I go to AA meetings." He tapped his feet against each other.

"Okay. Do ya wanna get high before ya go?" I motioned to the car I was in.

"I don't get high. I'm sober." He glared at me.

What had they done to him? I didn't know what to say. We stood there, staring at each other in awkward silence.

"Look, I can't talk to you. It's not good for me."

"You've got to be kidding me. Since when are you better than me?"

"I'm not. You wouldn't understand. Just leave me alone." He opened his car door and jumped in without looking at me.

I didn't understand then, but once I was in treatment it was easy to see how he'd been brainwashed. The counselors and staff were good at trying to convince you to get sober. They promised you'd be happy if you did. They said you needed to stay away from your old friends because they only used you to get high and didn't really care about you. The counselors tried to find your weak spot and break you down. They called it, "getting through your denial."

Staff members told me over and over again, "Elizabeth, you're going to die. You're a chronic alcoholic and drug addict."

Their death threats meant nothing to me. For a death threat to be effective, the person threatened has to want to live and I'd been intent on destroying myself for a long time.

The whole treatment structure was foreign and

bizarre. I was furious because not only did I not have any drugs, I wasn't allowed to smoke cigarettes. My head pounded and my stomach rotated between waves of nausea and shooting pains. I wanted to crawl into bed and sleep until it was time for me to get out. Much like everything I wanted to do, it wasn't allowed because there was a strict schedule to follow.

I was awakened each morning by seven and instructed to get out of bed. They expected us to eat breakfast in the cafeteria by eight, but I couldn't get my body out of bed. It ached and shook. It hurt to lift my head off the pillow. While the other kids filed down to the cafeteria, I lay in bed, pulling the pillow over by head whenever staff came in to wake me up.

After hours of staff coming to my room and trying to get me up, I'd grudgingly get out of bed. I didn't bother to shower or get out of my pajamas. Mornings were spent listening to different people lecture about the effects of different drugs and booze on the body and mind. I wasn't interested in anything the speakers had to say. I already knew drugs were poison and messed you up—that was the point of using them. I'd curl into a chair in a corner of the room and fall back to sleep.

After our lecture, I plodded in my pajamas upstairs to a makeshift classroom. I hated going because I didn't go to school on the outside and didn't see why I should have to go while in treatment. It didn't resemble any form of school I'd ever seen. The two teachers could be better classified as advanced babysitters. All they did was pass out worksheets that nobody ever completed.

Next came lunch. We walked through an underground tunnel that connected the treatment center to the regular part of the hospital. Filing in line with our trays, our nametags announced to everyone else that we were the kids in treatment. We ate in a room off to the side of the cafeteria, away from the doctors and nurses. I couldn't eat. Every time I tried to put something in my stomach, I ended up running to the bathroom and throwing up. It'd been about a year since I'd started to throw up blood. I hated the way it hung from my throat before it dropped in thick globs into the toilet. It was easier not to eat.

Group therapy filled the afternoon. This was where the serious mind games took place. The main counselor, Dave Bateman, led group. He was a short, stocky man with black hair slicked back into a tight ponytail. He wore jeans and T-shirts and looked young enough to pass for a patient. Long, dark lashes framed his huge blue eyes. His eyes were striking, as if they could look right through you. His face was serious but easily broke into a smile and laughter. He introduced himself as a recovered drug addict and an alcoholic.

He opened the brainwashing sessions with, "Let's go around the room and check in."

One by one, we'd go around the circle introducing ourselves and talking about any issues that had occurred since the last group. It didn't take long for me to learn that issues were a big deal in treatment. They were the things the treatment staff thought we needed to talk about to feel better. Supposedly, we all had them and anything could qualify as one. The Strawberry Shortcake girl, Amy, always went first, and it was the same routine every time. She'd burst into tears after she identified herself as an alcoholic.

"What's wrong, Amy?" Dave would ask.

"I can't talk about it," she'd sniffle. Her short, chubby friend, whose name was also Amy, would put her arm around her and hand her a Kleenex.

Dave would encourage her. "C'mon. You can talk about it. Talking about it takes the power away."

I didn't understand what he meant when he'd give his speeches about taking the power away from our issues. What kind of power could our issues possibly have? And how could talking about our feelings change anything? I didn't see the point to all the whining and crying.

I'd roll my eyes and slump in my chair whenever Amy cried. It wasn't the sort of crying that allowed you to still hold on to some of your dignity. It was the ugly-face cry that scrunches up your face in a way that looks like you've been constipated for years and snot drips everywhere. Amy always said she couldn't talk about what was bothering her, but it was only a few minutes before she started rambling. She always had a problem. Some days it was a letter she'd gotten from a friend or boyfriend, other times she'd had a bad dream, or wanted to get high. The list of her problems was endless. Her problems seemed trivial and juvenile. I figured she was a spoiled rich girl whose parents found out she smoked pot and put her in treatment. I felt the same way about most of the other kids. I had my own routine for checking in when my turn came around.

"Elizabeth, how are you today?" Dave would ask, shifting the focus on me.

"Fine," I'd reply, crossing my arms across my chest.

Inevitably, the next question from his mouth was, "How are you feeling?"

"Just waiting to get outta here. This whole thing is stupid."

Silence would follow while everyone stared at me. I stared back at them with no expression on my face. I worked hard at making sure my face was a blank slate. Slowly, they'd all look away, except for Dave. His eyes remained glued to me.

"Anyone have any feedback for Elizabeth?" Dave would break the silence, still staring at me, watching for any sign of weakness that he could jump on. I gave him none.

Usually, one of the Amys would speak up. "I don't like Elizabeth's negative attitude. All she talks about is getting high. It threatens my sobriety."

"Why don't you tell her?" Dave asked. "Tell her how it makes you feel."

It was such a comical part of group. The kids

talked about people as if they weren't there. Everyone spoke to Dave first like they needed his permission to speak to the person they had a problem with. The focus was always on feelings. It nauseated me. I lived to get as out of touch as possible with my feelings and saw no good reason to feel them. The only feeling I was comfortable with was anger and that was the one feeling we weren't supposed to express. Supposedly, it wasn't a real emotion but rather a cover-up for other emotions.

I laughed at the Amys who were so threatened by my negative attitude. "Too bad. If you really wanted to be sober, you wouldn't be bothered by me talking about getting high. I can't help it if you still want to do it. Maybe it's your problem. Anyone got anything else to say?"

My challenge was always met with silence. The other kids were scared of me and didn't like me. However, everyone had to meet with Dave a few times a week on an individual basis, and it was much harder to remain cold and aloof when we were alone. His office was small, with two windows behind his desk. His desk was covered with papers and the thick binders that counselors and staff wrote in. There were two blue chairs in front of his desk for patients. Every inch of wall space was lined with bookshelves overflowing with titles like *Of Course You're Angry* and *Learning to Live with Addiction*.

The door would shut behind us and there wasn't enough air for me to breathe. Dave would lean back in his chair behind his desk, arms folded behind his head. His eyes bored into me. I wanted to jump through the window behind him and run as fast as I could down the street. I couldn't, which only increased the panic of being trapped. I hated our sessions, but there was also a part of me intrigued with Dave.

"The others on the unit are threatened by you. Do you like that?" He asked during one of our sessions.

I shrugged my shoulders. "I really don't care. It's not my problem."

He leaned forward in his chair. "Doesn't it ever get tiring trying to be so tough all the time?"

I shook my head.

Don't trust him. Don't trust him.

"You know being tough is going to kill you, right? His eyes filled with sadness that looked genuine.

"I don't care." I stared out the window, watching hospital workers walk across the sidewalk.

"I happen to think you've got a lot to live for." He stood up. "You want to know what I think? No, I don't care if you want to know or not. I'm going to tell you. You don't fool me for one second. I don't buy your tough girl routine. I think you're in a lot of pain and inside of you is a little girl whose heart is breaking."

My head began to swim. I felt dizzy. He walked around his desk and stood in front of my chair. I refused to look at him, looking down at his tennis shoes instead—worn, black Converse.

Stay unaffected. He's just trying to break you. This is what he does. It's his job.

"I care about you and I'm not just saying that. I think there's a huge part of you that just wants someone to listen and understand you, but you're too damn afraid. You've been hurt a lot, huh?"

"You don't even know me." I switched my gaze to the carpet on the floor, trying to disappear into the gray design.

"I think I know a lot more about you than you

think." He laid his hand gently on my shoulder.

I wanted to pull away, but I was frozen. His touch scared me. I didn't know what to do. I wanted to pull away, but there was a small part that wanted to start to cry and let him hold me like I'd seen him hold the other kids. But, men couldn't be trusted. His touch had to mean something. He pulled his hand away and walked back to his desk. I breathed a sigh of relief, but for a second, I had the urge to tell him to come back.

"What do you want to talk about?" he asked, sifting through the papers on his desk.

"Nothin'," I said having a hard time speaking around the lump in my throat.

"All right. You can go then." He motioned towards the door.

I got up, turned away, and shut the door behind me. I froze there, my head swimming and swirling around. I wanted to open the door and yell at him that I hated it in this place and wanted to leave. I wanted to tell him I didn't want to live and I'd felt that way long before I started doing drugs.

Instead, I walked down the hallway and wandered back to my room, feeling as if I wasn't connected to the body carrying me there. Without drugs, it was as if I was only a mind racing and running wild, disconnected from anything around me. My head raced, my heart pounded, and I couldn't sleep at night. I had to get high.

Getting high was difficult because everything in treatment was structured to prevent it. I started stealing glue from the arts and crafts room when staff had their backs turned. When I met with the psychiatrist, I rummaged through her desk while she was out of the room and found White-Out in her drawer. For some reason, the nurses gave me pills every day. I'd pretend to put them in my mouth and then drop them into the pockets of my jeans. I chopped them up as best I could with a knife I'd stolen from the cafeteria. New patients had to have their bags searched when they got admitted. The nurses would pull out any product that contained alcohol and set it aside. I'd stand by the nurses' desk, watching and waiting to make my move. When they turned their backs, I'd grab the aerosol hairspray or mouthwash, tucking it down my pants.

I accumulated a stash of household products that I hid in the ceiling tiles in my room, shoving things into the space above it. At night and during the day when I couldn't get caught, I'd take something out and go into my bathroom. Dousing paper towels with whatever chemical I had, I'd stick them in the bottom of an empty toilet paper roll, put the cardboard roll into my mouth and take big, deep breaths. It was a cheap buzz that made a vacuum sound in my head, but at least I was getting high. It made me feel somewhat normal, and the sense of an impending breakdown lessened.

On my third week of treatment, a new guy, Ryan, was admitted to the unit. I came out of my room on the way to group and met him in the hallway. He had long blond hair that hung in his face, a Grateful Dead T-shirt, baggy pants, and sandals.

"Hey." He drew out the word like a pothead.

"Hey."

"How long you been here?"

"Too fuckin long," I said.

The door next to us opened and the two Amys appeared, their arms linked together. The Strawberry Shortcake doll shot me a dirty look as they walked past. I flicked them off.

"I hate them."

"You're not too happy to be here, huh?" Ryan

laughed.

"Are you crazy? I hate this place. It's a fuckin' waste of time and space. Everyone always messing with your head and shit. I can't wait till I get out of here so I can get wasted."

A smile spread across his face. He leaned towards me and whispered, "I've got weed."

I grabbed him by the shoulders. "Are you serious?"

He nodded his head. I grabbed his face and brought him towards me, kissing him on the cheek. "Dude, you're my new best friend."

That night I waited until after the second bed check before I inched along the wall to his room. We crammed ourselves into his bathroom that was the size of a small closet. I stood on the toilet while he sat in the sink. He'd rolled a joint using a piece of paper torn out from a Bible. I'd done a lot of things with God's words, but this was the first time I'd ever smoked them.

We smoked quietly, listening for anyone coming. We blew our hits upwards, but with no fan, the smoke quickly filled the bathroom in thick clouds. We coughed and before long tears streamed down our faces.

"See, this is all they needed to do to get me to cry," I said.

But I was disappointed. I expected it to feel like the first time I smoked since I hadn't smoked any weed for three weeks. Instead of uncontrollable giggles, the numbness took over my mind and dulled my senses without giving me any real enjoyment. We had just stepped out of the bathroom when there was a knock at the door. I hid underneath the bed as a nurse walked in.

"I see your feet underneath the bed," she said with her hands on her hips—the same stance every adult has when they've caught you doing something wrong. "You've been smoking pot in here." She walked over to the bathroom door and opened it. Smoke rushed out. I burst out laughing and crawled out from underneath the bed, running back to my room.

The next morning we were both kicked out. I found myself in the office of the counselor with wide hips, signing my discharge papers.

I shook my fist at her. "God, you're a bitch. All you people. You say you care about me? Fuck you. You people don't care. You're all full of shit."

She looked up from her papers. "You've wanted

to leave since you got here. Now you can. I just hope you don't die out there."

"Shut up. You don't care if I die. Fuck you and fuck this stupid place!"

I stormed out of her office, slamming the door behind me. I stomped to my room where my bags lay on my bed, then climbed up on the windowsill, hugging my knees to my chest and staring out at the trees.

What's wrong with me? What just happened? Why am I so pissed? I'm getting out. I've counted every minute since I've gotten here until I could leave. I should be happy. C'mon, Elizabeth, pull yourself together.

I wanted to cry. As much as I hated treatment, there was a part of me that liked having people say they cared about me. There was comfort in knowing that if I ever chose to talk about what my life was like and how I really felt, they'd listen. They might even help me. For a second, I thought about rushing back into the counselor's office and begging her to let me stay. I quickly pushed the idea aside and assured myself that I'd just been brainwashed.

EIGHT

I was released into the care of my parents after I got kicked out of New Hope. I took off in search of Strom as soon as our blue minivan parked in the driveway. I told my mom I was going for a walk to enjoy my new freedom. I spotted his Chrysler LeBaron on the street outside of his parents' trailer. I ran across the street, knocked on the door, and sprang into the trailer before he answered. He was sitting on the brown couch underneath the window in the living room.

"I'm back." I plopped down on the couch next to him.

"Hey kid, I missed ya," he said, tousling my hair. "Like five minutes after you left that morning, the cops showed up at my house."

"Did you get busted with anything on you?"

"I only had like a half on me. Lucky we got rid of the last of our shit to Charlie. His place got raided, too. He'll be goin' to jail for a long time. Sucks for him, but my ass is free." He was rolling a joint on the coffee table.

"Did you know some chick called my mom and told her that all this shit was going down?"

"Yep, some stupid bitch is a narc. That's how they got a search warrant." He threw me the joint. "If I find out, I'll bust up her face. I don't care if she is a chick."

"I'll do it. What kind of trouble are you in?"

"The pigs brought me down to the courthouse and I had to piss in a cup. Let's just say I failed." He laughed. "I did ten days in jail. My court date is coming up. I think I'm gonna use the treatment card. Just go to outpatient or some shit."

"I'd rather be in jail. Seriously. They try so damn hard to sober you up. It's just like Bobby said. A lot of whining and crying." I lit up.

"Was it really that bad?"

"It sucked. I don't even wanna talk about it. Can ya chop me one?"

Meth had become my favorite drug since I'd done my first line. It brought clarity to my mind and made me feel invincible and untouchable. I'd dreamt about it while I'd been away. I'd awakened many nights covered in sweat and tasting the familiar putrid drip in the back of my throat. I needed it now. I'd find some answers once I was high. Everything would become clear while the tingling energy flowed through my body.

I sat next to Strom on the couch, doing lines while we watched TV. I kept waiting for the rush and the startling clarity to hit, but it didn't. My mind moved faster and faster, but none of it made sense.

You can't even stay sober for two hours. Big deal, I never said I was gonna try. The cops are gonna come. They're out to get you. Everyone is in on it. Talk to Strom. I don't know what to say. It's Strom. You always know what to say. What's wrong? I'm paranoid. It's been a long time since you were this high.

I tried to quiet my mind by focusing on the TV, but it was useless. The images passed by my eyes without registering. Strom chatted on as if nothing was unusual, telling me stories about who'd gotten into trouble while I was gone. I couldn't concentrate on anything he was saying. After a few more hours, I had to go home even though I didn't want to. It wasn't a good idea for me to disappear for days. While I was in treatment, my parents had received lots of education on drugs and the signs to watch for. I had a sinking suspicion it wasn't going to be so easy to fool them anymore.

Strom brought me home, dropping me off a block away like he always did. I cheered myself on as I walked the block. *Act sober. Don't look at her. She doesn't know you're high.* My plan was to make my parents trust me again and eventually be able to do whatever I wanted to.

"You're high," my mom said when I walked into the house. "You just got home."

"I'm not high."

"Yeah, right," she huffed, walking away. I walked downstairs to my bedroom and flopped on the bed.

I can't stay here all night. I'll go insane.

I looked around at my familiar walls, and the candles burned down to the same familiar spots. I stared at my Jerry Garcia picture, wishing I'd been born twenty years earlier when doing drugs was more acceptable. My mom stuck her head in and handed me the phone.

"It's for you."

I took it from her and waited for her to shut the door behind her before I answered. "Hello?"

"Hi, Elizabeth," a deep voice said.

It's Dave Bateman, Ohmigod. Why is he calling?

The silence stretched out before he spoke again. "I was upset when I came to work today and found out you were gone."

What do I say? Should I just hang up? Why does he care?

"I was really hoping if you stayed long enough, you'd begin to trust me. You might have even started to believe life could exist without drugs. I wish you would've given it a shot."

"I did."

Why'd I just say that?

"Did you stay clean and sober today?" he asked.

"Pretty much. I just drank a little and got high a couple times.

Why am I lying?

A long pause followed. As usual, I couldn't deal with the silence.

"I'm gonna stay off the hard stuff," I blurted

out. "Just a little weed and I'll probably drink some, but I'm not gonna get all strung out again."

You're already wired.

"Hmm," he said. "Good luck to you, hon. I care about you and I'm not going anywhere."

I responded quickly, "Thanks, bye," and hung up the phone.

The night dragged on. I paced my bedroom back and forth with the music from Courtney Love turned up in an attempt to silence my thoughts. I lay on my bed trying to sleep, but it was no use. I was afraid I was going crazy. For the first time, I wanted to come down.

What's wrong with me? They messed you up.

I left my room as soon as I heard the sound of footsteps upstairs. I trudged upstairs. My parents were sitting at the table in the kitchen eating breakfast. They looked rested and refreshed. My mom's hair was tightly curled and her makeup was impeccably done. My dad's dark hair was still wet from the shower. I didn't know why he wasn't dressed in his work clothes—neatly pressed pants and a collared shirt—since it was way past the time he usually left for the hospital. He was an orthopedic nurse who'd devoted his entire career to one hospital.

"Eat something," my dad said. "We're going for a drive after breakfast."

"I'm not hungry." My stomach was in knots, twisting and turning. I didn't think I'd be able to swallow. I went outside and sat on the front steps smoking cigarettes until they were ready to leave wondering where we were going. I hoped we weren't going to the courthouse to meet with Rubin.

"Where are we going?" I asked after we'd piled into the minivan.

"You'll see," my dad said.

As we drove out of town, I looked over my shoulder and saw my black duffel bag on the seat behind me.

"Hey, wait a minute. What the hell is going on? Where are we going?" I asked.

My dad stared straight ahead, refusing to speak.

"Mom?"

"You need help," she said.

"I don't need help. I just need to be left alone."

We kept on driving, hitting the interstate and heading north. I wanted to jump out of the car, but was trapped. We drove to Minneapolis, parked in a ramp, and walked across a skyway into a hospital. The elevator took us to the fourth floor. When the doors slid open, there was only one metal door in front of us. The sign on the door instructed us to press the intercom to be let in. The sign above the intercom said: Redview Adolescent Locked Unit.

My dad spoke into the intercom. "We're here with Elizabeth Garrison." There was a buzz and the door swung open, leading into a room with a receptionist's desk. There were doors on each side of the room.

A big Latina woman stood in front of us. "I'll take her with me," she said and took my bag from my mom.

"Can't we even see the place?" my mom asked, looking around at the cold gray walls.

"I'm sorry. You'll have to go now," the women said without an ounce of emotion in her voice.

My mom reached towards me, wrapping her arms around me. I could smell the vanilla spray from Bath & Body Works that she always wore. I stood there, unmoving, with my arms at my sides. My dad touched her shoulders and pulled her away. "C'mon," he said. "Let's go."

The woman punched a code into a pad next to

the door and let them out. My mom looked over her shoulder at me, waving her fingers in a meek gesture. The tears that had been in her eyes for hours rolled down her cheeks as the door slammed behind her.

"Come with me," the woman said, leading me through one of the doors on the left and into a hallway. She opened a door on the right with a key, revealing a tiny bathroom with pea green tiles. It had a bench against the wall and a shower with a flimsy white curtain pulled around it.

"Take your clothes off," she said.

"Take your clothes off," I said.

"Listen, we'll sit here as long as it takes for you to get undressed." She sat down on the bench and stared at me, arms folded across her chest, resting on her swollen stomach. I stared back. We stayed locked in our stare down for what seemed like forever, before she spoke, "If you don't get undressed, you'll spend your first day here in the seclusion room."

"What's that?" I asked.

She smiled. "An empty locked room. It's just you in there. You can't see, talk, or hear anything other than yourself. How's that sound? You'll stay in there until you can follow the rules. I don't know where you've been before, but in here we follow the rules."

I sat there contemplating my choices and it didn't take long before I started undoing my jeans. "Can you at least turn around?" I asked, sliding my jeans down to my knees.

"Nope," she said with a grin. "Gotta make sure you're clean."

I stripped down to my bra and underwear, covering my chest with my arms.

"Take it all off."

"You've got to be kidding me."

She shook her head. "We don't play games."

"You don't have to be such a bitch." I wanted to slap the grin off her face. I did as I was told—pretending that being naked in front of her didn't bother me in the least even though I was mortified.

"There." I put my hands on my hips. "Pretty damn sexy, huh?"

"Turn around and bend over."

I turned around and bent over. "How do you like this view, lady?"

This is so humiliating. It's got to be against the law.

"Spread your cheeks."

I want to die. Right now.

"Do you want to lick me where I pee too, dyke?" I asked.

She looked me over from head to toe and in every crack while I willed myself to disappear into the nasty green tiles. Once she finished, I had to take a shower while she watched. She handed me a towel as I stepped out. I wrapped the towel around me. She handed me a pair of blue scrubs like surgeons wore at hospitals.

"You can get your clothes back when you earn them."

Every door in the place was locked. All the rooms had to be unlocked by a staff member and we had to knock and wait for a staff member to let us out. We went to bed at eight and woke at six to file into a long hallway. We stood in a line while staff ordered us to do jumping jacks, sit-ups, and push-ups for the next half hour. Besides our morning workout, we were locked in our rooms except for meals and groups.

Each room had two beds bolted to the floor and a long cabinet to hold our clothes. Every wall was bare and painted white. My roommate was named

Danielle and she laughed at me when I asked if there was any way to get high.

"Girl, the most high you'll get in here is flushing bananas down the toilet with me. And another piece, don't go 'round askin' people 'bout getting high. No one wants to be here and talking 'bout that shit makes ya stay longer."

I trusted what she said since she'd been locked up three times. There were twice as many staff members at Redview than there'd been at New Hope. The staff were either big black men who looked like bouncers at a club, or white men who looked like washed-out hippies. Whenever we were out of the rooms, they circled us like vultures, waiting to catch us doing anything that was against the rules or mimicked street behavior. Street behavior was acting like we did on the outside. Any gesture, speech, or clothing could be labeled street behavior and increase your stay.

"Pull your pants up, Markus! That's street behavior."

"Put your hands down, that's street behavior."

"You're being threatening, that's street behavior."

It went on and on. If you didn't quit doing what

you were doing, you were only asked one more time to stop. If you still refused, you were thrown into the seclusion room. The woman who'd checked me in had been telling the truth about the room. It was padded without any windows. You weren't allowed to eat while you were in there. You stayed in there until you apologized for whatever bad thing you'd done. One time a kid spent six hours locked in there, screaming and cursing at staff.

Most of the other kids were in gangs. They flashed signs to each other and threatened to kill each other on the outside when the staff weren't looking. I was ignored and left alone except for the time I doodled GD on my notebook during group. On the way out, a small girl with wild bristly hair grabbed my arm.

"What you claimin', white girl?" she hissed in my ear.

"I'm not claiming anything." I jerked my arm away.

"You claimin' GD. I seen you write it on your notebook. Don't be lyin' to me, bitch," she sneered.

"Look, Maleeka or Makeela, whatever the fuck your name is. GD stands for Grateful Dead. The band? Jerry Garcia?"

She stared at me, trying to figure out what I'd said as if I'd spoken a foreign language. Finally, she threw her head back and started laughing. "That's some funny shit. You white chicks are strange." She thumped me on the back with her hand. "Anyway, the name's Maleeka."

I spent the majority of my time sleeping in my room or staring out the barred windows, daydreaming about getting high. After two weeks, staff decided to transfer me to Park Meadow. Park Meadow was a treatment center focusing on chemical dependency, not like where I was at, with kids who'd stabbed other kids and were waiting for their sentences. I felt lucky to be getting sent to treatment because I was sure most of the other kids' fates would be a lot worse than mine.

Park Meadow was a huge mansion at the end of a long gravel road with trees surrounding it on all sides. It was painted red with white trim, and if I hadn't known better I'd have thought I was being brought to a vacation home. But the inside of the facility was anything but homelike.

The house had three levels. The main level had a massive room in the center, lined with cafeteria tables and a bay window that took up an entire wall on the north side. Two group rooms were to the left of it. They were filled with couches and soft padded chairs, a welcome break from the hard aluminum chairs at Redview. Across from the group rooms was a medicine room where a nurse worked and doled out the medication to kids who needed it. To the right of the main room, a hallway led to all of the girls' bedrooms. The upper level of the house, where girls were never allowed to go, was where all the boys stayed. Downstairs was a game room with a pool table, a makeshift classroom for school, and the counselors' offices.

My room was big and had a sliding glass door that couldn't be opened but let in a lot of sunshine. There were five wooden bed frames with mattresses on top of them. Two of the beds had teddy bears lying on the pillows and the others were unoccupied. I chose the bed in the corner, closest to the sliding glass door.

I had two roommates. Goldie was a tall Native American girl who was only twelve-years-old. She'd never done any other drugs besides huffing spray paint, but she already had enough brain damage to make her eyes cross and roll around involuntarily. My other roommate was Rio Mae, who always had a smile on her face even though she'd been abandoned by her parents when she was two and had spent her life living in various foster homes.

I'd been sober for almost a month. It was like coming out of a deep sleep and being halfway between waking and dreaming. The longer I stayed sober, the more awake my brain became. It was strange to remember my days, endless with so much awake time. The nights were terrible because my body had become rested since I'd spent most of my time at Redview sleeping and couldn't sleep anymore. My mind replayed things that had happened during the day and fragmented pieces of my past. My thoughts whirled, trying to make sense of everything, but I didn't let anyone know I was having a hard time.

To all outside appearances, I was the same angry, defiant girl. I walked around cold and defensive, ready to do battle. I didn't let on that I didn't mind some of the parts about being there. My favorite part was being able to go outside. Spring had arrived and the air smelled fresh and clean with the promise of summer. Birds chirped and squirrels chased each other up and down trees. It'd been a long time since I'd noticed nature.

There was a paved court with a basketball hoop and the guys let me play with them. It was the only time we were allowed to push and shove without getting reprimanded. I still had a good shot. For the first time in a long while, I thought about when I used to play basketball and it made me sad to think I'd given it up.

My mind became a battleground of thinking and at the same time trying not to think. Without drugs, it became harder and harder to push away and ignore the thoughts that were serious or disturbing. Because of this, I hated group. My ability to remain disconnected was tough the longer I stayed sober and in the midst of such intensity. I was uncomfortable when people cried. Unlike the kids I'd sat in groups with at New Hope, the kids at Park Meadow were a lot like me.

Hank, the counselor, was a stocky man with a neatly trimmed beard and fake teeth that clacked together when he talked. He took his job seriously and rarely smiled. He'd perfected the art of intimidation, but I refused to let him intimidate me. The focus of group at Park Meadow was the same as it had been at New Hope and Redview: our issues.

"What are you running from, Tyler?" Hank

began one day.

I crossed my arms and slid down in my chair. It was like he was talking to all of us, even though he used Tyler's name.

"Nothin,' I don't think." Tyler twisted his ponytail.

"Really?" Hank leaned forward in his chair. "What about what we were talking about in group earlier today?"

Tyler shrugged his shoulders and wrung his hands on his lap. His lower lip quivered. Hank scanned the room.

"Do you guys remember?" he asked.

We all nodded.

"Tyler, what was it like for you at home when your dad got drunk and hit you?" He moved his chair closer. His chair was the only one on wheels and he scooted around the group to be directly in front of whoever he was trying to break.

"It sucked," Tyler said softly, focusing on his hands in his lap.

Hank's voice got louder. "Say more about that. How did it feel? How did it feel when your dad beat you, Tyler?"

Tyler blinked rapidly to keep tears from

spilling onto his cheeks. "It sucked."

Hank slapped his leg. "C'mon, it sucked? You can do better than that. Did you laugh? Did you cry? Were you pissed? Shit, I'd be pissed if my old man beat the shit out of me. Christ, he was your dad. I bet he hit you all your life."

I clenched my hands together in tight fists. *Stop! Shut up! Leave him alone!* I wanted to choke Hank to get him to stop. I tucked my hands under my legs.

Hank went on as he always did. His voice getting louder and louder. I wanted to cover my ears. "What did it feel like when you were a kid? When you were small—what was it like before you got so damn tough?"

He gulped. "I hated it. I felt like I did something wrong. Like I always tried to be good, but it was never good enough. I always did something wrong." He couldn't hold back his tears anymore.

Hank softened. He moved his chair even closer, so his knees touched Tyler's and then he placed his hands on Tyler's knees. He spoke gently, "It wasn't your fault."

Tyler broke down sobbing, which sounded like

big hiccups as he gasped for air. The kid next to him on the couch handed him a Kleenex. He gulped. "I just wanted to die."

I looked away. I couldn't stand the raw pain, the air so thick with it that I couldn't breathe. I felt his pain as if it were mine and realized I'd thought the same things he'd just spoken out loud.

But my dad didn't beat me like Tyler's dad. He's hit me and thrown me around, trying to punish me and get me to obey. It was just me being punished, wasn't it? It's not like he beat me for no reason. I deserved it. But I feel like Tyler does. Is it still wrong?

I thought about the only time I'd seen my dad cry. I had a flash of myself as a little girl sitting on my dad's lap in my bedroom. He was apologizing for hurting me and saying he'd never do it again. A tear rolled down his right cheek. One tear.

What happened that day?

I couldn't remember what came before or after. But I did remember other days from my childhood. I recalled the day my dad had thrown my brother off his chair at the dinner table for laughing. He'd grabbed him by his throat while he was on the floor, and they knocked other chairs over in their struggle. My dad wrestled my brother into the bedroom for the paddle by pulling him along by his shirt. I'd grabbed Sarah by the hand and ran with her downstairs to my bedroom. I held on to her while she cried.

"I'm scared," she'd sobbed.

I'd taken her chubby, doll-like face in my hands and looked into her big, blue eyes. "We have a mean daddy. Sometimes he can be nice, but other times he's mean. Do you understand?" She nodded her head. I cautioned softly in my nine-year-old voice, "We have to be careful of the mean daddy, okay? You don't have to be scared. I'll protect you."

Without my permission, memories from my childhood flashed through my mind in group each time one of the other kids talked about what it was like for them growing up. The fragmented images bothered me. I willed them to stop, but they were stronger than me. I hated the way Hank attacked the kids and crumbled their insides. I was terrified he'd come after me with one of his attacks.

"Why do you always have to make everyone feel like shit?" I asked him in one of our private sessions.

"Because kids like you guys have a lot of pain."

"But what's the point in talking about it and feeling like shit? I don't see how it does anything good."

"I think you're just scared." He moved his chair closer to mine.

"Don't come near me!" I pushed my chair back against the wall. "Seriously, stay away."

"Whoa, whoa." He moved his chair back, further than it'd been. "What are you so afraid of?"

"I just don't like people in my space."

"Okay." He leaned back. "Kids don't run away if there's nothing to run from. Drugs help you run away. If you deal with what you're running from then, maybe you won't have to run anymore."

I do drugs because I like them. But why does it scare you to live without them? I just like my life better that way. Really? Do you really like puking, getting into trouble, losing time, and being up for days? It's not that bad. Oh yeah, do you really like the guys who put their dicks in your mouth when you're passed out in the back of a trailer someplace you don't even know? Shut up!

At that moment, I split into two distinct voices in my mind. The voices argued back and forth with each other. I didn't know whose voice was the real me or if they both belonged to a part of me. I just knew that two voices were born. They began a dialogue that would torment and haunt me until I sat with the barrel of a gun in my mouth, contemplating pulling the trigger to shut them up.

Garrison

NINE

It was hard to believe I could hate anything more than regular group, but I detested family group. Family group was the same format as regular group except the families of all of the kids in treatment were brought in and Hank performed his usual rituals with everyone. I knew my family was going to present the image of us as a picture-perfect Christian family and report that I was the only trouble in our house. According to them, I'd been fine before I got on drugs and if I got off drugs, then everything would go back to normal.

I'd been talking to my mom once a week since I'd gotten to Park Meadow and she ended each phone call the same way. "Elizabeth, Satan has gotten a hold of you through drugs. You need to turn your back on him. Once he's out of your head, you'll be fine. But it's going to be hard because he's really got you."

I was sure I'd get the same response in family group so I wasn't looking forward to my parents and Sarah making the two-hour drive to Park Meadow to attend our first group together. Daniel didn't come because he still wasn't talking to me. He'd quit talking to me after Christmas the previous year because I'd accidentally punched my mom in the face that night.

The night had started out well. I came home for dinner on time, which put a huge smile on my mom's face and made her eyes sparkle. She beamed to have the whole family sitting together around the table since it seldom happened anymore. She scurried around serving the cookies and treats she'd been slaving over for weeks and making sure our glasses were filled with her special green Christmas punch. I hadn't seen her so happy in a long time. After dinner, we all worked on a jigsaw puzzle together, laughing and reminiscing about family vacations we'd taken in the past to Phoenix and Nova Scotia. Next, we moved into the living room and sat around the twinkling Christmas tree—so pretty it could've been in a magazine—while my dad read the Christmas story out loud. He led us in a prayer after he finished.

My family always went to bed early and Christmas Eve was no different. They started to get ready for bed at nine and I started putting my shoes on.

"Where are you going?" my mom asked, coming out of the bathroom, where she'd been washing her face. The smell of Noxzema followed her.

"I'm gonna go out for a while."

"Elizabeth, no," she cried, the happiness disappearing from her face.

"Mom, you're all going to sleep so I'm just gonna go out for a while. You know I can't go to bed this early. I'll be back, don't worry."

"No, you won't. You never come back." Her eyes filled with tears. "It's Christmas. Why can't you just stay with us for one night?"

"I'll be here in the morning." I went to the closet to get my jacket. She looked as if she going to cry but swallowed her tears. She turned around and met my dad in the hallway as he was coming out of their bedroom.

"What's wrong?" I heard him ask her.

"Elizabeth's taking off."

I had my hand on the doorknob when my dad pulled my shoulders from behind. I turned to face him.

"You're not going anywhere," he said.

"Yes, I am."

The familiar battled followed. He yelled at me to stay and I screamed that I was leaving. We wrestled back and forth, vying for control of the door. My mom stood behind him, pulling on his shoulders.

"Please, hon. Not tonight. Don't do this. It's Christmas."

As always, he ignored her. He came at me again, ready for a fight. I swung at him in response. At the exact moment of my swing, my mom stepped between us. Instead of connecting with my dad, I connected with her face. Her mouth dropped open. She stared at me in shock, bringing her hand up to her nose. She looked at me as if I'd just taken a knife and plunged it into her heart.

I felt as if I was in a movie. My dad stood frozen behind her. I had to get away. I flung the door open and ran into the night. Crisp air met my lungs with a sharp pain. I took off sprinting down the street, my feet pounding against the icy road.

My throat burned and my lungs ached, but I ran until I couldn't run anymore. I stopped, leaning over, gasping for air. Snot mixed with tears dripped onto my jeans. I hadn't realized I was crying. I felt on the verge of hyperventilating like I did at cross country meets when I forgot to take my inhaler before the race.

I just punched my mom on Christmas Eve. I'm a fuckin' monster. What the hell is wrong with me? Calm down, Elizabeth. Breathe. I need to get high.

I fumbled in my pocket, searched for coins, and found enough to make a phone call. I started walking up to the phone booth outside of the grocery store to call Strom.

A car turned a corner and the headlights moved toward me. I didn't realize it was my brother's blue Mustang until he was almost in front of me. He slammed on the brakes and jumped out of the car.

"Get in the car." He pointed to the passenger side.

"No." I took a step back.

"What the hell is wrong with you?" He stepped towards me and grabbed both of my arms. "For God's sake, Elizabeth, just get in!"

"No!" I jerked my arms free and swung at him wildly with my fists. He wrapped his arms around me in a tight bear hug.

He hissed in my ear, "I am not Dad. This is your brother, remember?"

I went limp in his arms. "Okay, let me go. I'll get in."

He walked me to the car and I slid into the passenger seat. He got behind the wheel and drove a few blocks without saying a word. Finally, without turning to look at me, he said, "I don't know how you do it. You come home for one night and end up punching Mom. You've got dad pissed as hell, storming around the house, and Sarah's locked in her room bawling her eyes out."

"I'm sorry. I didn't mean to do it."

"Look, just come home." Daniel turned a corner, still focused on the road. "All you've got to do is apologize and everything will be fine."

"I'm not gonna apologize. It wasn't my fault. Dad shouldn't have come at me."

"Christ, for once, can't you just give in?"

No, I can't. If I say I'm sorry, then that means I'm admitting to being the bad one. Like it's my fault. He'll win again. I won't do it.

He stared at the road, and I stared out the window at the passing trees covered with snow and icicles. After a few minutes, he broke the uncomfortable silence. "What else are you gonna do?"

"I'm gonna go find Strom and-"

He cut me off. "Get high all night?"

"Yeah, but only for a while. I'll be back."

He slammed on the breaks, sliding on the ice before the car stopped. "Get out."

"But I-"

"Get the fuck out of my car," he hissed through gritted teeth, turning to look at me.

I opened my door. "I'm sorry. I really am."

"You're a fuckin' loser. Go get high with all of your loser friends. You make me sick." He motioned to my door. "Go. I can't even stand to look at you."

I slid out of the car. He reached for my door and pulled it shut before peeling off. I stood on the side of the road, waiting to see his taillights turn around and head back toward me, but they just kept getting further and further away. I went in search of a phone booth to make my call.

It was the last time we'd talked. After that, it

was as if I ceased to exist like he'd somehow erased me from his mind. I found myself wondering what would happen if he came to family group, but I didn't invite him because I was afraid he'd say no. My mom didn't even bring him up in our phone conversations. There was no mention of him coming to family group. It was as if I no longer had a brother.

I knew Sarah would come because no matter how I acted, I was still her big sister and she'd always looked up to me. Her love for me was unconditional. She sent me cards and wrote me long letters, begging me to get sober and telling me how much she missed me. It was hard to read them because even though she never tired of telling me I was the best sister, I hadn't done anything in a long time to deserve the title.

My family arrived right as group was starting. Sarah took the seat next to me and eyed the room without saying a word. Her eyes were video cameras recording everything to play back later and try to understand.

I'd been in two other family groups previously and had figured out there were two types of parents. There was one type that spent all of their time crying and wallowing in guilt about their children being in treatment because they felt completely responsible for it. Hank would work with them at easing their sense of responsibility while also challenging them to be accountable. The second type seemed oblivious to having played any part in their child's dysfunction, but after going one round with Hank they quickly realized they'd been involved and affected by what their child had been doing. They soon turned into the first type. Most of the time, if both parents were there, they'd each take turns talking, alternating between blaming each other and blaming themselves.

My parents didn't fit into either type. They were in a category by themselves. First, because they were the only couple in the room that wasn't divorced or remarried, and second, both believed I was solely responsible for being where I was and weren't going to be convinced otherwise. My dad did all of the talking in the introductions while my mom sat next to him, with her hands folded in her lap and a set smile on her face.

Every family had a turn with Hank. He focused his attention on my dad when it was our turn.

"I don't know why you're asking me questions.

She's the drug addict. Talk to her."

"We just want to get an idea of what things are like at home." Hank clacked his fake teeth together as he spoke. "It helps us to understand how we can help her and what problems we're up against."

"Problems? She's the problem," my dad said. My mom touched him lightly on the knee. "There's nothing more to understand."

Hank turned to look at my mom. "How do you feel, Robin?"

My mom smiled back at Hank with one of her plastic Christian smiles and looked up at my dad, waiting for him to speak. "My wife feels the same way I do. There wasn't any problem with Elizabeth or anything else until she got into drugs."

Hank raised his right eyebrow. "I find that hard to believe."

My dad straightened his back and glared. "I really don't care what you think. You don't know anything about us."

The room got quiet. Every person in the room stared at us as if they were watching a suspense movie on TV.

Here we go.

Hank smiled. "You're right. That's why I'm

asking questions. I don't understand why you're so defensive."

My dad pressed his lips together and made a sound like a horse sputtering. "Listen, my daughter is a drug addict. She's completely out of control. My family has nothing to do with it. She's had nothing but a good Christian upbringing by two parents that love her."

I looked over at Sarah, trying to get her to meet my eyes so I could send her a message that it was going to be okay. She stared back and forth between my dad and Hank. She looked terrified. My head began to swim and swirl, feeling as if it was going to roll off my neck.

"Your daughter is very angry or haven't you noticed?" Hank scooted his chair closer.

Knock it off, Hank. You're gonna piss him off. Just shut up.

His usual tactics weren't going to work with my dad. I'd known this before group started. There was no way he was going to get my dad to talk about anything other than how messed up I was.

"Of course, I have. She's on drugs. They've messed up her mind. She was never angry before."

Yes, I was. He's lying. I was angry all the time.

I just couldn't show it. I clenched my teeth together.

"I find that very hard to believe. Your daughter is too pissed not to have a reason. I-"

"Listen, buddy." My dad narrowed his eyes to slits and leaned forward, challenging Hank. "You need to talk to *her.* I'm done. You leave me and my family alone."

They locked eyes with each other as if they were two kids having a stare down.

Do something, Hank. Say something.

Someone coughed. Hank clasped his hands together and cracked his knuckles. He opened his mouth and shut it again. He turned around in his chair, looking at the others. "Anyone have any feedback?" No one said anything. My dad had just silenced an entire room. "Let's move on then."

My family continued to come to family group every week. We sat in every group, but were never counseled again as a family. I watched the other families work with Hank. The endings were always happy no matter how much pain came before. If Hank couldn't help us, then we were hopeless.

Hank had tried many times to get me to talk about my family and childhood in his private sessions with me. He tripled his efforts after his battle with my dad.

"What was it like growing up in your family, Elizabeth?"

I gave my standard response for almost anything: "It sucked."

"Your dad seems pretty frightening. Are you afraid of him?"

You are. He shut you up. What do you think?

"No, I'm not scared of anything."

"I'd be scared of him. Does he make you mad?"

"I'm only pissed 'cause he blames everything on drugs. Like everything was so fine before or something. Yeah, I used to not get into trouble. I was a good little fuckin' girl. But ya know what? I've wanted to die since I was eight years old. I used to daydream about hanging myself from the swing set in the backyard."

I shouldn't have said that. Damn. Why'd you do that? I don't know, it just came out. I wasn't thinking. Watch your mouth.

An image of me as a little girl swinging up and down on the metal swing in my backyard flashed through my mind. I wore my ripped jean shorts and my favorite blue tank top. I flew up and down, staring at the back of the house, singing a song I'd heard on the radio. I only knew the line, "Even though inside I feel like dying, you know you'll never see me crying." I just kept singing the words over and over again, pumping my legs back and forth, trying to get myself to go higher.

Hank's voice broke into my memory. "Elizabeth?"

"What?"

"Where'd you go?"

"I'm right here," I said, shifting my weight in my seat.

"I was asking you a question and you just disappeared." He leaned forward.

"I guess I just spaced out," I mumbled.

"Do you space out a lot?" He brought his arms up to the desk and rested his chin on his hands.

"I don't know." My head swam as if I'd just been shoved underwater. Everything looked fuzzy and his voice was muffled and far away.

"I'm just gonna ask you. Does your dad abuse you?"

I was suddenly rocketed from Hank's office to Keith's truck a few years before. I was sitting in the passenger seat. We'd just left my parents' house and were headed out of town to cruise the back roads while we drank beer. Keith had been silent since we'd left my house.

"I need to ask you a question." He took a left onto the first gravel road and pulled over on the shoulder.

"What do you want to know?"

He shut the car off. "I want you to tell me the truth. This is serious. Promise me you'll tell the truth?" He turned to look at me.

I nodded. He was going to ask me if I was cheating on him again and I was so tired of answering that question.

He cleared his throat. "I don't really know how to ask this ..."

I waited for him to finish.

"Okay." He exhaled, taking both of my hands in his.

Ohmigod, he's gonna ask me to marry him. What am I gonna say?

He took another deep breath. "Does your dad fuck with you?"

I stared at him. "Well, yeah. You already know that. He's a controlling prick."

Keith looked down at my hands. "That's not what I mean. I mean does he mess around with you? Like, you know ... I mean ... Christ, does your dad fuck you?"

It took a moment for his words to register in my brain. I jerked my hands away. "What? Ohmigod. I can't believe you just asked that. You're seriously messed up in the head! I ... what the ... I ..."

"Settle down." He reached for my hands again and I pulled them away. "The only reason I'm asking is because I see the way he looks at you. Every time we walk into your house he checks out your tits and ass. He stares at you like I do, but he's your fuckin' dad. It's sick."

Puke rose in my throat.

He sees the way my dad looks at me. Maybe I'm not crazy. But I've got to be crazy.

"So, does he?" Keith whispered. "Because if he does, I'll kill the bastard."

This can't be happening. This can't be happening.

The life left my body. My brain pulled the plug and brought me to a place of numbness and nothingness somewhere in the sky. I closed my eyes tightly then opened them slowly, back in Hank's office. He was sitting in the chair next to me with his hand on my shoulder. My legs were pulled up to my chest and my arms wrapped around them.

Hank spoke into my thoughts. "You've given me enough of an answer."

Did I talk? I don't remember talking. I was just thinking. What's going on? What did I say? What the hell is happening? Get a grip, Elizabeth. You're losing it.

I didn't remember how our session ended or leaving Hank's office. I found myself back in my room, sitting on my bed in a trance, twisting and turning a wire hanger until it snapped. Robotically, I broke it into small pieces. I watched myself begin to rub the sharp end up and down my arm rhythmically until my skin was raw and started to bleed. As if someone had flipped a switch in my head, I rubbed harder and harder and faster and faster until my arm was a bunch of jagged lines creating a twisted web on my arm.

I came to with a jolt.

What did I just do? I don't know, but it felt good. Shit. Clean it up. People are gonna think you're a freak. Stupid ass, why'd you do it on your arm? How are ya gonna hide that? Don't worry. What did I just do?

I jumped up from the bed and frantically collected the pieces of the wire hanger. I buried them in the garbage underneath papers and trash. I walked to the doorway, trying not to let any blood drip on the floor or my shirt. I peeked my head out and saw there was no one in sight. I sprinted to the bathroom. I stuck my arm underneath the faucet, watching the water slide off my arm like liquid rust. I blotted it dry with a paper towel.

I took a long-sleeved shirt from my dresser and put it on when I got back to my room. I lay down on my bed, crossing my arms across my chest the way vampires sleep in movies. My breathing was relaxed and my head cleared. The memories were gone. I told myself it was going to be okay over and over again until sleep came.

A few days later, Hank came to my room and knocked at the door. "I need to talk to you. Meet me in my office in five minutes."

I sensed something was wrong when I walked into his office because he was pacing back and forth across the room instead of sitting in his usual position behind the desk. I sat in my spot in the right-hand corner of his office, across from the desk.

"I need to tell you something. I had to do something because it's required by law." He continued to pace. "I'm a counselor and part of my job is being a mandated reporter. What that means is that if I'm told about abuse going on, or if I suspect it, then I have to report it to the authorities. I want you to know how much I've struggled and agonized over having to do this. First and foremost, I struggled because you've been one of the most untrusting kids I've ever had to work with. It has taken so long for you to open up in the least. You're at the very beginning of talking. I didn't want to jeopardize that. Second, I've debated trying to get around reporting it because you haven't told me that there's abuse going on. Personally, I don't think you are even aware of a lot of things. I think you've been running from the truth for so long that you don't even know what the truth is. But your reactions to your family, and the things you say send me millions of messages that you've been abused. You show every single sign. I had to go with my gut."

I sat in my chair, absorbing the words he'd just spoken, registering them without any emotion like I was a computer downloading information.

Hank told someone I was being abused.

He sat down across from me. His eyes were warm.

"What are you saying?" I asked.

"I'm telling you that I made a report to the authorities in your county that I suspected abuse was going on in your home." He looked into my eyes, searching for a reaction. "I don't know what they'll do with it. What happens from here is completely up to them. As much as I didn't want to, I had to do it or I'd risk losing my job. Do you understand?"

I nodded my head even though I didn't understand anything happening right now.

"Are you angry with me?" he asked.

I shook my head. I couldn't talk.

"Do you have any questions?"

I shook my head again.

"Are you okay? Is there anything I can do?" he asked. His eyes were wet and glossy. He worked his jaw back and forth,

"I'm fine," I said, not recognizing the sound of my voice.

"There's one more thing. Some people from the county might be coming to talk to you and ask you some questions. They might not, but I just want you to be prepared."

"Okay. Can I go now?"

"Are you sure you're okay?"

I nodded. I walked back to my room in the same trancelike state I'd been in a few days earlier.

What in the hell is going on? Abuse. I don't wanna talk about my family. I wanna get high. There's nothing. What will my mom say? Nothing is wrong with my family. Everything is wrong with my family. Ohmigod, if people come, what do I say? You say nothing. I'm crazy. All of this is crazy. What is happening? This isn't happening.

My eyes turned to my closet and the wire hangers inside.

It worked last time. Shut up. It's sick. Remember how good you felt?

I jumped up from my bed and threw open the closet door. I grabbed a hanger and tore it to pieces, hurriedly scraping the jagged edges along my arm.

I still feel crazy. Rub harder. This is insane. Rub harder.

And I did, this time bringing more blood. With each trickle that left my arm, the pressure in my head subsided until all the thoughts that I didn't understand were gone.

TEN

I thought I was going to be one of the kids who had to stay at Park Meadow for nine months. When Hank brought me into his office and told me I was being released after only two, I was surprised and excited, but also confused. Hadn't he just told me he thought I was being abused, and now he was sending me home? It didn't make any sense.

"I really don't think it's a good idea for you to leave. We recommended you stay in extended care for at least another six months, but your funding from the county has run out. The best we can do is to set you up with a really strict aftercare plan." Hank pulled out the folder from his desk that held my file. "You're going to be monitored closely by your probation officer. He'll be giving you drug tests. You'll have to go to at least three AA or NA meeting a week and-"

"Man, I hate those meetings."

Every few weeks we had people come to Park Meadow from Alcoholics Anonymous. They droned on and on about how everyone needed to find God or else they'd drink again. Their stories were far too similar to the stories my mom used to tell me about how she and my dad used to drink and do lots of drugs until they found God.

"I don't care if you hate those meetings," Hank said. "It's the only way you'll stay sober."

"Shit," I muttered, slumping down in my seat.

"You're also going to be enrolled in an aftercare program at New Hope Treatment Center-"

I cut him off. "Aftercare program? I'm done."

Hank raised his eyebrow and clicked his teeth together. "You haven't even gotten started. You'll go there three nights a week."

"I can't. I got kicked out of that place."

"I spoke to Dave Bateman. He's willing to have you back now that you've completed a treatment program. He'll be your counselor once you leave."

"And what if I don't do all of this?"

"You'll end up getting sent away again, but it won't be to treatment. Next time, it'll be juvenile jail."

I got home and was expected to step back into my life as if nothing had changed. My parents acted as if I'd gone away to treatment and gotten fixed. But my entire concept of the world had been shaken at Park Meadow. I'd look around at my family and wonder who they were. My head twirled and spun every time I walked through the door.

My dad's eyes followed me everywhere. I couldn't get away from the thick tension of his stare. It was like we were engaged in a silent war of I-Dare-You-To-Speak. My head hammered with anger each time I returned one of his looks. I refused to question why I was so angry. It was too dangerous to go there.

I watched my mom as she bustled around attending to her daily routines and chores like everything was fine. I searched her face for clues as to what was going on. Did she know what Hank had said about our family? About the report? If she knew, why wasn't she saying anything? Did she hate me for it?

There was so much I didn't understand. If Hank had made the report, then why was I still at home? Was it only a matter of time before someone showed up at my door and took me away? Would they just take me? What about Sarah? I couldn't even bear to think about Sarah. And Daniel? He never even acknowledged I'd been away. That was how my family functioned, but now I questioned the conspiracy of silence that Hank had broken, that I'd somehow taken part in.

I didn't know what was real. Everyone around me continued to believe and behave as if nothing was wrong in our house. It made me wonder again if I was the crazy one. Nobody ever came from the county to get me or talk to me. I wasn't sure what that meant. I didn't know what to do or how to feel so I did the only thing that ever made me feel better—I got high.

It wasn't easy because my life was filled with court regulations and restrictions. Hank's threats had been real, and he'd set everything up exactly like he'd said he would, but I couldn't follow through on any of it. I attended aftercare at New Hope Treatment Center for two weeks before I quit going. I didn't go to any of my required Alcoholics Anonymous meetings. Each week, I had to go down to the courthouse and pee in a cup, but I never passed the drug test. I got into trouble with the law for drinking underage, being high, breaking curfew, shoplifting, stealing, and having drugs and paraphernalia on me.

I started living from court date to court date. Each time I appeared, the judge ordered me to stay sober and follow the rules of my probation. My punishment was hours upon hours of community service, which piled up because I refused to do them.

I'd spent the majority of my time at New Hope and Park Meadow wanting to get high, desperate to return to some sense of normalcy. But once I got out, it was if I couldn't get high enough. All of the physiological responses took place, but the magic was gone. Instead of filling my void, I was left feeling emptier.

As we sat in a cramped hotel room, strangers filling every inch of space, I announced to Strom, "They brainwashed me in treatment. I feel all weird like I can get high, but not really."

"Here. Do more of this." He passed me the picture he'd taken off the wall. He'd heaped the glass with piles of different colored powders. We'd been passing it around the room for the last five hours. "This is good shit."

We balanced the picture on our laps. I took a chunk of yellow powder and dropped it into the beer I was drinking and then finished the beer quickly. I stuck my finger into the white powder and rubbed it all over my gums. I reached for one of the straws and brought my face down to the long trails, filling my nose with the familiar burn. I passed the picture to the next person in line on the bed.

The mixture of coke and heroin sent tingles through my body. My gums numbed as if they couldn't hold my teeth in place. I broke out in a wet sweat. For a second, my stomach heaved, threatening to come up, which signaled I was getting off. My heart started to race and for a second my mind was clear. But as quickly as the good feelings came, they were gone. I looked around the room, anxiously eyeing all the tall, skinny men rambling on and on to each other while their pupils danced back and forth.

I'm the only girl. So, what does that mean? Maybe I shouldn't be here. These people are old. Don't talk like this. This is where you belong. But what if I don't? Shut up! If you don't belong here, you don't belong anywhere. Quit thinking this way. I can't help it. I don't even know these people. Big deal. You don't need to.

My eyes darted to the bathroom door, slightly ajar. I could see movement through the crack—a tattooed arm with a belt tied around it. I jumped up from my spot next to Strom. He grabbed my arm and pulled me back down next to him.

"Where are you going?" he asked, streams of sweat dripping down his face and falling off the crest of his chin.

"To the bathroom."

He shook his head. "You're not gonna stick a fuckin' needle in your arm. Do ya hear me? If I ever catch you shooting that shit, I'm cutting you off. Seriously. You'll kill yourself. I know you."

The excitement of anticipation left me. If Strom said something, he meant it. I couldn't lose him or my supply. Mechanically, I reached into the nightstand next to the bed, pulled out the blue Gideon Bible, and stared as the words crossed and swerved in front of my eyes.

"You gonna save us all?" Strom asked, looking at me with empty eyes. Without a word, I took my lighter and brought it down to the pages, igniting them. The chatter in the room stopped, and everyone stared at the Bible in flames on my lap. A guy standing in the doorway started to cry like a baby. A voice yelled from the corner, "Shit. Make her stop. That's fucked up." I kept on burning the pages, watching them disappear into ashes and float around the room.

Someone else cried, "She's freaking me out."

Strom grabbed his beer and poured it on the fire. He took the charred remains from my hands and sat it back on the nightstand. "Why'd you do that?"

I shrugged my shoulders.

People began asking me why I did the things I did. Why I started fires or all of a sudden threw whatever I was drinking at the wall or someone's head. There were times in the car with Strom when I'd roll down the window and climb out to sit on the edge of the car door. Other times, I'd whip open the door and stick my feet out, hysterically laughing as I threatened to jump.

I didn't know why I did the things I did. From out of nowhere, I'd be gripped by a powerful anger and an overwhelming compulsion to destroy something. I didn't know where the outbursts came from or how to stop them. They were out of my control.

The only rule I followed was meeting with Dave Bateman every week. At first, I dreaded our meetings, but for some reason, I felt better every time I left. He radiated an inner peace and happiness. He talked to me like he was talking to another adult and was genuinely concerned about me. He shared his pain about losing his mom to a stroke when he was ten and what his life was like when he'd been using. He'd almost blown his head off, and it had led to him getting clean. He'd been sober for almost ten years, now.

He was married and had five kids. Their drawings and pictures covered his tack board. His eyes filled with love and his chest puffed with pride whenever he spoke about them. He seemed so put together, so real, and alive. A part of me was scared by his energy, but another part was intrigued and attracted by it.

I was becoming more and more convinced that I was going insane. The two voices in my head waged war against each other and never shut up no matter how much I willed them to. I didn't know who I was anymore. My mind was filled with blank spaces where memories should've been. I didn't want to think, but that was all I did. My head pounded with confusion, and my anger had turned into a volatile rage that scared me. I was afraid to tell anyone what was going on, but I took a chance with Dave.

"I think I'm crazy," I whispered.

"What? I didn't hear you."

I cleared my throat and tried again. "I said I think I'm crazy."

"I don't think so. I think your head is filled with chemicals that don't work anymore. You've lost control and you're trapped. That would make anyone feel like they were nuts."

"But you don't know what goes on in my head. There's like two different people talking to each other. They have actual conversations back and forth."

"You're not crazy. You're just a junkie. Sorry to disappoint you. It's a lot easier to be crazy than to be a junkie."

"But it was never like this before."

He laughed. "Of course, it wasn't. It never starts out that way. Every junkie reaches a point where the drugs quit working."

Using had taken a turn on me that I'd never

expected. For so long, drugs had been the only things that made me feel good and alive, and those feelings were gone. Now, I lived the same day over and over again. It terrified me.

I was convinced there had to be a way to reverse whatever was happening, so each day I dumped a buffet of chemicals into my body. I smoked meth, did lines, drank, smoked weed, and dropped acid with a mission to prove they still worked. But to my dismay, I couldn't get any higher. I was as high as I was ever going to get. I needed more, but there was no more to be had. I'd done every drug and there'd be no more first times.

More and more, I avoided people other than to get or sell drugs. I wasn't interested in pretending to be friends and carrying on conversations was becoming difficult. I rarely slept and paranoia gripped me. I trusted no one except Strom. I spent most of my days and nights locked in his bedroom at his rental house in the country. The shades were sealed shut at all times and candles provided the only light. There was a mattress on the floor against the wall in one corner and piles of dirty clothes in another. The only other piece of furniture was a stereo that filled the room with music at all times.

"You need to rest," Strom said one morning as the sun came up.

We never slept anymore, but we had to rest our bodies by keeping them still, or they'd physically shut down. We'd lay our aching bones next to each other on the old mattress, listening to the Counting Crows playing through one more time on the stereo.

"I've got some weird rash all over my legs," I said.

"Don't worry. It's nothing. It's just the red in your veins. Your circulation is all fucked up." He rolled over to face me and propped himself up on his elbow.

"You ever get tired of this?" I asked.

"It's our life, sweetheart. We don't have a choice. Only the good die young." His eyes saddened as he stared down at me.

"Sometimes I think we're already dead."

"We are." No emotion in his eyes.

"Do you think there's a God?"

"Yes, and he hates us." He took a long deep breath. "I don't wanna talk about this shit. You freak me out when you get all deep."

Dave was the one person who I could get deep

with, and I started looking forward to my meetings with him, although I always pretended I didn't want to be there like it was a big inconvenience. But for an hour in his office, I felt like I wasn't a lunatic. Unfortunately, every time I left the confines of his office, my mind became cluttered with chaos again. When my head started spinning really fast and I thought I might snap, I began comforting myself by telling myself I'd be able to talk to Dave soon. I just had to hold on until our next appointment.

I started telling him about crazy things I'd done to see how he'd react. He'd told me time and time again that he cared about me and I was stuck with him, but part of me still didn't believe him. I wanted to test him.

"How was your weekend?" he asked on a Tuesday.

"I slept with a guy that has HIV," I said nonchalantly as if I was making a statement about what I'd eaten for dinner,

"Really?" He tilted his head to the side. "Why'd you do something like that? Did you use protection?"

I shook my head. I'd never used a condom.

"Do you want to tell me about it?" he asked.

"We were having a party at Red Oak Park. It's this huge nature place in the woods. The police came and I took off with Chris. We drove around for a while and then headed back to the park. I fucked him in the weeds like ten feet from his girlfriend. She was yelling for us the whole time. How crazy is that?"

"How do you know he has HIV?"

"His ex-girlfriend told me. He's a slut. Like two years ago, he and his buddies had a competition to see who could fuck the most girls. They had a stupid point system and everything. I guess he got it then. No one will touch him now. Well, except for me."

Dave frowned. "That makes me so sad."

I swallowed and looked at a spot on the wall behind him.

There you go. I'm a slut. How do you like me now?

"I still care about you," he said. He had an uncanny ability to answers the questions I was asking in my mind. It was frightening.

I ended up at detox a few days after our session. I didn't remember getting pulled over, but the police report said we fled from the cops. The driver got a DUI, I got hauled to detox, and Strom walked away unscathed. What I did remember was coming to in the backseat of the squad car, my rage boiling. I felt like a caged animal. As soon as the door opened, I took off as if a gun had just been fired like my life depended on getting away. The officer ran after me and tackled me to the ground. When he lifted me up, I kicked him right between the legs. He dropped me and fell to the ground moaning.

I ran blindly again, hollering and screaming as if physical chains still bound me. My heart felt like it was beating on the outside of my body. My brain howled. Cops got behind me and surrounded me on all sides. As I watched myself from above, I kicked and flailed about like a mustang that had been captured from the wild. It took four officers to get me into the building. They carried me by my arms and legs down the familiar hallway. They unlocked a metal door, took off my handcuffs, and threw me inside a cell. I spat at them, cussing and hollering as they locked the door behind them. I picked up the thin mattress, the only item in the room, and threw it against the wall. I screamed to be let out, pounding on the steel door until my knuckles bled and I exhausted myself. I sat in the corner hunched over, biting my nails and rocking back and forth.

Is this really how you want your life to be? They told you it'd get worse. How fun is this? This is your life. It's always gonna be this way.

My stomach heaved, and I violently sprayed vomit all over my lap and arms. I puked until globs of blood came and created a nasty design on the green and yellows. I threw up the blood until nothing else came and then kept right on gagging.

"Please God, let me die," I begged out loud. "I can't live like this."

The next morning staff unlocked me and allowed me to come out of the room. A guy I'd seen around before came up to me. "Man, you are one crazy chick." He laughed. "We were all sitting in the smoke room last night while you screamed bloody murder coming down the hall. I've never seen so many cops needed just to bring in some scrawny ass little girl. You really put up a fight, huh?"

I nodded and smiled, proud it'd taken so many officers to get me inside.

He winked at me. "But, here's the funny thing. This morning when I got up, I peeked through the glass into your room, and there you were curled up in the fetal position and sucking your thumb. The badass sucks her thumb while she sleeps." He tilted his head back and roared.

Mortified, my face grew hot. "Fuck you. I'm going to take a shower."

The next week I went to see Dave at our normal time. I told him about my detox experience, omitting the facts that I'd been so ill and prayed to die. I boasted about the fact that it'd taken four cops to get me inside.

"I didn't know why I was so pissed. But Strom told me the next day that when we saw the cops, we ate all the meth we had and man we had a ton of rocks. I can't believe we ate it. Shit, it's no wonder I was out of my mind," I said.

He seemed unimpressed. "What kind of trouble are you in now?"

"God, too much. They put me on a court-ordered curfew. I have to be at my house at ten every night and I can't leave until eight. That's messed up."

"You can't blame them. They've got to be getting tired of you. How many times have you gotten arrested in the last two months?"

"I have no idea. I've lost count. My PO and

everyone else in the stupid system is throwing a fit 'cause I kicked the cop. They're trying to get me for assault on a police officer or some shit like that."

Dave rolled his eyes. "You kicked him?"

I smiled proudly. "Yeah, but still, it's not like I actually assaulted the dude."

"Have you passed any of your drug tests?"

"Nope. I haven't passed one. I tried to tell them I took diet pills, but I don't think they believe it. I've tried everything to pass those stupid things. I even drank that black tea and man-"

"Why don't you just quit getting high?" He stood up and walked towards me.

"Are you serious?" I asked.

He better not turn on me now.

He hopped up on his desk, swinging his legs in front of me. "I want you to listen to me and hear what I'm saying. Okay?"

I nodded.

"I like you. A lot. I mean that. You have to know that by now. I know you're messed up and I know you need help. But I can't help you if you keep getting high. I-"

"Why?"

"Because I'm not helping you. I'm keeping you

sick. Your life is a mess. You're like a huge gaping wound. You go out and bleed all week and then come in here for me to put a Band-Aid on it. Then, you go out and do the same things over and over again."

I sat back in my chair, pulling my legs up to my chest.

You can't leave me now. There's so much I wanna tell you. You help me. See, he's just like everyone else. He's had enough of you.

"You look like you're going to cry," he said softly, moving from the desk to sit in the chair next to me.

Don't cry. Don't cry. You'll be fine. You don't need him. Yes, I do. You should never have trusted him. I don't want to lose him.

"Can I hold your hand?" he asked.

I nodded, unable to speak. I gazed at his desk, searching for a pattern hidden in the wood. He took my hand and held it in his. The clock on the wall ticked.

Say something. Please.

"Here's the deal. If you quit getting high, we can still meet."

"What if I can't?" My voice squeaked out like a

little girl's.

"We'll start small," he said, dropping my hand. "Will you look at me?"

I turned my head towards him, peeked at his eyes and quickly dropped my gaze to the floor, wishing I could disappear into the blue design. My hair fell over my face. He reached out and tucked it behind my ears.

"We meet on Thursdays. For the three days before you come to see me, I want you to stay clean and sober. You can do whatever else you do, but from Monday until after we meet, no drinking or getting high. Can you do that?"

I nodded.

"I want to hear you say it," he said.

"I can do it."

ELEVEN

I'd never imagined not getting high, but believed if I wanted to badly enough or if I had a good enough reason, I could stop. I took my promise to stay sober seriously because meeting with Dave was the one bright spot in my life and I didn't want him to stop seeing me. I met with him on Thursdays and every Monday I'd wake up determined not to do any drugs. I'd stay in bed as long as I could, take my time in the shower, and draw out getting dressed as long as possible because I had nothing to do once I was ready. My life revolved around getting, selling, and doing drugs. Without that, I was lost and there were only empty hours that seemed impossible to fill. The day stretched out endlessly in front of me.

Cleaning my room was the only activity I had to do. When I ran out of things to clean, I'd rearrange the furniture, moving my bed from side to side. If my mom hadn't been such a meticulous housekeeper, I would've continued my frenzied cleaning in the other rooms in the house.

Once I'd cleaned my room, I'd sit on the edge of my bed and reach down to pull out my Ziploc bag full of green buds. I'd stare at it, rolling the plastic around in my fingers over and over again. I'd open it up and sniff the sweetness. I'd go to tuck it back under the mattress, but before I did an argument would begin in my head.

Pot's not a big deal. It's nothing. Just smoking a little weed isn't really getting high. It doesn't count. I mean you're still basically sober. But Dave said nothing. I'm sure he didn't mean weed. Yes, he did. You know he did. Well, still. I'm just smoking weed. It's still better than doing what I usually do. It's improvement. Shit, he'd probably be proud of me. Anyways, there's always tomorrow. I'll stay completely sober tomorrow.

The game was on. I'd leave my house and end up at Strom's. Once I smoked weed, it was inevitable I'd start drinking. I'd grab a beer from the fridge or my bottle of Captain Morgan without a second thought. Before long Strom would start chopping up lines. He'd slide the mirror towards me. I began staring at the lines before doing them.

I don't have to do it. You know you're gonna do it. Yes, but I don't have to. I just want to. I've already ruined staying sober today so I might as well. It's not like today even counts anymore. Next week I'll do it. Next Sunday. I'll stop.

The next week would come, and it was the same as the week before. I considered lying to Dave about it, but could never bring myself to do it. I didn't know why he was the only person I couldn't lie to. I was sure each time I came to see him it would be the last, and he'd tell me we couldn't meet anymore. Finally, after I'd hung my head and mumbled that yet again, I hadn't stayed sober at all, he suggested, "How about just trying to stay sober and clean the day before you come to see me?"

I agreed.

One day isn't a big deal. I can stay sober for one day. Anyone can stay sober for one day.

On the day before our meeting the following week, my skin crawled like it always did when I wasn't high. I scratched my arms as I paced back and forth in my bedroom, treading a worn path on the blue carpet. Everything in my room reminded me of getting high and I stared at my mattress, knowing my stash was only a few feet away. I had to get out of there.

I called Strom and told him to meet me at our designated spot.

I just need to get out of the house. I'm not gonna get fucked up. I'm not gonna do anything. I won't. I can't.

Strom always picked me up no matter what he was doing or where he was. Sometimes I'd have to wait for a few hours, but he always came. Part of Strom's job was to take care of me, and he was strangely fulfilled by it and teaching me his secrets. I, in turn, kept his secrets. All of them. I got to see the man behind the hard exterior and masks. I'd held him in my arms while he cried over another friend of ours who'd died.

He pulled up on his motorcycle and I hopped on. He handed me a bottle. "Tuck this. I picked it up for you on the way."

I shoved the bottle of Captain between us, assuring myself I didn't have to drink it today. I'd put it in the cupboard when we got to his house and drink it the following night after I'd met with Dave. We made a few drop-offs before we reached his old house and headed through the back door. We never used the rotting front porch because more than one person had fallen through. The back door led us into a kitchen with old pizza lying on the counter and macaroni and cheese crusted in a pan on the stove. We walked into the living room, which consisted of a big pool table and ratty couches. A few bodies occupied the couches, each guy staring straight ahead. We walked by them to the bedroom. They didn't notice as we walked through. We shut his bedroom door behind us.

"It was crazy here last night. Those dudes are from Stillwater. They were so messed up last night. They've all got wives and are scared to go home all geeked out." Strom laughed. "They've been sitting on the couch like that for hours." He pointed towards his mattress, at the mirror covered in piles lying next to it. "That's why. Remember like a month ago when we got that shit from the Mexicans? Well, I got it again."

"I can't," I said, turning around to play with the stereo, flipping through the CDs.

"Got a piss test tomorrow?"

"Somethin' like that." I took out the CDs and started putting in new ones.

"Shit, girl. You're missin' out. This shit is pink."
I listened to him snorting.

Pink Floyd filled the room. I turned around and walked towards the spot where he sat on the floor with the mirror in his lap. He blinked rapidly as tears streamed down his cheeks. Sounding as if he had a pound of snot clogging it, he said, "God, my nose is so fucked."

Don't do it. Don't do it. I knelt down next to him. *Stop. You're staying sober. You don't want to do this. Stop.* I picked up the straw on the mirror. *You're staying sober. Don't do it.* I brought my head up, my eyes burning and my throat constricting.

We stayed in his bedroom for the next two days, only leaving to go to the bathroom or change the CD. A stream of people came in and out. I didn't go home, which wasn't unusual, but I missed my appointment with Dave. Hunched over in the corner, by the stereo, I took whatever was passed in front of me. I was locked in my head, thinking the same thoughts over and over again.

I can't stop. I can't. I really wanted to. I did. I can't. Not even one day. I'm sixteen. I'm a junkie. I can't stop.

Somewhere along the way, I'd crossed an invisible line that meant I could never go back. I'd keep getting high in the same way you know that every day you'll have to go to the bathroom.

Every night in the secrecy of my bedroom, silent sobs gripped and shook my body. My love affair with chemicals had turned into a nightmare I couldn't wake up from. I'd traded my teenage years for an education on the streets and an opportunity to get high every day. I'd given up every relationship from my childhood that had meant anything. Those I called my friends were only fellow junkies who I knew nothing about, other than that they liked to get high as much as I did.

I'd turned my back on everything I used to value. The worst part was that drugs no longer even made me feel good. They'd betrayed me. I was sure I was as low as I was ever going to get but things kept right on spiraling downward. I kept getting into trouble with the law, and it was only a matter of time before I got sent away again.

And then I met Chad. He'd just moved to town from Arizona. He was at a party where I stopped by with Strom to make an exchange. We ended up staying there all night, and Chad and I hit it off. He was funny and let me shave his head bald in the early hours of the morning.

I thought being involved with a guy might make me feel a little normal. I hadn't been in a relationship with anyone since Keith. Chad made me laugh, and I'd been having a hard time finding anything to smile about so I called him up a few days after we met and asked if he wanted to go to Strom's house with me. I walked to his place, not far from mine. He was renting the basement of his aunt and uncle's house until he could save up enough money to get his own apartment.

I knocked on the door.

"Come in," he called.

I opened the door, stepping into the entryway of a split level house.

"I'm downstairs."

He met me in the hallway then led me into his bedroom. His bed took up almost every inch of space. Clothes were scattered on the floor. I perched on the edge of his bed.

Feeling cramped and confined, I said, "Let's go."

"What's the big hurry?" he asked, sitting down next to me and putting his arm around me. "I want to take a shower before we leave."

"Get on it, then. We're supposed to be at Strom's in an hour."

"Settle," he said, moving closer, almost sitting on top of me. "What's your deal with him anyway? I mean I know he keeps your nose supplied, but he's a loser."

I moved away.

"Hey." He scooted closer. "Sorry." He wrapped his arm around me again and kissed me on the neck.

I cringed. I only had sex when I was wasted or didn't remember it. It was the only time I could tolerate someone touching me and no matter what, I never enjoyed it. Sex repulsed me.

"Chad ..." I sighed. "Get in the shower so we can go."

He reached out and pulled me towards him, squishing me against his chest. He smelled like chicken noodle soup. He buried his head in my neck, slobbering me with his wet tongue as if I was water and he was the dog.

"Knock it off." I pulled away.

"C'mon, don't be playing games," he said, cocking his head to the side to look at me.

I stood up, feeling his clothes under my feet and kicked them away. He stood, towering above me. My stomach flipped over. I didn't have enough oxygen. He stared at me for a second and then threw me on the bed as if I weighed nothing. He jumped on top of me, pinning me down.

"Stop it. You're freaking me out," I cried.

"You're such a tease," he sneered, looking into my eyes without seeing me.

"I'm not. Knock it off. I don't want to do this."

He brought his mouth towards mine. I clenched my teeth together and pinched my lips shut. He thrust his tongue through my lips, pushing it against my teeth. I jerked my head back and forth, wanting to scream but knowing if I did, he'd gain access to my mouth.

No! No! No!

He gripped my wrists with one of his hands, bringing my arms above my head while he unzipped his pants with his other hand. I closed my eyes, not wanting to see what came out.

"Stop! Please Chad, don't do this. Please, don't. Please."

It was as if he couldn't hear me. His eyes bulged out of his head, and a bead of sweat formed on his forehead as he peered down at me. I screamed as loudly as I could. He clasped his hand over my mouth, muffling the sound. I couldn't breathe. I bit his hand, and he jerked it away.

"Go ahead and scream. Nobody's here. No one can hear you."

The excitement grew in his eyes. I wriggled my body underneath his while he laughed. In one quick movement, he reached down and pulled my shorts to the side. He pried my legs apart with his.

"Please, stop. Please."

He refused to look at me. He shoved himself inside of me in one powerful thrust. I felt my insides ripping and tearing apart. I cried out. My head began to swim.

Don't fight him. Don't move. It will only make it worse. You've been here before. It'll be over soon. Don't fight.

He violently thrust in and out of me while I disappeared into the ceiling, watching the ceiling fan move around, getting lost in its spin. He yelled as if he was in pain, arched his back, and collapsed on top of me. I could feel his heart thumping against my chest and smell his stench of chicken noodle soup. I lay there lifeless and immobilized under him. Suddenly, he pulled out of me and jumped up. He hurriedly zipped his pants.

"I'm sorry," he muttered, furtively glancing towards the bedroom door. "I'll take a shower, and then we can go."

He turned around, walked out of the room and down the hallway to the bathroom. I sat up, listening for the sound of water pounding and the shower door shutting. Once I was satisfied he was in it, I leapt off the bed, sprang up the stairs, flung open the door, and ran into the sunshine. I ran through the neighbors' yards, not wanting to be on the streets where people might see me.

I didn't have any memory of reaching my house or going downstairs. My next memory was sitting on the toilet and seeing blood between my legs. I got in the shower, furiously rubbing the washcloth all over my body to get rid of his filth even though it stung and burned. I scrubbed between my legs until I was raw. In clean clothes, I curled up in my bed, pulling the covers over my head. I lay in my bed for the rest of the day in darkness, listening to music, and wanting to die.

"What happened to you yesterday?" Strom asked the next day.

"I went to Chad's to wait for him to get ready. I guess he thought I wanted to have sex, but I didn't. Anyways, he did and-"

"What the hell do you mean by that?" Strom interrupted.

"I mean like I said no but, I don't know ..."

"You mean he raped you?"

"I guess you could say that."

He jumped up from his spot on the floor. "Get up. C'mon."

"What are you gonna do?" I asked.

"Don't worry about it." He marched into the living room where Jen and Rich sat next to each other on the couch. "Jen, I want you to bring Elizabeth to the parking lot of the Main Motel in two hours." He motioned for me to sit next to her.

"Strom, really, it's not a big deal," I said.

"Not a big deal?" The vein in his forehead pulsed. "Nobody fucks with you. C'mon, Rich. I need you to drive."

Rich followed Strom out the door. I sat down next to Jen. I didn't know her very well. She'd started to come around with her boyfriend, Rich, and never said much. She was the quietest tweaker I'd ever met.

"What's going on?" she asked.

I shrugged. We sat in silence, staring at the images on the TV until it was time to go. She drove a big blue Cadillac covered with rust spots. We drove through town until we reached the Main Motel parking lot. I spotted Chad's blue jeep parked next to Rich's brown Tercel.

"Ohmigod. Turn around. Get out of here!"

"What? Strom said-"

"I don't fuckin' care! Please, leave."

She whipped the car around skillfully, leaving the parking lot. We sped away and took the nearest gravel road out of town. I was shaking.

Chad must've denied the whole thing. Strom must've believed him. They were gonna call me a liar.

Jen handed me a pill and pointed towards her water. "Here, take this," she said. "It'll calm you down." I took the pill and gulped it down with water. "What's going on?" she asked.

"Chad kinda raped me."

"Kinda? That shit doesn't kinda happen." She threw her hair over her shoulders. "That fucker."

We drove in silence for a few moments, each of us lost in our thoughts.

"I understand why you had to get out of there," she said.

"You do?"

"Believe me. I get it." She lit a cigarette and took a long drag. "It's like when my uncle messed with me and my mom found out. All these people came from the county to talk to me and I freaked out. I don't know why. It's like you want someone to do something, but when it happens you get totally paranoid like they won't believe you."

She understands. Ohmigod. She gets its.

"It's like when I saw Chad's car there with Strom's. I know Chad denied it and I freaked out that Strom would believe him, ya know? I couldn't handle that."

"I believe you," she said, her long, pale fingers ashing her cigarette. "Men suck. Always wanting a piece of ass and they'll take it any way they can get it. Happens to me all the time. The fuckers."

Later on that night, I found out that Strom had believed me and was going to make Chad kneel down, kiss my feet, and tell me he was sorry. Before the parking lot, Strom had enticed him to a gravel road in the country by promising to get him high. Once they were there, Strom had pulled out his nine millimeter and held it against Chad's temple. Strom threatened that if Chad ever touched me again, he'd kill him. Chad had wet himself.

After that day, I shut down completely and became a spectator of my life like I was watching a movie. I no longer cared what happened to me. I wanted to die, but I'd been taught that people who committed suicide went to hell and burned forever. I was trapped, biding my time, and hoping the next funeral I attended would be my own.

I kept going to see Dave every week, but I stopped being honest with him, and our sessions no longer made me feel good. I felt worse each time because the happiness he exuded was always going to be out of my reach. He suggested I check myself into treatment. I toyed with the idea, but couldn't bring myself to do it. However, the decision was made for me when I went to my next court date in September.

I sat on my aluminum chair at the big wooden table with my parents on the left side of me. Rubin was on my right and next to him was the district attorney. Behind the table, my social worker and guardian ad litem sat whispering to each other. I didn't know what either of them did on my legal case and didn't care to find out. The judge's massive desk towered above us. He got a comfortable, black padded chair. An old lady with gray hair and glasses perched on the tip of her nose typed everything being said in the courtroom and sat in a desk next to the judge.

I slouched in my chair, vaguely aware of the sound of Rubin's voice telling the judge what trouble I'd gotten into since my last court date and all the things I hadn't followed through with. The judge would give me more community service hours that I wouldn't do and sentence me to go to meetings that I wouldn't attend. It was the same boring routine, and I'd lost interest long ago. The rap of the judge's gavel startled me.

From his position above me, the judge said loudly, "Elizabeth, I'm talking to you. Do you understand what a stay of sentence means?" I shook my head. He frowned down at me. "I need you to answer."

I sat straighter in my chair. "No, I don't understand."

"This is how it works. The court takes all the charges you've accumulated and puts off sentencing you for one year." He spoke slowly and purposefully, enunciating every syllable. "Provided you don't accrue any new charges or violate your probation in any way for the next year, the charges will be dropped from your record. You must comply with all of the court's requirements decided upon today and not get into any trouble."

What sort of requirements? What did I miss?

I looked over at Rubin for some type of clue, but he just stared back at me.

"Do you understand everything I've just said?" the judge asked again.

"If I don't get into any trouble for a year, then all of my charges are dropped, right?"

"Yes, but the other part is you must follow through with everything we set in place today. Rubin has recommended long-term chemical dependency treatment and I agree with his recommendation. From here on out, you must follow through with whatever Rubin deems appropriate for you. If you don't, we'll be back in court." His voice echoed through the empty courtroom. "I hope that doesn't happen. I'm tired of having you sit in front of me."

"What happens if I screw up?" I asked.

"You'll be charged with everything and we'll be

looking at sending you to a long-term correctional placement. Anything else, Rubin?"

"No, your honor."

"Court is adjourned." He tapped his gavel on the desk, and we rose from our seats.

My parents drove me to New Hope Treatment Center the following week. Rubin had made arrangements with Dave for me to go back there. We pulled into the parking lot of the big brick treatment center that had become so familiar to me. We walked down the sidewalk to the door to be buzzed in. I had a half-ounce stuffed in my shoe to get me through my stay. Suddenly, without thinking, I stopped and pulled the bag out from my sock. I walked up to the garbage can next to the door and tossed my bag of weed in, and then hurriedly rang the buzzer before I changed my mind.

Garrison

TWELVE

I was skilled at performing as the character of Elizabeth. It'd taken me years to perfect, but I had it down because I'd written the rules to govern her behavior when I was seven. I'd sat at my desk in my bedroom and put them in a numbered list. The first and most important rule was the foundation that kept all the other rules in place: *Don't let anyone know they hurt you.* If people knew they'd hurt you, it gave them power. Not being hurt was the one piece of power I had and I held on to it no matter what. It was the reason I never cried no matter what my dad did to me. I cut off every painful emotion. Anger was the only emotion I allowed myself to show others because it scared and controlled them.

The second rule tied in with the first one: *Don't trust anyone.* My mom claimed to be honest and trustworthy, but I'd seen her watch things happen and then deny she ever saw them occur.

"I don't know what you're talking about Elizabeth," she'd said on so many occasions, "that never happened."

Like when my favorite cat, Tiger, pooped on the floor because he was sick and my dad took him outside and shot him. Whenever I said something about how awful it was that he shot Tiger just because he had diarrhea, my mom would laugh and say, "Oh Elizabeth, quit exaggerating. That never happened." Even though she was standing next to me while we watched him walk down the driveway with his rifle and Tiger, but only come back with his rifle. If I asked him what happened, his response was always the same, "I took care of it."

I'd played my role for so long, I no longer knew it was a character. I slipped into her out of habit at New Hope. Angry and hostile, I moved through treatment ready to fight. I was cold and aloof, evading the serious talk about our issues or anything else emotional. I heard the same things in group I'd heard so many times before.

"Elizabeth is so negative. She threatens my sobriety."

"I'm scared of Elizabeth. She's got such an attitude. It seems like she doesn't really want to be here."

But I knew I was in trouble when one of the boys in treatment came running down the hallway to my room. He stood in the doorway because boys weren't allowed in girls' rooms. "Your bag is at the front desk. I think they're kicking you out."

I ran down the hallway to the nurse's station. I leaned over their desk and spotted my bags lying next to one of the chairs. I turned around to see Dave and the other adolescent counselor, Janice, walking towards me, neither of them smiling.

"Come with us." Dave pointed to the door leading downstairs to their offices.

I took a seat in Janice's office in front of the desk, and Dave shut the door behind us. Janice sat on the blue love seat across from me and Dave sat in the chair next to her. Both faced me head on.

I crossed my arms. "What's going on?"

Janice looked towards Dave. He said, "You're going to have to leave. We called your probation officer. He's going to come get you and take you to a group home. You'll-"

"Are you serious?" I sat straight up in my chair.

"You can't follow the program," Janice said.

"It's not fair to the other kids who are here to get better," Dave said.

A red light exploded in my head. "Fuck you, Dave! You're a goddamn liar. Always saying you care about me and all that bullshit about helping me. Now, you're just gonna kick me out on the streets. Fuck you!"

He jumped up from his chair and strutted back and forth between the door and his chair. He chewed on his bottom lip, and narrowed his eyes. I was afraid he was going to open the door and leave. Finally, he sat back down still breathing heavy.

"You really piss me off. I love and care about you. More than you probably even know. I've gone to bat for you many times. If anyone is in your corner, it's me. You would've been kicked out of here a week ago if it wasn't for me fighting to keep your ass here. I keep telling the staff just to give you a chance and that it will take some time for you to get comfortable, but you give nothing but attitude. There's nothing more I can do. It's up to you, and you seem perfectly content to destroy yourself. It breaks my heart, but I've got to let you go."

A lump lodged in my throat. I twisted my

hands together. The room was silent except for the sound of our breathing and the ticking of the round clock on the wall. I couldn't find my voice.

Dave broke in, turning to look at Janice. "Okay. Let's sign the discharge papers."

"Wait." My voice squeaked out.

"What?" Janice asked.

"I don't want to leave." I didn't recognize the sound of my voice.

"Why?" Dave asked.

"Because … I… I just …" My tongue felt too big for my mouth. "Because I'll die out there."

Janice and Dave stared at me, waiting for me to go on, but I couldn't.

"Let's talk about it," Dave said. "Tell me more."

I took a deep breath and tried again. "If I leave here, I know I'll get high. I don't know how not to. I'll never get sober if I go back out there and I want to see what it's like."

Their eyes bored into me. I felt naked and wanted a blanket to wrap around me. I brought my knees up to my chest.

"I think that's the first honest and real thing I've ever heard you say," Janice said. "This is the stuff you need to be sharing."

"What are you willing to do?" Dave asked.

I shrugged my shoulders. "Anything, I guess."

"Okay. Then, let's start talking, right now. Let's talk about your family and why you do everything you can to get out of that house."

I didn't know what happened next. I talked without knowing what I was saying, and they must've thought I did well because I was allowed to stay. But it was one of my mental blank spots. Whenever things got intense or I felt scared, I went to some place in my mind—one I couldn't name—and was never able to remember what happened. Anything dealing with my family was sure to cause it.

About a week later, I was sitting in my room drawing when Dave knocked at my door.

"What?"

"It's Dave. Can I come in?"

"Sure." I focused on the drawing I'd been working on since the night before.

He walked in and stood behind me at the desk, looking over my shoulder. "Nice." I continued working on the curve of the person's nose. "Some people are here to see you."

I stopped drawing and looked up at him. "What

people?"

He cleared his throat. "There's a sheriff and two women from the county. One of them is a social worker and the other one is a victim's advocate."

My mind spun. "What are they doing here?"

"I made a report to the country that I suspected abuse was going on in your house. They're just here to help. They just want to ask you some questions. All you've got to do is talk to them like you're talking to me. I'll be with you the whole time. Okay, honey?"

"No!" I grabbed a book from my desk and hurled it at the wall. "I won't. You can't make me. Ohmigod, I'm not going down there."

"C'mon. Don't make this difficult. I know you're scared."

"Fuck you. You don't know how I feel! Shit! Fuck! God dammit!"

I grabbed my pencil and stabbed it through my paper.

This can't be happening. This isn't real. No one will believe you. They'll talk to your dad. Mom will say you're lying. What if they believe you? I'm crazy. I lied. I told the truth. This isn't happening.

"Let's go. C'mon, they're all waiting. You have

to do this," Dave coaxed, moving towards me.

I pulled away, grabbed a chair, and flipped it over. I climbed onto my desk and jumped onto my bed behind it. I curled into a tight ball in the corner between the wall and the bed, shaking uncontrollably.

This isn't real. Just make it stop. Go away. Everyone needs to leave me alone.

Dave took a step towards me.

"Get. Away. From. Me," I said.

He stopped in his tracks.

"Sweetie-"

"Don't call me that. Leave me alone." I wanted to grab the pencil and stab his eyes with it to make him stop looking at me.

He didn't say a word, just watched me hunched over in the corner breathing rapidly. He stood there for a long time, hoping I'd change my mind and go downstairs, but I couldn't. He had no idea how terrified I was. I'd only talked to him about my dad because I was trying to make sense of the craziness in my head. I'd never told Dave or anyone else that my dad abused me. Never. They couldn't make me say he did.

"Okay," he said quietly. "I'll tell them you

refuse to come down."

He turned and left my room. I jumped off my bed and crawled under it to hide. Flat on my back, staring at the wire mesh inches from my nose, I pretended I was in a coffin, just like I used to do in my bed at home when I was little. I practiced being dead. My space was transformed from wire springs holding a mattress to the top of a wooden coffin lined in purple satin. The hard floor became a soft cushiony pillow holding my dead body while I slept in a world different than the one I was in.

I kept opening up to Dave even though he made a report to the county. He'd only done it because he had to just like Hank had done. It was a weird part of their job that I didn't understand, but on some level, I'd started to trust Dave in a way I'd never trusted anyone before. As angry as I was that he'd made the report, I was also grateful because he'd protected me by getting the people from the county to go away and to leave me alone.

As the days at New Hope grew into weeks, I became engaged in a constant battle between my character and myself. I didn't have a sense of self without my character. I'd look into the mirror above the small sink in my bathroom, and wonder who the person staring back was. I felt no connection to her.

Nights were the hardest. Either I couldn't sleep or woke screaming from nightmares and drenched in sweat. As soon as I was awake, I quickly pushed away the images from my nightmares. And then, the nightmare nights became sleepless nights.

One night, lying in my safe place underneath the bed, I contemplated untangling the wires from the springs above me and using them to make a noose so I could hang myself in the bathroom. I didn't care anymore if I was going to hell. At least in hell, I could focus on the physical pain of burning rather than focusing on the emotions tormenting me and the voices in my head would finally be silent.

Dave's deep voice broke into my thoughts, "Hey." I turned my head to see him lying on his side next to the bed, peeking in at me. "Bad night again?" he asked.

I didn't respond.

"Wanna come out from underneath there so we can talk?"

I shook my head.

"Do you want to hold my hand?"

I shook my head again.

He stuck his arm underneath the bed and stretched his hand out to me. "Will you, at least, hold my pinkie?"

I reached out and hooked his pinkie with mine.

He sighed. "You're not alone in all of this, sweetie."

We lay like that for a long time. It was at that moment I decided he'd be the one I'd let see me or rather, the me that wasn't there. It felt good to let someone else have a peek into the inner workings of my life, a place uncharted by anyone besides me. I didn't know what to do with myself, or with the chaotic mess I'd made of my life. I started to let Dave make decisions for me because I didn't know how to.

First, he decided it would be a good idea for me not to have any contact with my dad for a while. "I don't think you're going to be able to work through your issues with your dad if you're going to have to worry about seeing or talking to him."

I agreed not out of a mutual understanding to work through my issues with my dad, but because I really didn't want to see him. "But what about my mom?"

"I'll talk to her," he said.

I was surprised when my mom showed up for our family session alone. She rarely went anywhere without my dad because he controlled where she went and who she went out with. Even though her friends were church members, she rarely did things with them outside of church. Her time away from the family was limited to grocery shopping and running other errands. It was a huge step for her and I was amazed she took it. I couldn't imagine any scenario where she'd lie to my dad about where she was going, which meant she'd had to ask him permission to visit me by herself. There was no way the conversation had gone easy for her, and she would've had to stand her ground against him—something I'd never seen her do.

She was visibly nervous when she walked through the door of New Hope and looked out of place being outside of the house without my dad. There'd only been a few times I'd seen her in public without him nearby. She'd lost weight since the last time I'd seen her. I wasn't sure if it was intentional or stress since she was continually dieting—not as if she needed to. The women in our family were blessed with good metabolisms that kept us lean with minimal work. She'd recently gotten a perm because the curls were tight around her head like they were when it was fresh. She'd been getting the same perm for years. Her clothes looked different too as if she'd taken time and care to dress up for the occasion. She held her purse in front of her with both hands like a shield. We greeted each other like strangers as we awkwardly hugged before taking our seats in family group.

Much like other family groups I'd attended, each family got a turn and when it was ours, Dave instructed me to ask my mom if it was okay if we could have a relationship without my dad being involved. I didn't think I'd ever get used to talking in the third person even when the person you were referring to was sitting in front of you.

I nodded at him, still not looking at my mom.

"Go ahead," he said.

My hands shook. I was scared to tell her because it would hurt her and might bring up the things we never spoke about.

"Mom, I'd like to have a relationship with you that doesn't include dad." Dave sat in the chair next to me, squeezing my hand tightly, and I borrowed his strength as my own. "I need some time to be away from him, but I'd like to start working on my relationship with you. I want a relationship with just you. If you can't do that, then I don't think I can have a relationship with you either."

I couldn't believe the words had come out of my mouth. I was shocked. I'd never said something so direct, straight-forward, and honest to her.

She pursed her lips together, sucking her small upper lip underneath until it disappeared. "I can do that."

"Okay, great," David clasped his hands together. "I think this is going to be really helpful for your relationship."

My mom kept her promise and started coming to visit me by herself during visiting hours on the weekend. It was weird and uncomfortable talking to her without my dad or the threat of his presence. We had no idea how to do it. Our conversations were halted and forced like an awkward first date. We tried to stay away from anything serious. We talked about Sarah and how her homeschooling was going or craft projects my mom was working on. Other times, we talked about anything funny going on in the treatment center with the other kids until one day as we sat at a picnic table outside she announced, "I need to talk to you."

I nodded.

She had a look in her eyes I'd never seen before. Her face was taut and her expression grave. "I don't really know how to say this ..."

"It's okay. I'm listening." My palms were sweating. My heart started to thump.

"All the questions ... Everyone is asking me about whether you've been abused."

Who's asking her? What does she say? Ohmigod. Stay here, Elizabeth. Don't go anywhere. You need to hear this. Listen. Don't leave. Stay.

It seemed like hours passed before she spoke again. "Everyone keeps asking me if you've been abused. They don't ask me directly about your dad, but I know he's who they're talking about—they think he sexually abused you." She paused, watching my face.

A surge of panic shot through me. My body started to shake and I felt dizzy. I gripped onto the picnic bench to steady myself, scared I'd fall off if I didn't. My voice disappeared.

When she spoke again her voice was shaky and weak. "I asked him. He cried and said he never touched you. I have to believe him."

Of course, she believes him. That's nothing new. He cried? I can't believe she even asked him. He knows? I'm going to throw up.

"Elizabeth?" I refused to look at her. Instead, I anxiously searched for a garbage can to run to. "Is it your dad?"

Fear curled in my stomach like a fist. My mouth felt as if it was filled with cotton, preventing me from swallowing. I couldn't breathe.

"Is it?"

I looked down at my hands, but they didn't look like mine. "I remember weird things. I can't explain them. I have pieces. Images. Weird shit goes on in my head. Dad looks at my ass." My words made no sense, not even to me.

"What kind of things?" She asked, eyeing me quizzically.

The words I'd wanted to say to her since I was a little girl burned their way up my throat in a fiery ball. I'd never said the words out loud, and if I didn't get them out now, I'd shove them back down again until they dissolved like acid in my gut. Before I could second guess myself, I unleashed them.

"I was terrified of a monster coming into my room at night when I was little. And someone or something was definitely there. I don't know if it was a demon or what, but I saw it. Never the face, only his dark body. But I don't remember anything after that. Everything goes blank."

I looked up to see her reaction to what I'd just said. She was looking at me without any expression on her face. Her face was a blank slate. I didn't know what it meant.

"Anything else?" Her voice was as flat as her emotions.

"I have nightmares. Stuff about really gross, sexual things. Sometimes dad's in them ..." My food from lunch came up my throat, and I swallowed it back down. I clenched my teeth together.

"They're just nightmares. They're not real and they don't mean anything. You can't control what happens in your dreams. I wouldn't even worry about it." She folded her hands on the picnic table. "But, I do think you probably had a demon in your room at night. People see demons all the time, and Satan's number one attack is on the family."

"Dad touched me underneath my shirt when he was tickling me. He touched my boobs," I blurted out.

She laughed. "Oh Elizabeth, I'm sure it was an accident. He didn't mean anything by it."

I'd run out of steam. We sat in a stony silence until I couldn't take it anymore.

"I'm sorry. I'm just trying to figure it all out," I said.

"I don't understand why you have to figure it out. Why it even matters." Her eyes flared with anger.

Is she mad at me? Why is she mad at me? What did I do?

"My grandpa sexually abused me, and it's not like it affects my life or anything. I'm fine." She reached across the table and laid her hands on mine. "Besides, even if it did happen to you, we have to forgive the people who hurt us. Christ teaches us to forgive. Even if your dad did do something to you, Elizabeth, I forgive him. I forgive him because God forgives us."

That's it? You just forgive him? Don't you want to know the truth? Can't you help me figure this out? What about Sarah? Don't you want to find out what he did to me? If he did something to me, don't you think he might do something to

Sarah too? She's still there with him.

"Do you have enough cigarettes for the week?" she asked, changing the subject and shifting back to her fake smile.

I walked away from our visit in a daze, not quite believing the conversation had occurred. I related the details to Dave, but it was like I was telling him a story about another girl. He sat in the chair next to me, putting his arm around my shoulder. "I'm sorry, honey."

Sorry? What's he sorry for? I'm sorry I ever talked about it. So, shut up. No more talking about Dad. But I ... shut up. There is no reason to go there. Never. Never again.

My mom kept coming every week, but we didn't talk about my dad again. It was like the conversation never happened. Dave suggested I talk to her about it again, but I refused. My mom and I went back to talking about lighthearted things. Dave kept trying to bring it up in our sessions, but I wouldn't talk to him about it either, but I did start opening up to him about what other men had done to me. It was why he kept me in treatment for so long.

Normally, kids stayed in treatment for twenty-eight days, but I stayed for fifty-four. Dave kept getting me extensions from the county, but eventually the day came for me to leave. It'd been decided that I would go to River East, a halfway house in Minneapolis, for three months. The place was kind of like treatment, but not quite as strict. I wasn't afraid to leave treatment, but I was terrified to leave Dave.

"I'm so proud of you," he said as we drove up the long gravel driveway to the halfway house. I always got uncomfortable whenever he said anything nice about me. I watched as River East, a small white plaster building next to a church, came into view. He parked the car in front of the building and turned to me.

"I want to give you something. Don't laugh, 'cause it's kind of cheesy." I smiled as he took off the white sweater he was wearing and handed it to me.

He cleared his throat. "Whenever you get lonely and think nobody cares about you, just put this on and think of me giving you a great big hug."

I took the sweater, blinking back the tears that threatened to spill down my cheeks. "Thank you."

Dressed only in a red T-shirt, Dave rubbed his

arms as we walked in trying to keep himself warm. A short man with a huge belly and chubby cheeks greeted us, sticking out his pudgy hand to me.

"I'm Bill. C'mon, I'll show you around." He waddled in front of us. We followed him through the building lined with linoleum like school cafeteria floors. Bill showed us the room where group was held every night, and led us down a flight of stairs to the dining room and kitchen. Every kid had a chore to do and rotated cooking duties. The guys' rooms were all downstairs and as usual, I wasn't allowed in any of them. We headed back up the stairs as Bill explained I'd be bussed to the alternative high school nearby.

"All of these are girls' rooms." At the end of the long hallway, he opened the door to a white room with brown carpet. There were two beds, one on each wall. "And this is your room. You're lucky. You've only got one roommate." Half of the room was bare except for the bed and nightstand. My roommate's side was covered in Snoop Dogg pictures. "I'll leave you two alone to say good bye." Bill shut the door behind him.

I turned to look at Dave, clutching his sweater in my hands. He put both of his hands on my shoulders. "You'll be fine without me." His eyes were wet and glossy. "You're going to do great here. Everything is going to be okay."

"I'm gonna miss you." My voice was barely audible.

"I'll miss you, too." He pulled me into a hug. I breathed him in and held on tightly, not wanting to let him go. "I love you and I'm so proud of you. I'm only a phone call away."

I love you, too. I couldn't say it, but it was true. He slowly pulled away.

"Okay." He coughed. "I'm gonna go. I'm just gonna go." In two seconds, he was gone and I was standing in the same place, still holding on to his sweater.

Imani was my roommate and we got along pretty well. She was a year younger than me and had created her own character that was similar to mine. Most of our conversations centered on trying to prove who was the toughest. We shared our stories about the drugs we'd done and the crimes we'd committed, continually trying to outdo the other.

Our tastes in music were completely different, but we worked out a system where we alternated nights. On Imani's nights, we listened to Snoop Dogg as we fell asleep and on my nights we listened to the Beatles or the Grateful Dead. But no matter what we listened to, I always followed the same routine. I'd lie in my bed and strain my ears for the sounds of her falling asleep. I got very good at listening for the exact rhythm she made when she was sleeping deeply.

Once I was sure she was asleep, I reached underneath my mattress and pulled out Dave's sweater. I wrapped it around me as if his arms were inside of it holding me. Sometimes, I swore I could still smell him lingering in the soft fabric. There were nights that I cried silent tears into it but, no matter what, I made sure I was the first one awake in the morning so I could hide it underneath my mattress until night returned.

Garrison

THIRTEEN

I had almost five months of sobriety by the time I got out of River East. It felt like a lifetime. I was adept at staying sober in an institution, but the real test would be whether I could stay clean in the outside world.

A CHIPS petition was filed in my county shortly before my discharge. I didn't know what it was. I thought it had something to do with me being bad, but found out later that it stood for Child in Need of Protective Services. All I knew was that I'd be going to a foster home located an hour away from my hometown.

Yvonne, my foster mom, was the opposite of Mrs. Morrison. She was a middle-aged widow, over six feet tall, with wide shoulders and a big chest. Her frizzy gray hair stuck up haphazardly all over her head. Her face, lined with wrinkles, also bore a skin disorder that spotted her face with weird blotches and bumps. Behind her ugly exterior, flashed warm and attentive eyes. I was impressed that she'd married a black man in the fifties. She had two grown daughters with families of their own and Jewel, who was only fifteen. Jewel lived in a small guest house in the backyard, her private retreat from the foster kids. Yvonne bought her a red convertible even though she wasn't old enough to drive.

"Here's the deal, kid," she began the day I arrived. She swayed in her whicker rocking chair. "I've heard an awful lot about you from your PO and social worker and most of it hasn't been too nice. They say you're nothing but trouble and probably won't last more than two weeks before I get sick of you. I've heard all this stuff about how you're disrespectful and will tell me to fuck off. Well, we're gonna get one thing straight. If you tell me to fuck off, I'll tell you to fuck off. I don't take any lip. Got it?"

I nodded my head, shocked she'd sworn.

"Okay. Just so you know, I've had lots of tough girls in my home. I've had every kind of girl come through here so you don't scare me in the least.

You're probably wondering why the hell I do this, huh?" She sipped her tea and set it down on the end table next to her chair. "It's pretty simple. Kids in foster care have never had a nice home or they wouldn't be in foster care. I just want to give every kid who comes through here a chance to experience what it's like to have a good, safe home. I feel like it's my job to provide that."

I didn't know what to say.

"You're a druggie, right?" She hadn't stopped rocking in her chair.

I laughed at her choice of words. "Yep, but I've been clean for almost five months."

"Good for you. Honestly, I don't know anything about those damn drugs. They seem just silly to me. I don't understand what possesses people to do them. You're the expert. There's nothing I could teach you about them that you don't already know."

I nodded my head, listening carefully.

"This is how I see things. You already know what's going to happen to you if you start using again. No one can keep you sober. I know that much. It's got to be your choice. Drugs are your business, not mine. I just have one request, and that is if you decide to start using drugs again, you don't bring them into my house. What you do when you leave here is up to you, but I don't want that shit in my house. Okay with you?"

"Sure," I said.

"It's pretty simple. You respect me, and I'll respect you."

Yvonne treated me as if I was an equal. I never felt as if she looked down on me. There were things she didn't understand, but she was always quick to ask questions rather than criticize. I loved living there.

I shared her with two foster sisters, Enalyn and Courtney. Enalyn was eighteen and had been at Yvonne's since she was twelve. She'd been adopted from an orphanage in the Philippines when she was a baby. Her adoptive brothers beat her and she was removed from the home because her parents refused to stop them. Enalyn was beautiful, with smooth brown skin and long, shiny black hair that flowed down her back. Even though she looked like an adult, she saw the world through the eyes of a child because she was developmentally delayed. It was impossible not to love her.

She was Yvonne's prized product of a good, loving home. She puffed with pride every time she talked about the condition Enalyn was in when she first came to live with her. She'd been out of control with boys. They took advantage of her developing body because she didn't understand it was wrong to lift up her shirt and let boys touch her breasts. Yvonne had carefully schooled her in manners and the appropriate ways to interact. Enalyn adored Yvonne and was eager to please her.

"Mom says after Jewel graduates, I can live in her house." Her eyes sparkled like they always did. "I get to live back there. All by myself. I can decorate however I want. She says I can."

Courtney, my other foster sister, was fourteen and had been with Yvonne for a year. She was a continuing frustration for Yvonne because no matter how much attention and love was lavished on her, she refused to accept it. Courtney had been removed from her home because her dad had been raping her since she was nine. Looking into her eyes was like staring into the eyes of an old woman. Courtney wasn't much older than Sarah, and she looked up to me in the same way she did. I hadn't been there long before she started dressing and talking like me.

"Looks like you've got yourself a little

Elizabeth," Yvonne said all the time.

I didn't mind, but I got tired of her stealing clothes from my closet. I would've lent them to her, but she never asked. She didn't have the ability to ask for things. She hoarded clothes in her room in the same way she stockpiled food from the kitchen under her bed.

Each of us had our own room. My room was next to Courtney's and across from Enalyn. It had slanted ceilings and a queen-sized bed in the center, topped with a black silk comforter and matching red and black pillows. I even had my own TV and phone—something I'd never had. There was a matching red and black artist's desk in the corner. I'd wanted a black and red room since I was a little girl. It was like Yvonne had known me before we ever met.

I didn't realize how unsafe my home was until I lived with Yvonne. People said you didn't know what you had until it was gone, but my experience was the opposite. I didn't know what I didn't have until I got what I had at Yvonne's. When I walked through the doors, I didn't feel a sense of impending doom like I did at my parents. I didn't have to remain alert and aware of everyone's presence at all times. There was never the suffocating anger underneath the surface.

I didn't have to cover up my body and try to hide from peering eyes. I could use the bathroom in private with no one intruding on me. While I showered at home, my dad had a habit of sneaking into the bathroom, standing on the toilet, and dumping cold water over me. My mom always said it was his way of joking around, just like when he pinched and slapped my butt. He slapped Sarah's too. She thought it was funny, but I didn't.

My mom came to visit occasionally. She started working strange comments and questions about my dad into our interactions. Like once when we were in the middle of shopping for jeans she announced, "I knew something was wrong with you when you were young. I knew someone was messing with you. But I really think it was the neighborhood boys who messed with you. I just think you put your dad's face onto it."

Before I could respond, she changed the subject. "Do you like these jeans?"

Other times she'd tell stories about my childhood that I didn't remember. The oddest one was the day she heard me screaming while she was upstairs doing dishes and ran downstairs to my room and found me with my dresser on top of me. She explained, "There you were on the ground with your dresser on top of you. Your dad was pulling it off. You wouldn't stop screaming. I remember being shocked because you never cried or got upset when you got hurt. So I knew if you were making a fuss then something was seriously wrong. But the weird thing was that you were naked underneath your dresser. You weren't screaming because you were hurt, you were just screaming for your clothes. What happened that day?"

I searched my memory for a recollection of it, for any small piece, but came up with nothing. It was the same when she asked about me being left alone with my dad while she was up north visiting her family.

"Did anything happen then?" she asked.

Once again, I just shrugged my shoulders and mumbled that I didn't know. I couldn't ever remember her going away and being left alone with my dad. I was always relieved when my visits with her were over. I wanted to leave everything about my old life behind, including trying to figure out what happened with my dad, and I couldn't move past it if she kept finding a way to insert it into our conversations.

Everything about my new life with Yvonne was foreign as if I'd been cut out from an old picture and pasted into a new one that didn't resemble anything familiar. I missed the rigid structure and rules I had when I was at River East. As much as I'd fought against them at the time, I missed them when they were gone. I felt like a baby who'd just learned to stand and was suddenly expected to know how to walk.

My feelings of being lost and misplaced were magnified when I started attending school at the Alternative Learning Center. Part of my probation was to attend school and I hated it. The ALC was at the far end of the regular wing of the high school, separate from the mainstream kids. We weren't supposed to interact with them like we might contaminate them if we got too close. We had one room where we sat from nine until noon every day.

There were three groups of kids and I didn't fit into any one of them. One group consisted of teen mothers who'd already had babies or were expecting them. The girls worked at their desks all morning, focusing on finishing the work packets we were given. Then, there was a bunch of Latino kids who spoke Spanish and broken English. They stuck with each other and rarely spoke to anyone else. The last group was the kids who were just like how I used to be. They'd gotten kicked out of regular school and couldn't go back even if they did the work assigned. They came to class with red eyes or messed up pupils, reeking of booze.

Yvonne waited for me to get home from school to talk to me about my day like she did for all of us. She'd sit in her rocking chair, drinking her tea, and ready to hear stories from our days.

"It's gotta be hard for you," she said one day, noticing my depressed mood. "You must be lonely. I wish there was something I could do. I'm sure you've got to get sick of hanging around an old bag like me."

She never pressured me to talk about anything I didn't want to, but she was right. I was lonely, like a five-year-old on the playground, watching all the other kids play and wanting to join in, but not knowing how.

The only other kids I was around were the ones who attended the aftercare meetings I went to at New Hope. Most of them didn't want to be sober.

The group was constantly changing because most people never came more than a few times before they disappeared, except for Kasey. She was the only other person besides me who came regularly and wanted to be sober. Dave encouraged me to be friends with her so I started making an effort to talk to her.

She was a tall, lanky girl with short blond hair who'd gone through treatment a month before me. They'd called her Peanut when she was using. She was desperately trying to get rid of Peanut and become Kasey.

"Why do they call you Peanut?" I asked.

We were smoking outside the treatment center. Usually on our smoke breaks, I went off to be by myself, but that night I'd followed her outside.

She shrugged. "I don't really know. They just do."

I burst out laughing. "You have a nickname and don't even know why?"

"I never thought about it. That's funny." She made a high-pitched squeal when she laughed.

We started hanging out together outside of aftercare meetings. Neither of us had any clue what to do with our time so we took to doing anything to get a rush. Shoplifting became one of our favorite things to do. There was an exhilarating high as we successfully walked through the doors of a store with stolen merchandise stuffed down our pants or buried in a backpack. We each got a new wardrobe and anything else we wanted that way. We raced her grandma's car up and down Main Street, and sometimes drove into things just to see what would happen. We pulled up our shirts, flashing truckers on the interstate. At night, we climbed the walls of buildings and flipped cartwheels on the roof.

Kasey lived with her grandma, and we alternated between sleeping over at her grandma's and sleeping at Yvonne's. It was almost like we were normal teenagers as we munched on Oreo cookies late at night and lay side by side in bed, whispering and giggling until the sun came up. It was at night that we let our guards down, shedding our tough skins to become frightened little girls. Kasey and I became inseparable. It felt good because I hadn't had a girlfriend in a long time.

We'd stop in at the treatment center together, and Dave took turns meeting with us. Sometimes Dave and I sat in his office and talked, but we spent just as much time in the gym shooting baskets, playing endless games of Horse. In the beginning, he was supportive of my friendship with Kasey and laughed when I told him about our escapades. But as time went on, he grew less amused at the things we did. "If you're going to act, talk, and spit like a junkie then you might as well go all the way," he'd say.

I'd nod my head like I knew what he meant, even though I didn't, but it was only a matter of time until I found out what he was implying. I learned how easy it was to slip back into old behavior shortly after another member joined Kasey and me on our adventures. His name was Sam, and he started attending aftercare meetings with us. I was thrilled when I found out his parents were enrolling him in the ALC for the rest of the school year. I finally had someone to hang out with during school. We both liked to do art and our teacher encouraged us to develop our talents. She worked out a way for us to use the art room every other day for an hour.

It was our second week going to the art room, and Sam was using rubber cement to glue pieces of tile onto a board when he complained, "This stuff reeks."

"Shit. That's nothing. Have you ever huffed it?" I continued trying to get the background on my painting just right. I'd been trying to do it all week.

"Huh? Huffing? I don't get it," he raised his head from his work.

"You've never done it?"

"Uh, no. I'm not a freak."

"Shut up." I gave him the finger, but I was smiling. "You'd be surprised. It's a trip. You get like this vavoom sound in your head."

"Really?" He stared at the tin can. "How do you do it?"

I put down my brush. "You just pour it into a bag. Then, you take the bag and hold it in your mouth and nose like you're hyperventilating." I demonstrated with my hands on an imaginary bag. "You just make sure to hold the bag tight and breathe in and out as fast as you can."

He clapped and looked around at the empty room. "I wanna try it."

"Seriously? We're supposed to be sober."

Sam winked at me and smiled. "It's not like it's a real drug. It's just messin' around." He stood up and pushed his chair under the table. "C'mon. We've only got like fifteen minutes. Help me find a bag."

I got up and rummaged through the art supplies closet with him until I found a Ziploc bag filled with stencils. I dumped the contents into another bag and shook it out.

"This'll work," I said. "Just don't suck in the plastic." I walked back to our table, unscrewed the top of the can and dumped the thick goo into the bag. Sam stood by the door, watching. I walked over and handed it to him.

"Take it into the bathroom," I whispered, even though there was nobody around to hear me. "Do it just like I showed you."

He grabbed the bag and skipped out the door. I picked up the lid to screw it back on the can.

Stick your face in there. What? I'm not sticking my face in there. It's not a big deal. Christ, it's only rubber cement.

I shook my head, trying to stop the thoughts. But before I knew what I was doing, I stuck my face into the jar. The stickiness clung to my chin and forehead as I took a few huge breaths. I jerked my head up, shocked and repulsed. I shoved the can down the table away from my reach. My head felt dizzy like I'd just gotten off a roller coaster. I tapped my fingers on the table, staring at my picture, unmoving, dazed.

It seemed like forever before Sam stumbled back through the door, clutching the bag in his left hand. He had a goofy grin plastered on his face, and his eyes were slits like he'd smoked a lot of weed. "Shit," he said, speaking slowly. "Everything looks like a cartoon."

Get out of here. Run. Run. But I couldn't move.

Sam burst out laughing, clutching his sides. "Ohmigod, ohmigod. I hear it. I hear that vavoom in my head. Aw-shit! This is nuts."

Mechanically, I stood up and moved towards him. *What are you doing? I know what I'm doing. No, you don't. Stop. Think about it. Shut up.* In slow motion, I took the bag from his hands and then brought the bag up to my face, pulling it around my mouth and my nose. *What are you doing? Shut up, this doesn't count.* I breathed in and out like I was running a race. The fumes invaded my lungs with a strange burn. In two minutes, I was high.

I grabbed Sam's hand with my empty hand. "Let's get out of here."

We ran out of the room and hit the nearest

door. The sunshine struck my eyes, crisscrossing in waves. We headed across the street to a church, where we sat down next to each other on the steps. We passed the bag of rubber cement back and forth between us until we blacked out and lay on the church steps, unconscious.

Addiction was like having a monster living in your mind. By staying sober, I hadn't fed the monster any food for almost six months. I'd made it weak, but huffing the rubber cement just that one time had reawakened my monster. As soon as I fed it, it attacked and set out to destroy me.

I called Dave that night, fully intending to tell him what I'd done. "I have something to tell you ..." I stammered. My hands were sweating, and my throat felt tight.

"What is it?"

What do I say? Tell him it was an accident. "I kind of got high ..."

"How is that possible?" I could hear the edge in his voice. "Is that like being kinda pregnant?"

He's mad. He told you that you'd get high. You just proved him right. He's gonna leave. He's sick of your shit. You're such a fuck up.

"I don't really know how it happened. Me and

Sam, you know how we go to the art room every day? I think I told you that didn't I?"

"Get to it."

I swallowed hard. "We were using the rubber cement and it's in this big can. Anyways, I had to put the top back on and while I was doing it, I got dizzy. I think I breathed in. I don't know if I did it on purpose, but I felt weird afterward. Kinda strange."

He laughed. "You didn't get high. Fumes will do that to you even a little bit. One time when I was painting my bathroom, I felt a little weird. I had to go outside in the fresh air for a while, but it's not like I got high. Next time just turn your head away. It's not like you stuck your head in the can or something like that."

I laughed. "You're right. I guess I'm just being paranoid."

From that point on, each night when Dave told me he was proud of me, I cringed inside. My secret ate away at me. I decided I should just get drunk so I could tell Dave I'd relapsed. It wasn't logical, but it made sense to me. The details of my relapse wouldn't matter. I could start over with a clean slate. If I could make the decision to start using again, then I could just as easily make the decision to stop.

On our way to group the following night, I told Kasey I wanted to get drunk.

"We should get a bottle," I said.

"Are you serious?"

"It's not like we're gonna do drugs or anything. I just wanna get drunk. Just once with you to see what it's like." I couldn't look at her.

Leave her out of this. What kind of a friend are you? She doesn't really want to be sober. I'm doing her a favor. Helping her along.

She lit a cigarette. "I don't know. I'm kinda scared."

"C'mon. We always talk about how much fun it would've been to use together. Let's just do it. Once. It'll be fun."

I turned to look at her. She stared straight ahead and her forehead creased.

"Kasey," I called to her seductively. "You know you want to. But hey, if you're too scared, I understand."

"I'm not scared," she snapped. "I can get someone to buy us a bottle."

Once I was drunk, I wanted to smoke pot. I'd

already relapsed and wanted to make it a good one. Kasey tracked down the friends she'd stayed away from while she was sober to get it for us.

Overnight, Kasey and I became two friends who got wasted together, instead of two friends staying sober together. Each time I used, I convinced myself it would be the last time, and I'd confess to Dave the next day. The next day would come and I'd put it off for one more day. The days turned into weeks. I quit going to aftercare groups or the treatment center to visit because I didn't want Dave to see me. He'd be able to look at me and tell I wasn't sober.

Kasey ended up revealing my secret for me. As she pulled into Yvonne's driveway to drop me off, she announced, "I talked to Dave a few days ago. I'm going back into treatment to do a relapse program."

"When?" If she'd talked to Dave, then he had to know I was using too. There was no way she hadn't told him. She stared out the window with the back of her head to me.

"Today," she said.

"Today? Why didn't you tell me?"

"I was afraid you'd talk me out of it. I didn't

want to tell you I couldn't handle all this. I hate this shit, Elizabeth. It's like I'm right back where I was before and I can't stand it."

We blew our smoke out the windows in thick white clouds.

"I should probably get going," she said, staring at the center of the steering wheel, still refusing to meet my eyes. "I still have to pack."

I nodded and opened my door. I wanted to give her a hug, tell her I understood and that I loved her, but I couldn't. I'd reverted to the character of Elizabeth and showing emotion was not part of her makeup. I turned to look at her. "Call me?"

She shrugged. "Sure."

She drove away without looking back. As I watched the car disappear, I knew I'd soon become a name on her list—the list you have to make in treatment of all of your using friends that you can't hang around anymore. Without Kasey, I didn't have any connections so I couldn't get high. I resorted to huffing household products again, but it didn't take long before the cheap buzz wasn't doing anything for me. I wanted the real thing. It wasn't long before I found myself punching in Strom's familiar digits and planning to meet him the next time I was in town to meet with Rubin.

I met him at the park across the street from his parents' house. He looked the same. His brown hair was greasy and sticking up. His skin still hung from his face, creating three rolls of chins when he looked down. He gave me a hug. We sat across from each other at an old picnic table as he packed a one-hitter for me.

He looked up as he did it, smiling. "It's been awhile."

I took it and started to smoke. "Yep."

"So, where do you live now?" He stared at me.

Did I look different? I felt different.

"Pervis," I said, exhaling.

"Hmm." He dug another one-hitter out of the pocket of his jeans and began packing it for himself.

Don't you want to know where I've been? It's been almost a year since you've seen me. Haven't you wondered?

I waited for him to ask questions, but none came. We sat in silence, smoking our pot, pretending to be interested in the baseball game going on in the park at the field across from us.

I've forgotten how to be with him. Or maybe this is how it's always been. But I thought we talked.

"How've you been?" I asked.

He shrugged his big shoulders. "Fine. Ya know. Same old shit. Different day."

I smiled. "Yeah."

"Anything exciting going on?" he asked, tapping his fingers on the top of the table.

"Not really."

"Oh ..."

The silence stretched out between us. Finally, I spoke. "I should get going. I gotta meet my mom soon. She's gonna bring me back to Pervis."

"It's good to see you. Ya shouldn't be such a stranger."

"I won't." I smiled at him. "Hey, I don't know anyone where I live and I can't get anything. I don't have any money, but do ya think you could give me a bag?"

Before I finished my sentence, he was digging in the pocket of his jeans. He handed me a baggie filled with green buds.

I tucked it into my pocket. "Thanks."

He shrugged. "Don't mention it. It's only weed. If you need anything else, lemme know. Gimme a call, whenever."

It was surprisingly easy to step back into my old life as if I'd never been gone. Calling up old friends and connections, it struck me that no one asked me any questions. I'd been away for almost a year, but it was like no one had noticed. I thought being sober had destroyed the character of Elizabeth, but in no time at all, I was back to the performance.

It was harder and took more planning to get hooked up because I was over an hour away from my hometown. I started staying out all night and skipping school. I avoided Dave at all costs. I quit spending time with my foster sisters and Yvonne. I locked myself in my room when I was home.

I avoided all of Dave's calls, but he finally cornered me on the phone. Usually, I let the other girls answer the phone to screen the calls, but I was the only one home, and I'd been waiting for a call from Strom so I answered it when it rang.

He didn't bother to say hello. "When are you gonna be done getting high?"

"I ... uh ... I don't know."

"Do you have any plans to get sober again?"

Do I? I don't know. Tell him yes. "Yes. It's just hard."

"Why don't you give me a call when you've made up your mind? I'm not gonna watch you destroy yourself." He hung up without saying good-bye. I clung to the phone until it began making the busy signal.

I paced my room as I waited for Yvonne to get home. When I heard her come in and turn on the TV, I walked slowly down the stairs. *What are you doing? You're gonna bust yourself. Stupid ass. Shut up. You don't want to do this. Yes, I do.* I stood at the end of the stairs and cleared my throat to get her attention. "I've got to tell you something."

She picked up the remote and turned the sound down.

"I'm getting high again," I said.

She looked at me without an ounce of surprise on her face. "I know."

"You do?"

She nodded. "I may not know a lot about drugs, but I'm certainly not an idiot. It's pretty obvious, kid. You're different. You're moody and irritable. Plus, all sorts of strange people keep showing up on my doorstep."

"How come you never said anything?"

"I wanted you to come to me when you were

ready. I talked to Dave about it when I first started getting-"

"You talked to Dave? What'd he say?"

He's probably talking shit behind your back. Shut up, he isn't. I bet he is.

"He said to be patient and let you have your consequences." Yvonne folded her hands together.

What the hell does that mean? Is he going to leave me? Is that my consequence? Everybody knows I've been getting high?

"Why didn't you do anything?" I was surprised at the sound of anger in my voice.

Yvonne raised her eyebrows. "Really, Elizabeth? What can anyone do to make you quit getting high?"

She was right. Nobody could stop me. We sat in silence for a few minutes before I spoke again. "I'm scared. My world is falling apart again."

She reached over and squeezed my knee. "I still love you. You'll get through this. I know you will. You've just hit a rough spot. It'll get better again."

I wanted to believe her, but I'd been given a wonderful opportunity to change my life, and I'd blown it. I had a beautiful home, living with safety and security for the first time in my life, and I was risking losing it. I'd lost the first real friend I'd had in a long time. I'd been given a chance to go back to school, and I'd blown that too. Was there time to stop the downward spiral or was I already too far gone?

I wanted to see if I could stop the descent back into madness again and couldn't do it without Dave's help. He allowed me to start attending aftercare groups again even though I'd relapsed. I began meeting with him whenever I got a chance and we started talking on the phone again every day. It wasn't unusual for me to call him at home in the middle of the night or for him to call me. It was against the rules for him to give me his home number, but I didn't care as long as he didn't.

I didn't believe I could get sober without him, and he didn't make me try. When things were okay, we played basketball in the gym or sat outside the treatment center at one of the aluminum tables, playing cards and smoking. When things were bad, we'd stay in his office with the door locked. He'd sit next to me, holding me in his arms and rubbing my back.

Sometimes we stayed in his office late at night. One night, I couldn't reach Yvonne on the phone to come pick me up so Dave offered me a ride home. I jumped at the invitation. I loved spending time with him. He pushed play on the CD player and Tom Petty's voice rang out. I listened to the sound of his words while I stared out the window, looking at the stars and wishing we could drive forever.

"Come here."

He patted the spot on the seat next to him. Without a thought, I slid over next to him. He invitingly lifted his arm. I laid my head against the side of his chest as he wrapped his arm around me. Breathing in his sweetness, I closed my eyes. *I belong here.* We didn't speak. It was like he could talk to my soul without using language. He moved his arm down and wrapped his fingers on the side of my lower stomach, squeezing me softly. He gently rubbed circles on my side. His touch sent tingles down my spine. I opened my eyes.

I want him to touch me. Ohmigod, Elizabeth. You can't think this way—he's your chemical dependency counselor.

But I couldn't stop. My body was alive with sensations I'd never felt before. A rush of energy flowed from my head down to my toes. I wanted to reach up and bury my face in his. My cheeks were on fire. I'd known for a long time that I loved him, but this was different. Somewhere along the way, I'd fallen in love with him.

When we pulled up to the stop sign a block from Yvonne's house, he turned to look at me. "You better slide over. I don't want Yvonne to think your CD counselor is goofy, but first you've got to give me a kiss goodnight."

My heart thudded. I lifted my head and brought my lips to his mouth, kissing him softly and then scooting away.

"I didn't mean like that. I meant on my cheek," he said with a strange look in his eyes that I'd never seen before.

We never talked about the night he gave me a ride home, but things changed between us after that. I was afraid each time he looked at me, he'd see how much I loved him. I wasn't supposed to love him like I did. I was terrified he was going to go away and leave me so I tried to keep my feelings a secret, but it was getting more difficult to hide them.

When we walked outside the treatment center late one night and he suddenly announced, "I want you to meet my wife," I felt like he'd just slapped me in the face. I knew he had a wife, but I'd never seen her which made it easy to pretend he was just mine. We walked to the driveway of the treatment center as his wife pulled up in an old station wagon. He opened the passenger door and said, "Kathy, I want you to meet Elizabeth," pointing to me.

Even in the dark without makeup on, she looked like a supermodel. My heart sank.

"Hi, Elizabeth. I've heard so much about you." She smiled sweetly.

"Hey," I said. In the back of the station wagon, two young boys, looking like various parts of their father, smiled at me. "I'm going back inside."

I tried to pretend as if nothing had changed and everything was okay, but I didn't have the strength. I was plagued by the idea that I was only trying to stay sober so I could have Dave in my life. It nagged at me constantly. Each day I was sober, the only thing that kept me from throwing it all away was knowing I couldn't be close to Dave if I kept getting high. I didn't care enough about myself to stay sober, but I wanted him to love me so I did it. Our time together was running out. Seeing his wife and two of his children had opened my eyes to reality. There would come a day when Dave would move on with his life. He had a life outside of me, a family and children he belonged with. I was only a kid he was trying to help. I wasn't as special as I thought I was.

My anger returned with momentum. I'd finally found someone I loved, but I'd never be able to have him. God had played another cruel joke on me. I wasn't staying sober because I wanted to. I was staying sober because I wanted him. If I couldn't have Dave, then I didn't want sobriety. After all, it wasn't my sobriety—it was his.

Garrison

FOURTEEN

Our monthly visit was almost up. For the last hour, I'd regaled Rubin with my usual stories of going to AA meetings, working a part-time job, and doing well in school. None of which were true, but I hadn't gotten into any trouble for a long time so they sounded believable.

"One more thing to take care of before I leave." Rubin reached into his briefcase and pulled out the familiar plastic container with a red seal on the cap. "It's been awhile, so I figured it's time. Can you go for me real quick?"

I sat on the toilet with Rubin waiting outside the door. My heart sank because my drug count would be off the charts. I'd been using all of my favorites on a daily basis for months. Failing my urine test would be a probation violation and all my charges that had been put on a stay of sentence would come reeling back into my face. I'd been caught within weeks of my time being up. I rushed to Dave's office as soon as Rubin left.

"I failed my piss test. They're gonna lock me up."

"Not if you check yourself into treatment first. They don't know how long you've been using. For all they know, you've been sober this whole time. If you check yourself into treatment, it'll look like you just had a minor relapse, realized your mistake, and decided to do something about it." Dave no longer expected me to stay sober and for some strange reason, he was okay with it.

"Can I come back here?" I asked.

"We're too close," he said, shaking his head. "I can't go back to being your CD counselor."

"What do you mean?"

He walked over and sat in the chair next to me like he'd done so many times in the past. "C'mon, Elizabeth." He brushed his hand across my cheek. "You know as well as I do."

Do I? What do I know? I don't know anything.

My head swirled. He took my chin in his hands and tilted my face towards his. I took a deep breath. *Ohmigod. Is he going to kiss me? No. God, you're losing it, Elizabeth.* He brought his lips to my forehead and kissed me softly before pulling away.

He spoke in a voice I'd never heard before. It was deep and husky. "I crossed the line of being your CD counselor a long time ago. Somewhere along the way, I started having feelings for you. I hate myself for it, but they're there and I don't think they're going away any time soon. I love you in so many different ways. Part of me is in love with you."

I looked away from his intense stare. *He loves me, too? He can't. I can love him, but he can't love me. Can he?* I'd fantasized so many times about this moment. How he'd take me into his arms and tell me he was in love with me too. But now it was happening and instead of making me feel good like I'd imagined, it made my stomach tighten into a knot. I wanted to get up and run out of his office as fast as I could. I kept my eyes averted until I could leave.

Dave had a plan for me and I followed it. He took me to a place called The Portico, an extended care treatment center for women. It didn't look like any treatment center I'd been to before—a sprawling mansion in the middle of a residential area showcasing old Victorian furniture. I sat next to Dave in the director's office without speaking. The director was older, with gold glasses perched on the tip of her nose and white hair permed just like my mom.

"Elizabeth needs your help," Dave said. "I understand this is an adult halfway house and she's only seventeen, but she doesn't fit with the adolescents. She's chronic and I really think you could help her."

The woman looked at me and back at Dave. "Normally, we don't do this, but I trust your expertise and I suppose we can make an exception. If she's really serious about getting sober then I want her here tomorrow."

"Not a problem," Dave said. "I can talk to her social worker and get a Rule Twenty-Five going. I'll bring her myself."

He took care of everything. He called my social worker and made arrangements for me to go the following day. He brought me to Yvonne's and explained the situation to her.

"Are you sure this is what you want to do, kid?" Yvonne asked, turning to look at me once Dave had finished.

I wasn't sure about anything, but nodded my

approval anyway. She peered at me, trying to read my thoughts, but I kept my gaze focused on Dave. If he said checking myself into Portico was what I needed to do, then I'd do it.

At eight the next morning, Dave returned in his station wagon and my bags were packed once again. Saying good-bye to Yvonne was harder than I thought it'd be. Somewhere inside me, a small voice told me it was never going to be the same.

"I'll be here waiting for you when you get out, kiddo." She hugged me tightly against her large frame. "You're welcome in my home anytime."

I didn't like The Portico because I didn't know if I wanted to get sober again and it wasn't worth the effort if I was only going to fail again like I'd done so many times in the past. I spent more of my time worrying about my feelings for Dave and his feelings toward me than I did about my sobriety. I couldn't shake the feeling that it wasn't right for him to be in love with me. But I loved Dave and he said I was special so maybe it was okay that he loved me the way I loved him. However, no matter what I told myself about it, I couldn't shake the one voice that resounded over and over, interrupting my thoughts: *He's old enough to be your dad.*

You're only seventeen.

The one thing I did know was that I didn't want to get sent to a juvenile detention center until my eighteenth birthday. I made the decision to act my way through treatment even if I didn't plan on staying sober once I got out. I knew what was expected of me to look like a model patient. The recovery lingo that used to be a foreign language had now become my second language.

I had a hard time fitting in at Portico. Not only was I the youngest person, but I was also the only one funded by the county. All of the other women came from a world of wealth. They'd never had to steal or sleep with old, nasty men to get high. They just blew thousands of dollars from their trust funds. They'd never been in any serious trouble with the law because they had rich parents or husbands who hired expensive lawyers to get them off. They wore sparkling jewels and a few had even flown to treatment on private jets. They'd been to the Betty Ford Clinic and Hazelden, luxury resorts compared to the places I'd been. I was Goodwill clothes among designer labels.

I spent most of my time in my room when I wasn't in group. I had a roommate, but we didn't talk. She pretended like I wasn't there and stayed away from me as if I had some form of a disease she might catch. Nobody included me in their conversations around the dinner table and when I did talk they looked at me as if I had a slight case of mental retardation. After a while, I didn't speak unless I was spoken to and even then, I kept my responses short. I'd been there for almost a month when staff called me into a meeting with the director.

I sat alone in a chair up against the wall, while they all faced me in their chairs— seven women neatly dressed and immaculately made-up, stared back at me.

"Mary's jewelry is missing," the director said.

"If you think I took it—I didn't." I refused to steal from them because it was what they expected and didn't want to give them the satisfaction.

"You'll never get better if you can't get honest," my counselor said. The others nodded their heads in agreement.

"Look," I said. "I don't know who took the jewelry, but it wasn't me."

"Why are you being so defensive?"

"Shit. I-"

Martha, the other counselor, interrupted. "Please don't use that language."

"I guess I forgot where I was. Have you ever thought maybe somebody else did it? Oh, of course not. It couldn't have been one of the princesses."

All eyes bored into me. I went from one pair to the next, trying to send my hatred towards them through some sort of telepathy.

The director let out a sigh. "Since you refuse to be helped, you might as well go. We'll let you know what we decide to do with this matter."

I stood up, holding back the urge to toss my chair at them. I stormed into the hallway, where a few of the women were standing and didn't even pretend not to be eavesdropping. They sneered at me and I returned their sneers. I made my way up the winding staircase to my bedroom and plopped down on my bed, staring at the ceiling.

Before long, I heard a knock on the door and Jill walked in. She was the technician who'd taken me to detox the week before. I wasn't wasted, but the Portico staff had been convinced I was. Once I'd gotten there, I'd passed every sobriety test, but my counselor made them keep me there overnight. Jill was holding my duffel bag over her shoulder, and I didn't have to guess about the decision they'd made.

"You're being discharged and going to jail. Your mother agreed to pick you up. She'll be here in ten minutes." Jill tossed my bag to me. "The police have already been called and they're waiting to pick you up if you don't leave quietly."

I didn't know what to expect when I arrived at the courthouse with my mom. She hadn't said a word during the drive, just stared at the road with her lips in a straight line and her hands gripping the wheel so tightly her knuckles turned white. I thought we'd march into court, but instead, we headed down the familiar flight of stairs leading to Rubin's office. Rubin sat in his usual spot behind the desk and his small office was crammed with bodies. The bodies of my committee—the ones who made the decisions in my life—occupied the rest of the chairs. My guardian ad litem, appointed by the judge a couple of years earlier, sat next to Rubin. She was supposed to be my voice in the courtroom, but I didn't know what that meant because I didn't have a voice. Ever. Next to her, Lynette chewed on a toothpick. My social worker had introduced Lynette to me as her friend who she thought might be helpful to me. But her cover had been blown when Lynette gave me her business card with the title "Victim's Advocate" in glaring black letters across the top. I wasn't a victim and didn't know what an advocate was, but I didn't need one.

Judge Hansen sat next to them, dressed in plainclothes rather than his usual black robe. As always, he twirled his glasses in his hand. I'd come to the conclusion they were more of a prop than a necessity since he rarely put them on his face. My social worker, Ruth, was next in line. Her arms were folded on her pregnant belly that stretched out so far it looked painful. Besides Rubin, she'd been part of the committee the longest. She took care of all the funding for placing me and was continually annoyed that I didn't express more gratitude to her as if she thought I should be happy they kept sending me away and locking me up.

"Isn't this nice that we're all back together again?" I said, sitting next to Rubin as my mom slid quietly into the chair beside me. Nobody cracked a smile, not even a fake one.

"Here's the deal. We've reached the end of the road. For the past few years, we've given you every break imaginable. Rather than punish you, we've repeatedly tried to help you." Rubin paused, making eye contact with everyone in the room. "You reach a point when you realize you've done all that you can do for a person and we've reached that point. We've run out of options and we've all reached an agreement. First of all, you are free to live wherever you choose. We're not going to put you into another placement because you're going to be an adult in six months. You're on your own."

"I don't get it. I'm free?"

This time, Judge Hansen spoke. "You're free from the adolescent court system. We're closing your social services file and your CHIPS petition. After today, your case is going to be handled by corrections only and we're going to begin the process of transferring you into the adult correctional system. You've used up all of your chances. Once all the paperwork is complete and filed, you'll be tried as an adult when you break the law and punished in the same manner as one. You're almost an adult now, and we're speeding up the process."

I took his words in slowly, letting each of them sink in. "So, I'm not going back to Yvonne's?"

Ruth smiled. "Nope." I wanted to punch the

smug look off her face.

"Where will I go?" I asked, looking toward Rubin.

He shrugged. "Wherever you want. However, you're not allowed to leave the state. You'll have to find a place to live on your own."

"It's no longer our responsibility," Ruth said.

For so long, I'd wanted out of the claws of my committee's constant orders, threats, punishments, watchful eyes, demands, and relentless questions. I'd spent hours dreaming about being free, but I'd just been let go from their restraint and felt nothing but lost. *Where will I go? What will I do? I'm gonna end up in prison.* I looked over at my mom, but she looked away, refusing to meet my eyes.

Rubin slid a document across his desk to me. I signed on the dotted line next to their signatures, and it was over. The committee filed out of the room. I followed my mom back up the stairs, feeling a powerful sense of impending doom.

I'm not gonna make it.

"I suppose you can stay in the back bedroom for a few days until you figure out what you're going to do," she said as we pulled out of the parking lot.

I didn't want to go back to living with my

parents. I hadn't seen or spoken to my dad in almost a year. How was I supposed to walk back into their house and act like nothing had happened? My presence had been erased from their house. I didn't even have my old bedroom anymore. A year before, they'd gutted out my bedroom in the basement and redone it with pink carpet and flowered wallpaper for Sarah. Sarah's old room had become the storage area for all my mom's arts and crafts supplies. Even though Daniel's room was downstairs and empty since he'd left for the Navy, she made no offer of his. I was an outcast and would soon find out what it was like to be homeless.

I wasn't homeless like the old men who wandered the streets, talking to themselves, and drinking cheap wine out of brown paper bags, but I had no place to go and nowhere to call my home. I succumbed completely to the ever-present desire to destroy myself, burying myself in chemicals. They didn't work anymore, but I didn't care.

Every time I thought it couldn't get any worse, it did. I spent endless days and nights driving with Strom from sunup until sundown because neither of us had anywhere to go. His house had been condemned, and he'd resorted to sleeping on his parents' couch. We became wanderers from trailer to trailer, from one apartment to the next, and off to the next dark basement as we dropped off drugs. As quick as the money came into our hands, it was gone. All we had to show for it was bloody noses, aching bones, and vacant eyes.

Strom had the luxury of being comfortable at his parents' house so whenever he needed to crash, he could. I tried going home but it wasn't any comfort. I'd lie in the twin bed my mom had moved into the back bedroom, among boxes of crafts, longing to sleep but unable to relax. My skin crawled and there wasn't enough air. My parents' bedroom was right next to the room and I heard every breath my dad took.

Put a pillow over his head. Just do it. What about mom? She's a light sleeper, she'll wake up. Who cares? Your life is over. So you go to prison. I don't wanna go to prison. Who ya kidding, you're gonna go to prison. It's only a matter of time. Do it. Besides, you can just kill yourself afterward. Where's the guns? The guns? Ya know, he hunts. Stick the rifle in your mouth. I can't. Yes, you can. No, I can't. You're a fuckin' wimp. Some tough girl you are. I'm losing my mind. It's already gone.

The voices had grown into their own personalities. I couldn't control them anymore or shut them off. They screamed constantly. I couldn't stay at my parents' house. The voices controlled me and I was afraid if I continued to stay there I would hurt my dad or myself. I had to have a place where I could stay after Strom and I had reached our limit of sleepless days and nights. A car was the perfect solution. My parents had tucked away a thousand dollars for each of us kids as graduation presents. My brother had gotten his money when he graduated, and if I could talk my mom into giving me my graduation money, then I could buy a car.

I came home the next day when I knew my mom would be alone. "Mom, do you still have the money from my graduation?"

"Yes. Why?" she asked, instantly suspicious.

"I was thinking if I'm ever gonna get my life together, I'm going to need a job. And I can't get a job without a car."

"I'm not giving you the money. You'll blow it all on drugs in a week."

"Listen mom, I have to have a car if I'm going to work. I have to be able to get there."

"That money is a reward for graduating high

school. That's why we saved it."

"C'mon, really? Do you actually think I'm ever gonna graduate high school? I'm supposed to be graduating in a few months and technically, I'm still in ninth grade. Can you honestly tell yourself that's gonna happen? Let's be real for just one second."

She stared back at me, looking twenty years older than she really was. Her lips quivered and her eyes filled with tears. *Look what you've done. Look at her. How can you live with yourself? You're a monster. Do you hear me? A fuckin' monster! Shut up. For God's sake, leave me alone.*

"I'll talk to your dad."

I went back a few days later and she handed me ten hundred dollar bills.

"Thank you." I moved to hug her.

She pushed me back. "Don't you dare thank me. Just go before I change my mind."

Within a few days, I had a car and my own home—an '87 Duster with red padded seats and a radio. It was all I needed. I paid seven hundred dollars for it and blew the rest on dope. Whenever Strom went to his parents to come down, he dropped me off at my car. I spent many winter nights curled up in the front seat shaking, trying to quiet my thoughts. I'd hoped the voices would stop when I was out of my parents' house, but they continued to torment me.

Did you hear that? They're coming. They're coming to get you. No one is coming to get you. You'll see. They want to kill you. They'll kill you. Drive. Get out of here.

I did what they told me to even if it made no sense. I drove endlessly, never getting anywhere, but always moving. The voices were more content when we were moving.

I didn't have money for food, but it didn't matter because my body had forgotten how to eat again. Sometimes Strom would bring me to restaurants on a mission to feed me. He'd set a plate of food in front of me and order me to eat. The most I could get down was half a bagel, and even that was hard to keep from coming back up.

I still went to my parents' occasionally for a warm shower, a clean set of clothes, and a chance to get rid of the fuzz on my teeth. I'd go while my dad was at work or late at night when both of them were sleeping. But it wasn't long until my mom confronted me, cornering me as I came out of the bathroom. "I can't watch you do this."

"Wha ... I ... just ... what did I say? I can't remember ... I just ..."

"Just look at you. You can't even speak. You used to be so smart and now you can't even talk. I cannot watch you destroy yourself. You wanna do drugs, fine. Do drugs. Kill yourself, but not under my roof. I won't have you die in my house."

She started locking the doors at night so I couldn't creep in whenever I needed to. I had no choice but to keep wandering, in and out of consciousness and different days that all felt like the same day. I lost track of whether it was night or day, where I was, where I'd been, what I'd done, who I'd been with, what drugs I'd done, when I'd slept, or if I'd slept. There was no escape from the torment.

The only way out was to die, and I watched as those around me continued to fall. The next person to perish from our group was Bryan. He'd crashed his truck drunk, flying out of the car. Like everyone else, he was dead on arrival. Strom, Bobby, and I had been drinking all day in preparation for another service. It'd only been a few weeks since we'd lost someone. That time it'd been Piss Pants. He'd been given his name after peeing his pants on a bar stool at a local bar. I had no idea what his real name was.

I hadn't gone to the memorial service for Piss Pants and didn't know anyone who had because nobody wanted to be questioned about how he died. We never talked about that night, the party, or how he'd left in a car with Hamilton and Justin and overdosed in the back seat. We didn't mention how they'd left him on the front steps of a church. Even though Hamilton and Justin were the ones to do it, we knew anyone of us would've done the same thing. We made sure not to talk about Piss Pants because saying something out loud made it a reality you couldn't take back.

I walked into the funeral home with Bobby and Strom at my sides wondering how many more funerals we'd attend before we were all gone and it was finally over. Bryan's face was heavily coated with makeup and unrecognizable. Thick paint couldn't cover the bruises—blue and purple shades still shone through. I followed his arm down to a plastic hand. He'd lost his real one in the accident.

His eyes were closed and he looked peaceful. I'd never seen him sleep or look peaceful. I'd only seen him with dilated pupils overcoming any signs of color and eyes bulging out of his sockets. His blond hair was combed nicely and I'd never seen that either. Usually, his hair stuck up haphazardly from running his hands through it over and over again.

I wanted to feel something as I stared at him, but there was only a hollow emptiness. I knew nothing about him. We'd spent many days together, but I didn't have any clue who he was. I didn't even know his last name. He could've been anyone. The people I called my friends were only fixtures who sat next to me as we got high. It wouldn't be long before I'd be surrounded by junkies who would look at me just like I was looking at Bryan and like me, they'd feel nothing. I walked to the back of the room and leaned against the wall, chewing on the nubs of my fingers since my fingernails were gone.

Bobby and Strom joined me. Strom pointed to the door, and we quietly exited, greeted by cold winter air. We tried to be nonchalant, but our walk was hurried. We got into the car, and each of us reached underneath the seats to grab a beer. We packed our one-hitters full of the pot we carried in our pockets, smoking in silence, staring out the windows, each of us in our private world. Strom started the car, and the radio blared. I drank another beer and smoked my one-hitter trying to get lost in the familiar voice of Neil Young. But my mind refused to leave.

We reached a farmhouse on the edge of town. The familiar smell of body odor mixed with old booze, urine and puke hurled up my nose. This time, I wanted to gag. There were ten bodies with faces I'd seen before. I sat in wetness and slime that still stuck to me when I moved further down the couch. I didn't bother to say hello to anyone and no one said hello to me. The pool table was littered with cans and dirty papers. Someone had cut out Bryan's obituary and tacked in on the wall next to all the others—the overdoses and car accidents. Strom picked up a set of dice from the pool table and started to shake them in his hand. "Should we roll to see who goes next?" The room filled with laughter. Any other time my voice would've joined them.

"What's wrong with you?" Bobby asked, plopping down beside me.

"Nothin'." They rolled the dice and laughed about whose number fell, then started their stories about how they'd die. They were the same stories we told every time, one last hoorah and out with a bang. Normally, I'd tell my fantasy about lying in a field under a tree with a creek running by, nothing but grass underneath and the blue sky above me. I'd shoot myself so full of dope that I'd go to sleep and never wake up.

But all I could think of now was that we didn't die romantically. We put guns in our mouths and blew our brains out. We died in car accidents that we caused, our hands severed. We stopped our hearts from beating with chemical potions and were easily discarded on doorsteps like bags of trash when we died. I guzzled the bottle of vodka in front of me, but my mind still ran on.

"I gotta get outta here," I told Bobby.

Bobby didn't ask any question. He just grabbed Strom and as quick as we'd come, we were gone—to another kitchen in another trailer park with a two-foot bong on the table. The owner of the trailer chopped up lines on a mirror and passed it around. Strom looked at me as if I'd lost my mind when I declined, but the last thing I wanted was to be up for any more days than I'd already been. I wanted my mind to shut down.

The conversation was full of the things we said

we'd do, but never actually did. I hit the bong over and over again, drinking between each hit. My body was wasted, but my mind was still sober. I hated it and hated myself even more. The man across from me had raped his own daughter. We'd all read about it in the paper and seen it on the news. These were who I called my people? No one but Strom cared about me. The others would kill me if I had something they wanted or if I stepped out of line. They'd rape me if they got the chance and some already had.

I jumped up from my chair and ran to the bathroom. I violently heaved into the toilet, wrapping my arms around the white bowl as it came in spastic waves. I couldn't get it out fast enough. I was contaminated with filth, disgust in every part of my body. I puked until there was nothing but blood and eventually that was gone too. I dry heaved with every thought that went through my head.

The worst part was that no matter how much I hated my life and myself, I couldn't live any other way. This was where I fit until my number was rolled. Every day was the same and it was always going to be that way. I was in hell and never getting out.

The one thing that had always kept me from committing suicide was the fear of hell. I'd spent my childhood terrified of the place. But at that moment, lying on the cold tiles of the bathroom floor with my head resting on the rim of the toilet, I only had two options left. I could go on living in the hell of my life or I could take myself to the next level of hell.

I stumbled out of the bathroom and asked Strom to take me to my parents' house where I banged on the front door until I woke up my mom. She'd always been a light sleeper and she came to the door quickly, frowning. "You look awful." I shrugged and moved past her. "You're staying here tonight?"

"Yes. I just ... Mom, I can't ..."

She patted my shoulder. "Just go to bed. We can talk in the morning."

In the shower, warm water pounded my skin, but I couldn't get warm. I couldn't even remember what it felt like to be warm. My bones ached. I scrubbed my skin, trying to wash off the filth. I stuck my finger into the back of my throat, trying to grab the glob of goo that hung there at all times. I caught a piece of the slime, gagged, and pulled it out in a long line, then watched the black mucous work its way through the small holes in the drain.

That's what you put in your body. You can't even get any more in. It's not working. You have to do something. My mom's pink Bic razor hung from the wire container over the showerhead. *Do it with that. But that never works. Cut deep. The razor sucks.* Methodically, I took the razor and scraped along my wrists, moving it up and down as if I was shaving my arms. I cut and crossed jagged edges. I bled, but only enough to look like a cat had attacked my arms.

The gun. There's a gun in Daniel's room. Use it. C'mon. Your life is over. I can't. Yes, you can. It'll be quick. I stepped out of the shower, dried myself, and put on the same dirty clothes I'd been wearing for days. I caught a glimpse of hollow eyes in the mirror. *That's not me. I'm not that girl.*

In the hallway, I put my head against the door of my parents' bedroom, listening for the sounds of them sleeping. I heard my mom's deep breaths and the weird clicking sound my dad made in the back of his throat. I walked through the living room and down the stairs, trying to keep them from creaking.

I didn't bother to turn on the light in my brother's room. My eyes adapted quickly. His room was just like I remembered it—the wallpaper with blue ships, posters of punk bands on the wall, the glowing edges standing out. I sat on the edge of the bed in a time warp.

Daniel, where are you? Do you miss me? Do you ever even think about me? Do you remember when we were little and promised we'd always be best friends? I couldn't stop the tears anymore. Sarah was across the hall in my old room. *What's her life like? God, she's got to be so disappointed. She's lost her big sister.* My eyes turned to the corner of the room where Daniel's hunting rifle stood, propped in its black case. I picked it up and unzipped the cover, pulling the long barrel out, turning it over and over in my hands. It was longer than I remembered. *You should call Dave. I can't. Yes, you can. No, I can't. Remember what he said?*

A few days before, I'd stopped in at Dave's office. Instead of taking a seat next to me, he stood with his arms crossed. As I started to sit in my usual chair, he said sternly like he was talking to one of his kids, "You have to leave."

"What do you mean?"

"Elizabeth ..." He gulped as two tears slid down his cheek. "I can't watch you die any longer. I won't do it anymore. It's tearing me apart."

"What am I supposed to do?"

"I don't know. But I'm just going to give you a kiss good-bye and then you're going to leave this office and not come back." He took my head in his hands, brought his face towards mine, and kissed me softly on the lips. Then, he pulled back and motioned to the door. I hung my head and walked away.

Nobody cares. You have no one. I picked out the Pink Floyd CD from Daniel's collection and slid it in. I programmed it to the song "Comfortably Numb" and pressed repeat before sitting back down on the bed. I put the gun between my feet. It was long enough to come up to my face. I put my mouth over the cold barrel. My mouth fit easily around it. I rested my teeth on the metal and my hand on the trigger.

How do I pull the trigger? How the hell do I do this? Can I do this? You don't have the guts. Yes, I do. I just want to make sure I do it right. I don't want to blow half my face off and end up still having to live.

I sat with the gun in my mouth as "Comfortably Numb" played all the way through, over and over again. I was in a trance as the voices argued. *Fuck it. Pull the goddamn trigger, you wimp. Blow your fuckin' head off. But God hates me. What if I miss? What if I only blow half my face off? Quit thinking about it. But ... Fuckin' do it.*

At some point during the night, a small, meek voice joined the other angry voices in my head. *What if you got clean? I can't get clean. I've tried. I'm doomed. But what if you're not? What if there's another way to live your life? There's not. But what if? You've never really tried.*

Still in a trance, I put the gun back in the corner. *Fuckin' wimp!* I didn't wait for the sun to rise. My mom would be up at five-thirty and she'd want to talk to me. I couldn't talk to her. I got into my car and drove. *I am so tired. I've never been this tired.*

A few days later, I had another court hearing to continue the process of transferring me into the adult correctional system. I had no idea what was happening with my case but didn't care. I'd quit paying attention. *Maybe they're locking me up today. Who cares?* I walked down the long hallway and up the stairs to the waiting room outside the courtroom. Hunched over in a chair, shaking my legs up and down and rocking back and forth, the mantra repeated: *I'm tired. I'm so tired.* The big wooden doors swung open and the bailiff called out, "Elizabeth. Elizabeth Garrison."

I stood up, swaying to one side. I started to walk towards the door. Right before I stepped through, I stopped. The small voice returned. I looked up at the ceiling and prayed silently, *"Please, God help me. Please."*

I walked down the aisle and sat in my usual spot at the wooden desk. The whole committee was there, sitting in their normal positions just like me. As always, Judge Hansen towered above us. I disappeared into my thoughts, oblivious to the talk going on around me.

"Elizabeth," Judge Hansen's voice broke in. "Do you have anything to say for yourself?"

I can talk? They want me to talk? I hadn't been allowed to talk in court in over a year. I opened my mouth and heard my voice speaking, but the words weren't my own.

"Please, give me another chance to get clean. I just wanna get clean. I'll do anything you want me to. I'll go to jail, prison, whatever. I don't care. I'll do anything. I just need a chance to get clean. You have to send me somewhere. Please." *What is going on? Shut up! Shut up! Shut up! What am I talking about?* I separated myself from my thoughts and kept talking, begging the judge and everyone in the room to give me one more chance to get clean. I didn't know what happened next and or why they changed their mind, but they took mercy on me. Rubin made arrangements for me to go to treatment within the next week.

The morning I was scheduled to go back into treatment for what felt like the hundredth time, I lay curled into a ball on the front seat of my car, praying for the sun to rise. I'd promised myself that when it came up, I was done doing drugs. Forever. The sun came up slowly. I turned my car on and began driving down the gravel road into town. *Get high. Get high. You can't get through this day without getting high. No! Shut up! I won't.*

I slammed on the brakes, spewing gravel. I rolled down my window, letting bursts of searing cold into the car. I dug frantically in my pockets for my bag of weed and folds of meth. I threw them out the window. I reached underneath the seat, grabbing pipes and foils in handfuls. I tossed them out the window. The wind caught some of the tinfoil and it fluttered through the air.

A primal scream tore out from somewhere deep inside me. I felt like I'd ripped off my arm and tossed it away. I wanted to jump out of the car and collect everything before it blew away. It took every ounce of energy I had left to put my foot on the gas pedal.

Garrison

FIFTEEN

Thirteen days before my eighteenth birthday, I checked into St. John's Hospital more exhausted than I'd ever been. I got my own private room next to the nurse's station to keep me away from the adults. I crawled underneath the thin, crisp sheet, laid my head on the foam pillow, pulled the coarse white blanket up to my chin, and closed my eyes. I lay in that same position, unmoving, most of my days there, feeling as close to death as I could be without physically dying. When I did get out of bed, I floated through lectures or group therapy.

After I'd been in the hospital for three weeks, Rubin transferred me to a place called Recovery House. It was an adult women's halfway house and since lots of the women had just gotten out of prison, the staff were equipped to monitor me closely. The court was waiting to see if I would stay sober before deciding how to proceed with me. I accepted the situation without putting up a fight, grateful to be staying out of jail even though the prospect of living in a house with twenty-five other women disturbed me. Memories from The Portico rushed through my mind.

But the women at Recovery House were hard-core just like me and except for the drunken housewives who never left the confines of their home, everyone had spent time on the streets. The house was filled with prostitutes, gang members, women just out of prison, and women who'd sold their souls in various ways to get high. We were women who'd lost everything, the ones the rest of society looked upon as the lowest form of human beings. The only competition that existed among us was arguing over who had the worst life.

I'd never met women like them before. They'd admitted defeat and were no longer fighting the battle to appear tough. They spoke openly, and when they cried, others gathered around to hug and hold them. I'd never have admitted it to them, but they terrified me. Not because of their lives, but I was scared they'd crumble my armor and it was the only protection I had left. I stood on the periphery of their circles, not letting them get close to me.

At night, one of my roommate's, Crystal, would curl up into the fetal position and cry harder than I'd heard anyone cry before. "E-E-Elizabeth?" she'd call out, lifting her head from the pillow. "Are you awake?"

I'd lay in silence with my eyes closed, pretending I was in a deep sleep and didn't hear her. She sobbed every night and never tired of calling out for me even though I never responded. I wanted to go to her and tell her it was going to be okay, but I couldn't lie to her. I wasn't sure we lived in a world where things were ever going to be okay. We had another roommate, Shaundra, who was braver than I was and she'd crawl into bed next to Crystal, curling herself around her small body.

"Oh, baby," she'd whisper in her southern drawl. "It's going to be okay. Really, honey, it's not that bad."

"I can't take this," Crystal would sob. Her baby had been taken from her three months ago when it was born addicted to heroin and she'd never been able to hold him. "It hurts. It hurts so fuckin' bad and all I can think about is getting high."

"I know, doll. I know," Shaundra would coo to

her, running her calloused hands through Crystal's dark hair. She wasn't lying. Shaundra had lost all three of her children to child protective services because she'd left them alone for three days with nothing to eat while she went on a crack binge. "Ya just gotta let the pain come. Ya just gotta let it move through ya." There were many nights when they cried themselves to sleep in each other's arms.

It wasn't only my roommates who consoled each other so unabashedly. All of the women comforted each other whenever someone broke. Their pain was raw and unflinching. I wasn't convinced that giving life to our demons made them go away. Anytime I'd let mine breathe, they'd devoured me. And besides, they were tearing themselves apart for nothing since most of us were never going to stay sober.

One day in group when everyone was being all touchy-feely, I announced, "We're not all gonna make it. Seriously, statistically speaking, in five years only two of us are gonna be alive and sober. The rest of us are gonna be either dead or fucked up."

Nakita jumped up from her chair. "Girl, I'm so fuckin' sick of you. Shut the fuck up! Maybe you think you're gonna die, but keep that shit to yourself."

I cocked my head to the side and looked at the counselor, Carla. "Tell her, Carla. You know the statistics. I'm not lying. Tell her. Tell her the truth that very few of us are gonna make it out of this hell."

Carla's eyes grew huge. "Elizabeth. Stop."

I jumped up from my chair, too. "Stop? C'mon, you want me to tell the truth. Isn't that what getting sober is all about? We're supposed to tell the truth. That's what I'm doing."

Nakita lunged at me. I ducked. Her arms circled the air above my head. "You fuckin' punk ass bitch. I'm gonna shut your ass up!"

I stood up to her, pushing my bony chest against her huge chest, feeling her breasts smash against me. I looked into her eyes without flinching. "Bring it on. You can try to kick my ass but it doesn't change the facts."

Carla leapt from her chair, grabbing Nakita's arm. "Nakita, stop! Elizabeth, sit down!"

Carla stepped between us, but we continued to glare at each other over her shoulders. Nakita's nostrils flared in and out. She hissed, "I'm gonna hurt her. Seriously. She needs to keep her negative ass mouth shut."

I spat at her, my fluid landing on her dark face. "I'm not scared of you. I have yet to get my ass kicked by a girl."

Carla grabbed my shoulders with both her hands and pushed me back. "You need to stop it. I mean it. In fact, you need to leave group."

"I don't-"

"Not another word! You need to leave. Go to your room and stay there."

I laughed. "You're not my mom."

Carla pointed towards the door, her face a deep red. "Go. If you don't leave now, Elizabeth, then you're gone. That's it. You cannot act this way."

"Fine," I snapped. "Fuck all of you."

I stormed out and stomped up the stairs to my third floor room. I threw myself face first on the bed, pounding my fists and kicking my legs like a two-year-old throwing a temper tantrum.

The women in the house left me alone after that and pretended I wasn't there. Before, they'd ask me to go with them on their outings to AA meetings or to get food, but the invitations quit coming. I pretended I was unaffected, but alone in the silence of my room, I writhed in agony. I was clean but felt like more of a mess than I'd ever been. The only relief came from cutting, and burning my arms and legs with cigarettes in a vain attempt to release the pain inside.

There was one phone in the house for everyone to share and never-ending battles over whose turn it was next. I was surprised one night when Crystal announced the phone was for me. The only person who called was my mom and I'd already talked to her earlier in the day.

I picked up the receiver. "Hello?"

A husky male voice said, "Hey, girl. Now this is gonna sound crazy, but I been watching you."

"Who is this?"

"My name's Reggie. I'm your neighbor."

My neighbor? Did he mean the apartment next door? We'd been instructed not to associate with any of our neighbors.

"How the hell do you know my name?"

"Look, before ya freak out, lemme explain some shit. Ya know ole girl, Kristine? She stays at your crib, right?"

"Mmm-hmm."

"We kick it sometimes and I been seeing ya in

the parking lot and wonderin' if I could get to know ya. I asked her 'bout ya. She hooked me up with this number. See, I know how hard this shit you're going through is. I been sober six months myself. Hardest shit I've ever had to do."

"Really?"

I began talking to Reggie regularly over the next week. I asked Kristine about him and she assured me he was a good guy. I agreed to meet him for coffee. Going out for coffee was what people in sobriety did, and although I'd never drank it before I'd gotten sober, I'd started drinking it all the time.

Our coffee date was much more complicated than it needed to be. Even though Reggie's apartment was only across our parking lot, I couldn't walk over there without someone seeing me. I'd be in serious trouble and I couldn't get in trouble. Instead, I agreed to meet him at a gas station half a mile away. A tall, skinny man opened the door and got into my car. He stuck out his hand. "Glad to finally meet ya, girl." He gave me a wide smile. His dark skin contrasted sharply with his white teeth.

I took his big hand in mind. "You, too."

"Nice ride," he said.

I shrugged. "Nothin' special."

"This is what I been thinking. I know we was gonna go to Perkins and have coffee, but how 'bout we just go to my place and I'll make us some? 'Sides, then I can show you the pictures of my kids." He'd mentioned his two little girls many times. He was just starting to be able to see them again.

"All right. But I'm gonna have to park a few blocks away, 'cause I don't want any of the girls to see my car."

"Cool," Reggie said, turning up the sound on the radio and rolling the window down. I peeked at him out of the corner of my eyes. He was average looking, not especially attractive. His presence had been so large on the phone, I'd expected him to be much bigger but even though he was tall, he was bony and his clothes hung on him. I parked my car a few blocks away and we started walking towards his apartment.

Looking around nervously, he said, "We should go in through the back door so nobody sees, huh?"

"For sure. They're pretty strict about us not hanging out with the neighbors."

"Can't blame 'em. There're some crazy people livin' 'round here." He smiled at me again.

We hurried towards the back of the brick complex, which was identical to the one I lived in next door. He opened the steel door, and I rushed inside. He pointed down the stairs and towards the end of the hallway. "Last one on the right."

I stood by his door while he dug in his jeans for the keys. He opened the door and motioned for me to go inside. I stepped in and my eyes darted around the room quickly, taking in the dingy walls and the dirty, shaggy yellow carpet. I heard the sound of the deadbolt being latched behind me. My stomach twisted. I took a step forward. I heard him breathing behind me.

"You should make coffee," I said. I didn't turn around to look at him.

He didn't move. I walked forward to the middle of the room. A bird cage hung by the draped window. It was a big cage, but there was no bird. I pretended to be really interested in it while furtively looking around. The only other piece of furniture was a brown, raggedy couch with the cushions hanging off. I spotted a crack pipe underneath it.

"Ya know," I said, trying to keep my voice steady. "Maybe we should go to Perkins."

"Why? This is fine." His voice sounded

different, lower.

"I'm scared I'm gonna get in trouble. Someone might have seen me come in here."

"Oh, nobody saw you come in here."

He was behind me. There wasn't enough oxygen in the room to breathe. My heart thumped in my chest and my head swam. *Stay here. Don't leave.* His hands were on my hips. *This can't be happening. Stay calm. Stay here. Don't leave.*

"Turn around."

"How come you have a cage with no bird?" My voice cracked.

"Turn around."

"Really, how strange is that? I mean a birdcage, but no bird. It's sad or something."

His hands tightened on my hips. He turned me around to face him. His eyes had changed. The pupils had grown larger and colder. "We didn't come here to talk."

Trying to move to the side, I said in a rush, "Listen, I gotta go. Really." He held me tight, squeezing his hands harder on my hipbones. I wanted to cry out, but I clenched my teeth together. *Don't let him smell fear. Don't leave.* "I didn't mean to give you the wrong impression. I should go. I really-"

His big mouth crashed down on mine. He tried to shove his tongue through my teeth and I clenched them together until my jaw hurt. He moved his head to my neck, licking all the way down to my shoulder. I pushed him back.

"Stop. I wanna leave. I have to leave now."

He lifted his head and tilted it back, laughing. "I told ya. Ya ain't goin' nowhere. You're mine now."

I smelled old booze seeping from his pores, mixed with putrid sweat. He crushed me against his chest. I pulled back, but he was stronger, and held tight. I screamed. He grabbed my hair and snapped my head back.

"Shut the fuck up, bitch." His spit hit my face. I gagged. He slapped me.

I struggled to get one arm free and pounded on his chest. I heard myself screaming from somewhere far away. He lifted me effortlessly and threw me over his shoulder like I was a bag of cargo. I beat at his back with my fists and kicked at his stomach wildly. He carried me into the bedroom and threw me on the bed. I scrambled up and he tossed me back down as if I weighed nothing.

What happened next was a blur filled with pieces of awareness and empty, blank spaces. I fought him on the bed with everything I had in me, which only excited him more. He pinned me on the bed and ripped my threadbare jeans apart as he breathed heavily in and out. I screamed until my throat was raw. No one came. Sometimes he'd slap my face with the back of his hand to shut me up. Other times he let me scream while he laughed.

As he struggled to get inside me, I writhed back and forth, trying to prevent it. I pounded on his chest, trying to pummel him with my fists. It made no difference. At one point, I freed myself and tumbled from the bed, cracking my head on the heat vent on the floor and knocking myself out.

I opened my eyes back on the bed. He was inside me again, pumping wildly, slapping my hips, shoulders, and thighs with his big hands.

He's going to kill me. He's going to kill me.

He finished and fell on top of me. I couldn't move under his weight.

Please fall asleep. Please fall asleep. I listened so hard to his breathing that a ringing began in my ears. Outside the room, birds chirped. Just when his breathing became relaxed, he raised himself to look at me.

His eyes were empty and dark as if I was looking into a tunnel with nothing at the other end. He looked right through me, unseeing. He was shiny from the dried sweat on his body. My body ached and screamed in pain. I throbbed between my legs, a hammer steadily pounded on my skull. He was naked on top of me though I couldn't remember when he'd taken his pants off. His lean chest was red from where my fists had beat it. He reached down to play with himself, never taking his eyes off me.

He's going to kill me when he's done with me. No one knows I'm here. This is it. No, I don't want this to be it. I will not die this way. I will not.

"Hey." My voice was raspy. It hurt to talk.

"I told you to keep your fuckin' mouth shut. You do what I tell you to. I'm not done with you."

"I know," I said, trying to sound convincing and forcing myself to look in his eyes. "I just thought maybe we could go in the living room."

"Nice try, bitch." He laughed, raising his arm again.

I said quickly, "No, really. I'll suck your dick out there. Really. I will. I want to."

He stared at me for what seemed like hours. "You better suck it good."

He got up from me and jerked me up by my arm. "C'mon. Move." He slapped my ass from behind.

I walked into the living room. *This can't be happening. Yes, it is. Do not fuckin' leave now, Elizabeth.*

I tried to sound excited. "Why don't you sit on the couch?"

He walked over and took a seat. I stood in front of him. He grabbed my head with both of his hands.

I cried out, "I'll do it. I said I would."

I brought my head down to his monster. *Do it, Elizabeth. You have to.* I put it in my mouth and began to perform, trying not to gag. He began to move with the motions of my mouth. I peeked up at him, never stopping what I was doing. His eyes were almost completely closed.

Now!

I jumped up, grabbed his head with my hands, and slammed it against the wall. I dashed for the door, unlatched the deadbolt, and ran as fast as I could, not looking back. I darted through the hallway, whipped open the door and ran into the sunshine. I raced all of the way through the parking lot back to Recovery House.

I hurried through the door and took the stairs three at a time. I shut the bedroom door and locked myself in the bathroom. I stripped off my tattered clothes and jumped into the shower. The scalding water scorched my skin. I took the soap and my washcloth, scrubbing on the inside, over and over, trying to remove him from every part of me. I dry heaved onto my feet and watched the yellow mucous slowly snake its way down the drain.

I didn't remember getting out of the shower and going into my room. I wasn't aware of my roommate finding me naked on the floor while I ripped open the cuts and burn blisters on my arms with my fingernails. I didn't remember the cops coming or the drive to the hospital.

But, I did remember the hospital.

The sterile white room and two male doctors with long white coats. Three male cops dressed in blue, standing against the door with their arms folded. A detective sat on the stool next to my bed, questioning me. He looked down at the notebook on his lap. "So, you're a drug addict?"

I nodded my head.

He snapped, "You have to speak your answers. I already told you once. We're recording your statement."

I cleared my throat. "Yes, I'm a drug addict."

"You live at Recovery House?"

"Yes."

"You say that your relationship with Reggie started on the phone?"

"Yes."

"Where were the two of you going?"

"For coffee."

"How did you end up at Reggie's place?"

"We decided to have coffee there."

The detective raised his eyebrows. "You didn't know this man, but you decided to go to his house. Is that correct?"

"I guess." I stared at the white tiles underneath his stool. *Smooth gray cracks between the tiles. Scuffed black shoes.*

"You say that he smokes crack. Is that correct?"

"Yes."

"How do you know that?"

"I saw the pipe."

"Did you see him smoke it?"

I shook my head.

He let out an exaggerated sigh. "Look, you need to speak."

The questioning went and on.

"How'd you get the marks all over your arms? Did he do that?"

"No." *There are white tiles on the ceiling, too. This whole place was white tiles. Gray cracks between them.*

"Then, who did?"

"I did them to myself."

The room was still.

"Okay, let me get this straight. You're a drug addict, but you claim you've been sober for three months. You talked to Reggie on the phone for a week and agreed to meet him at Perkins, but you went to his apartment instead. When you got into his home, you saw a crack pipe, but neither of you smoked it. Then, he raped you. Repeatedly. Allegedly. Have I got it right so far?"

There are little holes punched in the ceiling tiles. How many holes are in one tile?

I finally looked at him. He looked back with pure disgust, at something repulsive. "Yes. That's right."

"Supposedly, you screamed the whole time, but

no one in the building heard you. You performed oral sex on him voluntarily and escaped by pushing his head against the wall. You ran back to Recovery House. That's when the police were called. Now you're here, no semen inside you. All you have are cuts and burns all over your arm that you say you did yourself. And you want to press charges?"

I looked behind him. One of the cops smirked. The same one who forcibly held my legs open so the doctor could insert the metal into me. The tall cop next to him picked something out from underneath his nails. They wanted to finish up with me and move on to people who mattered. I wasn't one of those people.

No one will ever look at me like this again.

At that moment, it struck me how hard I'd fought for my life. Reggie intended on killing me and would've succeeded if I hadn't gone up against him. But, I had. I'd fought for my life which meant I wanted to be alive. But not like this. Never again.

Garrison

SIXTEEN

The police brought me back to Recovery House and the head counselor, Dawn, called an emergency session in the main dining room.

"The police arrested the man who did this to her, and I can assure you that you're all safe. The police are closely monitoring the house." Out of the corner of my eye, I saw her nod toward where I sat curled up, staring at the holes in my jeans. "I'm sure this incident will bring up past issues, and all of your counselors are available to talk to any of you who may need a little extra help in the next few days. I also want to stress how important it is that you are there for Elizabeth. Does anyone have any questions?"

No one said a word. After a few moments of uncomfortable silence, we stood, joined hands, and said the Serenity Prayer out loud like we always did. The other women formed a line in front of me. One by one, they came forward and hugged me. I kept my hands at my sides, but for the first time, let them circle their arms around me like I'd seen them do to each other so many times in the past. No one asked me for details about what had happened. They didn't need to because my experience mirrored their own. Some kissed the top of my head. Others had tears sliding silently down their cheeks as I let them cry the tears I couldn't.

I was committed to the vow I made in the hospital, but knew it was going to be the hardest thing I'd ever have to do. I wasn't entering into it blind. Everything was going to have to change—the way I thought, how I acted, my emotions, nothing could stay the same. The adjustments required to break away from the life of addiction were nearly impossible. It was why so many of us didn't ever make them and why so many of us died. I was determined to be one of the select few who made it.

I enrolled at the Adult Learning Center and started taking GED classes. I was going to graduate high school no matter what it took. Walking into the Center felt like my first day of kindergarten—a mixture of fear and excitement coupled with the desperate desire to perform well. I was surprised at how good it felt to hold a pencil in my hand. I couldn't remember the last time I had. I was even more shocked to find out my brain worked. I was worried I'd done too many drugs at a young age and given myself brain damage, but much to my relief, I discovered I could still read and write.

Every day after my noon AA meeting, I picked up a cup of coffee and headed straight to the Center. I took practice test after practice test, trying to build my confidence for the real one. I poured over the answers I'd gotten wrong to figure out where I'd made the errors and to make sure I didn't make the same mistake again. I sat down with the tutors provided by the Center to explain the materials I didn't understand. I carried books back to Recovery House with me to study. I hadn't had a book in my hand in nearly four years, and the crisp pages felt good underneath my fingertips.

On the morning of my test, Shaundra cooked me breakfast and set it before me. She'd never gotten past sixth grade and was as excited as I was to take the test. My stomach was already twisting and there was no way I'd be able to swallow a bite. I slid the food into the garbage when she wasn't looking so I didn't hurt her feelings.

I broke out in a cold sweat when I took my seat in the testing room. There were only four other students in the room and they all looked as nervous as I felt. My heart jumped in my throat as the instructor read the directions before passing out pencils and answer sheets. I gripped my pencil and tried to breathe slowly. I kept telling myself I'd studied a lot and had nothing to worry about.

Once the instructor passed around our sheets of paper, it was instantly silent—so quiet it made my ears ring. I took another deep breath and began. The reading comprehension parts were easy, and I flew through them but struggled with the math and science portions. I tried to remember and use the information my tutors had spent so much time teaching me. I had no idea how I'd done when I'd finished.

I was too afraid to open the envelope myself when the results came in the mail. I made Shaundra do it. She tore open the envelope.

"You passed! You passed, girl!" She jumped up and down, her wild, fiery afro bouncing up and down.

I grabbed the paper from her hands. My hands were shaking. I'd made the cut-offs. It was all there in black and white—I was officially a high school graduate.

"Oh my God! I did it!"

I raced through the house, up and down all the stairs squealing with excitement, trying to find anyone who as at home to share my good news with. I couldn't believe it. I was holding the first tangible piece of evidence that a different life was possible for me and I hadn't wrecked myself beyond repair. I hadn't done so many drugs that I was mentally retarded. I could still think and process. I could learn. Everyone in the house was so proud of me.

I didn't realize how proud they were of me until a few days later when I walked into the dining room and found it packed with all the residents, staff, and counselors.

"Surprise!"

I looked around in wonder. It wasn't even close to my birthday. What was the surprise? My counselor, Carla, walked up to me carrying a long black graduation gown and cap. She beamed with pride. "Put this on."

I lifted my arms as she pulled the gown over my head, smoothing it out as it fell. Next, Makita came up and handed me a small orange, plastic flower—one that you buy from 7-11 or the grocery store at the checkout counter.

"Every graduate needs a flower."

I reached out and hugged her tightly—the same women whose face I'd spat in months ago. She embraced me without reserve.

I took a spot at the head of the table as a few of the girls brought in a cake with the words, Congratulations, Elizabeth, scrawled across the center. My eyes filled with tears as the women gave me cards and small gifts. All of us survived on meager general assistant checks from the government and every penny mattered, but they cared enough about me to spend money on recognizing my accomplishment. It was the nicest thing anyone had ever done for me.

My first step towards recovery had been successful, and I'd cemented myself within a group of supportive women who'd welcomed me with open arms into their circle of healing. But even with the help of those around me, my growth was slow, awkward, and painful. For each move I made forward, I took another two backward. My mood changed by the hour. I rocketed from one emotion to the next without knowing why. My highs were so high I couldn't contain it and felt like the joy would explode from my body. My lows were so low that I felt trapped in a thick puddle of mud with concrete slabs tied around my ankles.

When I felt good, I was like a newborn baby taking pleasure in everything as if I was seeing it for the first time. I could sit enamored by the clouds for hours, aware of every breath coming in and out of my lungs, marveling at the fact that I still existed and was capable of thinking and feeling. I'd sit curled up on my bed or under a tree at the nearby park writing, filled with a burning desire to somehow express the emotions and thoughts raging through my body and mind. The words I'd trapped inside of me poured out and filled pages.

As quickly as the good feelings came, they were gone and replaced with complete despair. Sometimes there would be a trigger to set me off like getting into a fight with one of my roommates or hearing a song that reminded me of getting high, but there were other times when I plummeted into sadness without any reason. The worst part was being defenseless against the assaults. My walls were slowly being demolished and without them, my frozen insides began to thaw. I cried all the time, but always alone because even though I was making progress at letting people get close to me, I still wasn't able to let others see me so exposed. I sobbed alone in the silence of my room or car. Overwhelming grief passed through me in black waves. Each time I thought I'd die from the pain and made it through, I felt a little stronger for when the next wave came.

"You're in a state of mourning," Carol said during one of our sessions. "You've lost the one thing in life that ever made you feel okay and that is a real genuine loss. As real as any other loss."

There wasn't a day that passed when the craving to get high didn't grip me in its stronghold, screaming at me to return to oblivion. Each time I said no and didn't give in, left me feeling like a part of myself had been savagely ripped out. But it was more than that. The monster from my childhood bedroom and the demons from my past which used to be restricted to a tiny room in my mind set out to devour me and there was no place to hide. They threatened to pull me down into a dark pit of despair that crushed me until I could hardly breathe and felt like I might die. Any hope for relief was gone.

It was in those moments of agony and torture that I started to pray again. I did it in a way I'd never prayed before. I didn't pray in a submissive, humble, reverent voice to God. Instead, I screamed at him in a volatile rage. I wanted him to stand in front of me so I could bite the flesh off his face for allowing me to be hurt the way I'd been. He could've saved me if he wanted to, but instead he'd condemned me again and again. I wailed against him until the words were gone and replaced with guttural sobs snaking their way into the pit of my stomach.

My screaming sessions with God gave me more relief than any of the therapy or group sessions. When the torrent of feelings and screams finally stopped, I was empty and void, but strangely at peace. Nothing was resolved. Nothing had changed. I didn't have any more of the answers to the questions I'd hurled at God than I had before they started. But, I'd released some of the venomous poison inside of me and performed my own bloodletting. Without knowing it, I'd given myself what I needed.

SEVENTEEN

The mothers with custody rights were allowed to have their children stay for the weekend. I'd started rebuilding a relationship with Sarah and asked Dawn if she could come for the weekend since I didn't have any kids. Since I was now one of the senior people at the house and had followed through on all of the rules, I was able to function fairly autonomously within the overall structure at the house. I still had to be at all required groups and meetings as well as taking random drug tests, but more and more, I could come and go as I pleased as long as I was home by curfew. I was surprised when Dawn said yes. I wasn't used to the new trust people were beginning to grant me.

Sarah had come to visit me while I was at St. John's and I hadn't been able to stop staring at her.

She was no longer the chubby little girl with bouncy blond hair and big blue eyes framed by pink frames. She was a tall, skinny teenager who'd traded in her glasses for contact lenses. I'd missed every birthday she'd had for the last four years, and I swore I wouldn't miss another one.

My mom brought her to Minneapolis and dropped her off. It was awkward between us at first, but I was determined to get to know her. She loved garage sale shopping so I introduced her to thrift store shopping. We combed through row after row of jeans, racing through the sections to see who could find the best deal first since we both wore the same size. I took her out to dinner for the first time with the paycheck from the job I'd recently gotten.

Once I'd gotten my GED, I'd set out to find a job that would allow me to start saving money for when I'd be discharged from Recovery House. The only job I'd ever held was at the Dairy Queen so my options were limited, but I didn't care. I had a long way to go before I'd find a reputable job, but had to have something to start putting on a resume. I'd landed a part-time job as a telemarketer that consisted of pouring through the Yellow Pages to find businesses who I could sell ad spaces to. It was repetitive and mindless, but it was a start and allowed me to pay for Sarah's dinner.

"Really, Elizabeth, you don't have to do this. I'll use the money mom gave me," she said when I grabbed the black sleeve our waitress set on the table after we'd finished our meal.

I tucked my debit card inside the folder—the card from the first checking account I'd ever opened. "I want to. Really, I do."

I took her up to my room when we got back to the house. I wanted to protect her from any of the potential drama that could erupt in the house at any moment. One of the other privileges of being a senior member at the house was my own room. I shared a unit with two other women, but we each had our own private rooms. We played her favorite card game, Phase 10, before I created a make-shift bed on the floor for her with the pillow and sleeping bag I'd asked my mom to bring.

"You know this week when mom told you that I puked in my bed?" she asked as she lay on the floor of my room in her sleeping bag.

"Yeah, I remember."

"I didn't really get sick. I mean, I got sick … I puked in my bed. I puked, but that's not why."

"Were you drunk?" Besides the flu, it was the only other reason someone would throw up in their bed even though I couldn't imagine Sarah taking a drink.

"No."

I waited for her to go on. When she didn't, I pressed, "What then? What are you talking about, Sarah?"

"I like ... you know..."

"Spit it out. I told you I want us to be able to talk to each other. It's okay, whatever it is. I want to start being here for you. I mean it. You can tell me anything."

Earlier at dinner, I'd had the conversation I'd been waiting to have with her. I'd started by apologizing, telling her how sorry I was for never being there for her and missing out on so much of her life. I went on to explain how bad I felt for all of the fights she had to witness and how scared she'd been. I promised her I was going to be different and make it up to her. I told her I wanted us to be able to talk to each other openly and honestly.

"Promise you won't tell mom and dad?"

"Whatever you tell me stays with me," I said. I wanted her to trust me with anything.

"I took a lot of pills ..."

"What do you mean?" It still didn't make sense. Was she taking pills to get high? What kind of pills?

"I took a lot of pills."

I sat upright in my bed. "You took a lot of pills on purpose?"

"Yes," she said in the small, soft voice I remembered from our childhood.

"Why?"

You know the answer. No. Please, no. Not her. Not Sarah.

"Sometimes I just don't wanna be here. You know? I wanted to go to sleep and wake up in heaven. If it's so nice there like they say, then I wanna go there. I don't like it here. But, I puked everywhere. I was so sick."

It was as if I'd tripped and it was the second before the ground was rushing up to meet me. I didn't want to ask the question, but I had no choice. "Why do you want to die?"

Silence filled the room and stretched on endlessly. Finally, she spoke. "I don't know."

And I knew she didn't because if someone had asked me the same question when I was child, I'd never have been able to give them the answer. Now,

I had plenty of reasons for wanting to die—all I had to do was look backward and pick one. But in my life before my addiction, there was nothing on the outside that I could point to and say—that's it. She was haunted by the same ghosts I was.

I wanted so desperately to help her, but how could I help her when I could barely help myself? I didn't have any solutions. There was still so much I didn't understand. I wished I could ask her if a faceless monster lurked in the corner of her childhood bedroom too, but I was too scared to know the answer. And even if she said yes—what would I do?

"I understand how you feel." It was the closest I could get to telling the truth. "You should talk to someone."

"I can't talk to people," she said.

"I totally get that. I used to hate it with a passion, but it helps. It really does."

Silence once again. I reached down and ran my fingers through her hair. I wanted to hop out of my bed, wrap my arms around her, and hold her like I used to do when she was a little girl. But she was no longer a little girl, and I was no longer the big sister who protected her. I was the big sister who'd broken my promise to protect her and I'd abandoned her a long time ago. Left her alone in the house of family secrets.

After a few minutes, she said, "I'm fine." Her voice had changed back to normal. "Can we go to the thrift store again before mom picks me up tomorrow?"

"Sure," I said. She sounded like our mom. She'd just dropped a bomb, and now she wanted to talk about shopping. Even though she'd been able to step around the damage, the bomb kept exploding over and over again in my head. It was worse in the morning when I had to let her go back home, knowing that she was going back to the house with talking walls, and fires in the kitchen that everyone pretended weren't burning. What was going to happen to her?

I locked myself in my bedroom until group time in the evening because I didn't trust myself. I was afraid I'd trick myself into getting high. By the time it arrived and I took my seat in the circle, I was crawling out of my skin because my voices screamed at me to get high, drink, cut myself, hit someone in the face, drive my car into a tree—anything that would take me out of myself. I'd been telling them to shut up for hours, and couldn't hold on much longer.

Everyone had barely sat down when I spewed out the entire story about Sarah. I didn't realize I was crying until Nakita handed me a Kleenex. It was the first time I'd ever cried in front of anyone but family and Dave.

I pounded my fists on my thighs. "I want to get high! Dammit, I want to get fucked up so goddamn bad, I can't stand it." My chest hurt, like someone held my heart in the palm of their hand, squeezing it. "I think I'm having a heart attack."

Carla pulled her chair close to me. "Breathe, Elizabeth. You're not having a heart attack. It's just feelings. You've just got to let them come. Don't fight them."

I pulled my knees up, wrapping my arms around them, and hid my face. Silent sobs shook my shoulders and wracked my body. The intensity of the pain nearly drowned me.

"Look up. Look at me." Carla said. "There's no going away. I want you here."

I lifted my head slowly to meet her eyes.

Run! Leave! Get out! No. No, I'm staying. Leave me alone. Please.

"What does it mean to you that your sister tried to commit suicide?"

I gulped. "It means she wants to die."

"It's more than that. C'mon. What else?" Her eyes penetrated me.

"Because ... because, then maybe ... maybe I'm not crazy."

"And if you're not crazy, then-"

"I am crazy. I'm fuckin' nuts."

Carla shook her head. "If you're crazy, then you don't have to look at the truth. And the truth is that both you and your sister have some of the same feelings. Or maybe she's crazy, too."

"She's not crazy," I snapped.

"Well, then-"

I interrupted again. "I don't want to talk about it."

"You brought it up," Nakita said. She was sitting in the seat next to me.

I glared at her, wanting to jump up and have one of our fights. Instead, I looked away and began talking as fast as I could. "I've always thought I was crazy. Ever since I was a little kid. I can't even tell you all the weird shit that went on in my head. Way before drugs. My head is messed up. It's easy to believe I'm crazy."

"And what's the alternative to being crazy?"

I took a deep breath. "That some really awful stuff happened in my house and messed me up pretty bad." My voice grew softer, "Messed both of us up."

I'd answered the question people had been asking for so long. Bad things happened in my parents' house. The place was infected with a disease I knew intimately but couldn't identify by name. But the first words of truth were out, and I could never take them back.

EIGHTEEN

As my discharge date grew closer, it was a no-brainer that I couldn't go back to live in any of my old towns. I was going to have to start over somewhere else. I'd have to live far away from everything and everyone I'd ever known—my family, my streets, my Strom, my trailers, all of it. Nothing could resemble anything from my past. I didn't have a chance at a new life if I slipped back into any part of my old one.

My final weeks at Recovery House had been spent preparing to live alone in my first apartment. But nothing could've made me ready for the surge of anxiety and fear that surged through my body as I stood in the doorway of my new bedroom on my first night. Smaller than my bedroom at the halfway house, my new room was empty except for the twin bed my parents had given me, pushed against the wall with my burgundy sleeping bag unrolled on top of it. A dresser that used to be my sister's stood against the opposite wall.

I was eighteen-years-old, technically an adult, but with no idea how to live in the real world. I took a deep breath and instructed myself out loud, "Just stay focused on getting through this night. That's all you've got to worry about."

I'd dreaded this moment because sleep would be difficult. It'd taken me months to learn how to fall asleep sober. Without chemicals, I'd lie in bed for hours with my mind racing, replaying events from my life. Some nights the paralyzing fear would grip me, making my heart race. Sweet smelling sweat would ooze from my pores as all of my senses became keenly alert. The darkness carried ghosts of all the memories I'd tried to block out for so long.

I was scared about graduating from the halfway house. I didn't know what to do with my freedom. My structured environments and safety were gone. I could easily trick myself into getting high. The selves in my head were slowly becoming one, but they still battled. It'd been comforting to live with women who understood what I was going through, reassuring to know I wasn't the only one struggling to make sense of the contradictory messages in my head. But that night, my mind was my only company.

I yearned for my old room at the halfway house, for my bed under the window that was always opened a crack to let in fresh air. I wanted the nightstand next to it that held my journal, along with the white alarm clock that woke me every morning at seven to go to the telemarketing job I'd worked so hard to get. I wanted the walls covered with pictures I'd spent hours tearing out of magazines. I missed the stains of the ugly lime green carpet. I even missed the sounds my roommate made every night in the bathroom, sticking her fingers down her gagging throat after eating bags of chips, cookies, and candy bars. It was hard to believe I could miss the sound of her puking into the toilet, trying to rid herself of her demons, but at least, her sounds were familiar.

I missed listening to twenty-four women get ready for bed. The sounds of flushing toilets and sinks running. Female voices calling out good night, the patter of feet on the carpet, doors shutting and lights turning off. The faint smell of cigarette smoke from someone smoking in their room because she couldn't wait for the morning when the alarm was turned off. I missed it all.

Nothing in this room was familiar. Each creak was new. The only movement was my breathing. I walked towards my bed thinking about Linda, the overnight technician at Recovery House. She'd comforted me many nights when I couldn't sleep. I'd rise and slip quietly past the other rooms and down the stairs to the second-floor staff office to find her smoking on the balcony off to the side of the office, the only one not wired with an alarm.

Linda was a big woman, like Yvonne, over six feet tall with broad shoulders and a large chest. Her short gray hair, sprinkled with spots of white, closely framed her face. She wore a subtle red lipstick on small lips that easily moved into a smile. I'd knock on the glass and she'd turn her face, smiling. I'd stand next to her, leaning against the black railing, lighting one of my cigarettes.

"Another one of your nights?" She stared at the stars overhead.

"Yeah," I'd say softly.

In silence, she'd smoke her Virginia Slims and

I'd smoke my Marlboro Reds, the smoke curling its way up to the sky in twisted spirals. She always left the conversation up to me, listening if I wanted to speak and keeping silent if I didn't.

After our smoke, she'd sit on the wooden office chair underneath the overhead lamp, and pick up her knitting from the end of the table. I'd sit on the floor at her feet, with my legs crisscrossed. Her small white dog, Sushi, would run to my lap with her tongue sticking out and her tail wagging, licking my hands and face. She told me every time I played with Sushi, "She likes you. She doesn't like everyone, you know."

Sometimes I'd tell Linda about my day. I'd tell her about silly fights that we girls had gotten into over using the phone or what we had for dinner. I shared with her interesting stories from the AA meeting I went to everyday. At other times, I'd tell her about getting high and how I couldn't understand how I could love it and hate it so much, all at the same time. Sometimes I even talked to her about my family and what it was like for me growing up. There were times when I was quiet, content just to be in her presence and play with Sushi. But no matter what I said or didn't say, I always had one request, "Will you sing for me?"

She'd set her knitting back on the table and reach under her chair for the instrument. "Of course, darling." It looked like a keyboard except it didn't have any keys. There was a volume switch on the left and a small speaker on the right. It had a bunch of lines across the middle that she'd tap and sweep her fingers across. The lines made beautiful strumming sounds under the touch of her skilled fingers. The first time she showed me the small white board, she'd explained, "I never learned to play the guitar or piano. Then, I found this old thing, and I've been hooked on it ever since."

Her voice, filled with emotion and power, boomed from her chest. She'd flip her fingers back and forth across the board in smooth, quick motions, tears dripping down her face and onto the board. Her eyes shone and her face glowed like she had sunshine inside that was released when she sang. I'd sit at her feet mesmerized. She'd written all the music and lyrics, filled with sweet words about a God who loved her beyond comprehension, a God so different from the one I knew and my parents worshiped. The only song she played that wasn't her own was "Amazing Grace." It was my favorite. I wouldn't notice I was crying until I felt Sushi's soft pink tongue on my cheek, licking away the warm tears.

Alone in my apartment, I longed for her melodies. I sat on my bed, pulling my knees up to my chest, wishing I could believe God loved me. I wanted to know the God Linda knew. I'd give anything to have a belief in God that didn't include darkness.

One of her favorite things to say to me was, "You're alive for a reason. God didn't bring you all this way just to drop you on your face."

As I thought about her words, I recalled the first time I'd overdosed after getting out of my second treatment center. Strom had promised to throw me a party. I hadn't been able to use drugs for three months and every day I'd been away from them, I'd counted the hours until my next high. It was the only thing that made treatment bearable.

Our party consisted of Strom and me sitting cross-legged on his mattress, the only piece of furniture in his dark bedroom. The floor was covered with CDs, dirty laundry piled in one corner and moldy food and trash spilled out of a garbage can in another corner. The one window was covered with a sheet. A lamp burned dimly on top of the stereo, casting eerie shadows on the wall.

A buffet of drugs spread out in front of us: a mirror with chunks of yellow and white powder, an open bag of pot with sticky, green buds spilling out, my half-empty bottle of Captain Morgan and Strom's bottle of Windsor Canadian. We'd been at it for hours. I grabbed the rolled-up bill and brought my face down into the powder, inhaling another line. The familiar burn in my nostrils made my eyes water, and I grabbed my bottle to wash it down.

There was a knock at the door. A male voice called out, "It's Hamilton."

I looked towards Strom. He looked up at me and mouthed "eight-ball." I still remembered the routine.

"Come in!" I yelled back.

Hamilton looked like he'd lost ten pounds since the last time I'd seen him. His pale skin stretched tightly across protruding cheekbones. His vacant eyes bore black circles around them and sunk into his head. His black Metallica T-shirt hung on his body, and his jeans sagged.

I chopped a line on the mirror. Hamilton wrung his hands together and tapped his feet against each other as he watched. Strom eyed him from his spot in the corner. Hamilton took a seat on the floor across from me, rubbing his nose in anticipation. I pushed the mirror in his direction.

"Here you go," I said. "It's really good shit. You'll be up for at least two days, guaranteed."

His eyes lit up as he grabbed the tooter and brought his head down to the mirror. Strom dug in the wooden box that held his stash and pulled out a crumpled picture. He laughed at me. "Hey, look at this. You look totally geeked."

The photo showed my eyes bulging out of my head, about ready to burst out of their sockets. The blue was erased by dilated pupils. My matted hair stuck up on top from running my fingers through it. My yellowed skin was covered with filmy dirt, a result of days on acid. My mouth opened in a horrific yell.

"That was the night we couldn't even figure out how to play Go Fish, we were so fucked up. Remember?"

I turned away from the photo. "Christ, how could I forget? I look like I'm insane."

"Look like it? You are." Hamilton brought his face up from the mirror.

"Shut up. Do you like it or what?"

"Yeah, I want it. Gimme an eight." He stuck his hand into his pocket and pulled out a roll of bills.

"Gimme your money," Strom said, taking out a bag from the stash in the wooden box. He handed Hamilton the bag and took his money, then tapped my arm. "Turn down the stereo."

I jumped up, and suddenly felt like I'd stuck my finger into a light socket, only it was ten times more powerful. Electricity surged through my body, shocking me. I arched my back and tried to yell, but no sound came. I fell to my knees as brown liquid sprayed from my mouth and nose. My heart felt like it was going to burst through my chest in a violent explosion. I clawed at my shirt, trying to rip it off. I could see nothing but white lights blinking everywhere in front of me. My last thought, before darkness overcame the white and I floated into nothingness was, *please God, let me die.*

I shuddered at the memory of that night and how angry I was coming to in the bathroom with Strom by my side. There were so many times I should've died. Like the train. I'd never told anyone about the train story, but I told Linda because I knew she'd understand.

I was driving my parents' red Mazda truck, trying to get it home before five so my mom wouldn't know I'd taken it again. I was so wasted I couldn't work my feet on the clutch. My vision tripled and lights blurred in front of my eyes. I kept passing out at the wheel, weaving off the road, and then being awakened by the crunch of gravel on the shoulder.

I passed out one final time, only to be startled awake by the blare of a train horn and its white light glaring in through the window. I'd stalled the truck in the middle of the railroad tracks. The train roared toward me like a tornado, just yards from the truck. I covered my face with my arms as the thought flashed: *I'm dead.* A powerful force pushed the truck over the tracks as the reverberating thunder of the train sped past, its horn still blaring.

The truck was still not running, but I was over the tracks. I opened the door with shaking arms, my knees wobbling. I leaned against the stalled truck, then looked down at my pants, and saw I'd wet myself. I felt completely sober.

"Do you believe in angels?" Linda asked after I told her the story.

I didn't know what had moved the truck over

the tracks, but alone in my apartment that first night, I realized Linda had been an angel in my life, and she hadn't been the only one. All along my journey, there'd been people who'd intervened in my life and kept me alive. I got down on my knees next to my bed, a position I hadn't been in for years, and talked to God in my regular voice—the agonized screams towards him, gone.

"Dear God, I don't know how to pray. It's been so long and I don't even know if you're listening. I don't know why I'm still alive. But I've got to believe you're keeping me alive for a reason. I can't have been through all of this for nothing." Gut wrenching sobs gripped my body and I had to wait to continue until they subsided. "There's so much I don't understand. About you. About me. About my parents. My life. Why you let things happen. But I'm scared. I don't know how to live without drugs. I don't know how not to hate you. I've never been on my own like this. I feel like a lost little girl. I need help. I can't do this by myself. I've got to have some help or I know I'll never make it. Help me."

When I finally opened my eyes, the fear of the night had left me, and my mind was quiet. An overwhelming sense of peace filled me. For the first time in my sobriety, I believed there was a chance I'd be okay. I got up and crawled into my sleeping bag, pulling it up to my chin. I closed my eyes and took some deep breaths.

"Please, keep sending me your angels," I murmured, drifting into a peaceful sleep.

Garrison

NINETEEN

I walked down the wooden stairs into the basement of a church. I was never on time, but tonight I was early. I headed straight for the table with coffee and grabbed a cup of the thick, black liquid that always made my stomach ache in protest. It was an unwritten rule at AA meetings that the coffee had to be terrible. I wasn't a regular at this meeting, so I moved through unfamiliar faces to an empty aluminum chair.

I spotted Conrad, who acknowledged my presence with a wave and a slight nod. Last week, he'd asked if I would tell my story as his annual club banquet since I'd just gotten a year of sobriety. I'd never shared my story, and the idea troubled me. A story implied a beginning and an end, and I didn't have either. I watched my life and made sense of it all through videos in my mind that I spliced together to create some semblance of a whole. I constantly pressed pause, rewind, fast forward, and stop. The biggest change for me now was watching the movies of my life, and beginning to recognize more and more that I was the girl in the videos.

I look downed the aisle at five empty seats where my Recovery House girls should've been sitting: Jen, Maria, Brenda, Tonya, and Tammy. We'd been a crew for our first year, a strange bunch that never would've associated with each other if we hadn't ended up in treatment at the same time. Jen was two years older than me and my opposite. Whereas I'd taken my anger and thrown it in the world's face, she'd eaten all of hers. Then, there was Maria, an older version of myself, a forty-year-old speed freak who'd been shooting our favorite poison for twenty years and even though she was sober, still moved like a tweaker. Brenda was a retired hippie who'd traded in her needle for a bottle of booze. Tonya had damaged her brain from chronic alcohol abuse. On her good days, she resembled a fairytale grandmother bustling around the house taking care of people, but on her bad days, she stayed locked in her room, convinced everyone was out to get her in some elaborate conspiracy theory. Finally, there was Tammy, the classic picture of an alcoholic housewife. While the rest of us wreaked havoc in the outside world, she'd caused just as much chaos without ever stepping outside her front door.

We'd gotten out around the same time and made a commitment to stay together. Each Friday night we gathered back at Recovery House at five o'clock where we held a private group session that we each took turns leading. We all made it to one year of sobriety and threw a celebration for ourselves. Just when I thought we'd beaten the statistics, Tammy returned to the place we'd all worked so hard to leave.

Tammy was one of those people who came out of the womb with a day planner in her hand. If she said she'd be somewhere, she was. If she promised to call you back, she always did. When she didn't call me for three days, and even missed the Thursday AA meeting, I knew something was wrong. A few days later, my phone rang at four-thirty in the morning.

No one ever called at that time of morning just to say hi so my heart was already pounding when I answered.

"Hello?"

"He-H-Elizabeth ..." Tammy's voice sounded as if her tongue was trapped in a mouthful of mush.

My heart sank. "You're drunk."

"Yes. Yes, I am. I am," she slurred.

I was speechless. I wanted to ask her why, but knew that neither of us could ever answer the riddle as to why we used when we knew better than anyone just how crazy it made us and how it destroyed our lives. It was the most baffling part of addiction.

When Tammy opened her door to let me in that morning, I tried to keep the shock from showing on my face. Her usually neat blond hair was dirty and matted to the left side of her head. I'd never known she wore dentures, but there was a huge gap where her front teeth used to be. The right side of her face was scratched and bruised. She clutched a dirty white bathrobe around her small body.

I reached out my arms. "Come here."

She stumbled into my arms and held on, smelling like old booze and vomit. Sobs shook her frail body. I shuffled us into her apartment. Blinds shut tightly, blocking out any chance of light. Her immaculate apartment lay in ruins, the recliner tipped over, and the cushions tossed on the floor. Empty pints of cheap brandy randomly marked the room. Ashtrays overflowed with cigarette butts that spilled onto the floor. The floor was covered in rancid puke and urine, and I tried to breathe through my mouth. My shoes squished on the carpet as I walked over to the couch missing its cushions.

"I'm so ... emb ... embarrassed," Tammy said, throwing her body down next to mine. I held her and rubbed her back gently as she mumbled incoherently. I didn't know what to do with the person next to me. I'd never been on this side of the scenario. Between sobs and disconnected words, I caught the names of her son and daughter.

She'd only been drinking for three days, and already any semblance of her new sober life was destroyed. I felt the sickness in the room as if it was a real entity that could overtake me at any time. "Tammy, I don't know what to do. Can I call the Recovery House for help?"

She nodded. Staff told me to take her to detox. She sobbed while I drove. In the emergency room, the breathalyzer read .42. The nurse shook her head. "A point four means you should be dead. I don't know how you walked in here."

Tammy's drinking set up a chain reaction. Before long, I was meeting Jen late at night in the Denny's parking lot to tell her goodbye. She'd already been arrested three different times and was running to Oregon to hide. Maria was next in line. Her doctor wrote her a prescription for Ritalin because he believed it'd help mellow her out. In the next twenty-four hours, she filled a three-month prescription, boiled it, and shot all of it into her veins. Then, the part of Tonya's brain that was damaged from alcohol took over the part that still worked and she was committed to a state mental institution. Brenda stayed sober, but refusing to get hurt again, she cut herself off from any contact with the world.

I reflected on the statistics I used to spew in our group while I waited anxiously for the meeting to start. At the time, I never imagined I'd be the one to watch the numbers play themselves out or be the one still standing. There was a tap on my shoulder and I turned to see Charlotte's face. I scooted over one chair so she could sit in the aisle.

She squeezed my knee. "Hi, honey."

I smiled and watched her set her purse on the floor, turn off her cell phone, and begin the scanning routine. She scanned the room in the same manner I surveyed every room I entered. I'd met Charlotte early in sobriety, but was only recently letting her get close to me. She terrified me when I met her. It was hard to believe I could be scared of a sixty-year-old woman, but when she looked at me with her crystalline blue eyes, it was as if she could look right into my soul. Like Yvonne, Charlotte could take my broken spirit into the palm of her hand, caress it soothingly, and give it back to me comforted.

Finishing her scans of the exits, entryways, those in front of us, and those in back of us, she asked, "Did you go to your therapist this week?"

I rolled my eyes and huffed an exaggerated sigh. "Yes."

The court required me to go to therapy. The legal restrictions were lessening, but I had a feeling the therapy rule would be the last to go. My therapist, Patti, had been assigned to me during my first month at Recovery House so I'd kept her once I'd gotten out. At first, I didn't like her because she talked to me quietly like I might break if she spoke louder. I also didn't trust therapists because of what had happened with Dave. I couldn't imagine myself falling in love with a woman, but I never thought I'd fall in love with Dave either, so I was really careful. She sensed my hesitation and had gone to great lengths to gain my trust.

Our sessions focused on what she referred to as my disassociation. She explained to me that the things I did with my brain to disappear or pretend I was somewhere else were coping mechanisms children developed to deal with trauma. Nobody was born with these abilities. She assured me it was a normal reaction to abuse, and people used it all the time to detach from their physical surroundings and the emotional impact of what was happening.

Lately, she centered our time together on identifying the reasons for my disassociation and had honed in on my dad. She was convinced he was the root cause, but I wasn't convinced. For weeks, we debated the ways he'd punished us—the spankings, the violent outbursts, the wrestling matches to leave the house. My parents considered it within the realm of normal punishment for misbehavior because their religion supported and encouraged the idea. Part of me still believed they were right.

"What your father did to you was not discipline. He crossed over the line into physical abuse."

She said it again and again. We rehashed incidents over and over until I finally came to the place where I was able to admit she was right. My dad had repeatedly injured me on purpose, and my mom had done nothing to stop it.

Even though I was able to say my dad had physically abused me, I wasn't able to admit he'd sexually abused me. My memory was too full of holes and blank spaces. I wasn't willing to fill them in with something I didn't know for sure. All I knew for sure was that I'd been terrified about a monster coming into my room at night to hurt me. I'd seen the monster numerous times but had never seen his face because he didn't have one. The scariest thing about the monster was the ominous expressionless mask he wore. I wasn't willing to put my dad's face there. Maybe someday I would be, but not now.

Charlotte nudged my elbow, breaking into my thoughts. Everyone stood as the meeting opened. I took her hand and grabbed the hand of the other person standing next to me. We recited the words of a familiar prayer, not one from my childhood. The chairperson began to go through a long list of announcements.

The man leading the meeting looked like he used to be a linebacker in his day, but now all his muscle had turned to fat. His long hair was pulled into a ponytail that trailed to the middle of his back. He was losing the hair on top of his head and kept the rest of it long to stay in denial about it. He said beautiful words with his mouth, but I saw the look in his eyes, a look I knew not to trust. He probably went home and beat his wife.

His eyes triggered memories. My mind wandered off to another day and another table—the table of my childhood kitchen with the mustard yellow walls. The only picture hanging in the small kitchen had a murky orange background with a hideous tree, lumpy and dark centered in the middle of it. It was alive with evil. The branches become the arms of a skeleton that could reach out to grab me, or rip my sister out of her highchair. The black frame couldn't contain it.

I'd always wondered how my mom could go on eating her dinner no matter what happened at the table. Even as a kid I remembered thinking, *Why? Why does she just sit there?* Recently, my mom had begun to give me small pieces of the answer, tiny chunks of truth, to help put the puzzle together.

Each year in the fall my mom, her four sisters, and my grandma traveled up north and spent the weekend at a hotel in a small town, where there was a huge craft sale. This year my mom had invited me to go along with her and we had a room to ourselves. As we lay there in the darkness, listening to the hum of the heater, she asked, "Do you know why I always stayed up with you kids while you were sick?"

Whenever one of us kids had gotten sick, she'd lavish us with care, holding our hair while we puked or putting a cool washcloth on our fevered foreheads. One time, I had hives so bad that I scratched my skin raw, so she lay in my bed all night long, holding my hands tightly in hers so I couldn't scratch in my sleep.

"It's because when I was sick, my mom never took care of us. I had to be all by myself, and those were some of the loneliest nights of my life. One night both mom and dad were passed out drunk and-"

"What? Grandma drank?" I'd never seen my grandma put a glass of alcohol to her lips.

She laughed. "Oh heavens, Elizabeth. She was as bad of a drunk as your grandpa. They used to disappear all the time to go on benders. Back then you could do that. The only reason she doesn't drink anymore is because her stomach is completely shot and she gets deathly ill. She bleeds out of her throat. Anyway, I got really sick one night and puked all over the hallway on my way to the bathroom. I woke my mom up and told her I was sick. She just yelled at me to clean it up and go back to bed. I vowed then that if I ever had kids, I'd never make them be alone while they were sick."

"Was grandma nasty like grandpa when she drank?"

"She was just as bad as he was, maybe even worse. You should've seen the fights they got into." She was silent for a minute. "You had the same violent temper as my parents when you drank."

Her comment surprised me because the longer I stayed sober, the less she wanted to talk about it. She didn't even like to hear my apologies. Each time I'd tried to say I was sorry and to explain some of my behavior, she'd shrug me off, "Oh, Elizabeth.

Of course, I know you're sorry and forgive you. But that was the past, and there's no need to talk about it. It's all over now."

The clapping brought me back to the present. A woman walked to the front of the room where the big man embraced her and thumped her on the back. He pulled away and handed her a sobriety medallion. With a huge smile, she cried. "Thank you. Thank you so much. I can't believe I've stayed sober for ninety days. So much has changed in my life. I can't even find the words. I started drinking after I'd been sober ..."

I couldn't focus. Soon Conrad would introduce me to speak and my heart was racing. How would I explain my life to these people? I considered starting out with the desperate prayer I'd said outside of the courtroom. It seemed like ever since then, miracles had been happening, not the miracles in the Bible stories I read as a child, but things like surviving Reggie and me staying sober seemed nearly as dramatic as walking on water. I didn't know how I'd made it with so many wounds still bleeding. I simply refused to give up and kept holding on, trusting blindly that someday my wounds would become scars. I believed in the promise of a someday even if for now, I still bled.

Sometimes, I had to just pretend to be okay. If I got high again I'd die, and for the first time in my life, I didn't want to die. I'd never really been alive, and was beginning to hope that I might become a whole person. I still held on to my suicide card though, because I'd rather blow my head off and chance going straight to hell than live in the hell of my addiction for another day. Just keeping that option was somehow comforting.

The woman had finished speaking and Conrad walked up to stand behind the podium. *Ohmigod. This is really happening.* He winked at me. "I'm honored to introduce our speaker tonight. She's an incredible lady, a great example of the miracles that can happen if you just stay sober long enough to let them. I sat in many meetings with her in the beginning of her sobriety. Honestly, I didn't think she'd make it. But the person you see tonight is not the person that I used to sit next to in meetings. For one thing, her vocabulary has expanded. I've been a trucker for twenty years, and things used to come out of her mouth that shocked even me."

The crowd laughed. I tried to keep my throat from closing up. *Why did I say I'd do this?* Conrad continued, "Seriously, though. This girl should be dead, but God's got a plan for her. I've thoroughly enjoyed watching her grow and change. I'm constantly amazed and grateful to be part of it. If she can stay sober, anyone can. I'm sure you'll get a lot out of her sharing tonight. So, with that, I give you your speaker. Elizabeth?"

Conrad smiled and nodded at me as the crowd clapped. I stood, but my knees wobbled as if they might not be able to hold my body as I walked. All eyes turned to look at me. Charlotte reached up and touched my hand. *Run. Get out of here. Run now!* That voice of fear was the only one I needed to give me the strength to take a step past Charlotte and into the aisle. That voice was the part of me so scared to see and tell the truth that it'd rather die. This one had been there since the beginning and would probably be there until the end. All I could do was act against it. I took strides towards the podium, so far away.

Eyes bored into me and I could sense the questions. They wondered what a young girl, barely a woman, could share with them that might touch their lives in any sort of meaningful way. They didn't understand that although my body was young, it housed the spirit of a very old warrior. If they were to look into my eyes, they'd be able to see that I'd been to places I wish I'd never been, seen things I wish I'd never seen, done things I wish I'd never done. And even though I'd returned from the war, I carried the battlefields, and my fallen soldiers, within me still.

I stepped up onto the podium. *You can still get out of here. Run!* Conrad hugged me and I hugged him back. In front of the podium, I adjusted the microphone and faced all the strangers looking back at me. My voice caught somewhere in my throat. I couldn't find it. Then, I realized that these people were not seeing the girl people used to shudder to look at. I wasn't standing crooked and hunched over. I was standing straight and tall. My eyes weren't vacant and hollow with dark circles encasing them. They shone brightly. My face wasn't showing every bone, and my hair was no longer dingy and gray, or hanging in my face. My face was clear and fresh, my hair pulled back neatly. They couldn't see the young girl next to men ten years older than her, men who kept her high for a price she agreed to pay. They couldn't see any of it because I was no longer that girl. I was no longer a girl, but a woman. I was no longer high, and my soul was my own.

I took a deep breath and rubbed the one-year sobriety medallion in my pocket. Suddenly, I felt the eyes and the smiles of Linda, Yvonne, Hank, my Recovery House women, and the other shadowy angels hovering over me. From inside of me, they formed a new voice: *You have survived. Now thrive.* I looked at the eyes of the crowd, smiled, and began to speak.

"Hi. My name is Elizabeth, and I'm a recovering drug addict and alcoholic ..."

Garrison

EPILOGUE

Dr. Elizabeth Garrison has spent the last fifteen years devoted to the recovery community and working with children who have experienced trauma. Elizabeth went on to overcome all odds. She graduated summa cum laude from a small liberal arts college in the Midwest. She continued her education and earned her Ph.D. in clinical psychology, specializing in childhood trauma. She currently does research for the National Center for Child Traumatic Stress where she continues to search for solutions to prevent child abuse and developing ways to conduct therapy for children who've been exposed to all forms of trauma, abuse, and neglect. She lives in Los Angeles, California with her husband and son.

If you'd like to contact Elizabeth, she can be reached at lizgarrison22@gmail.com

CPSIA information can be obtained
at www.ICGtesting.com
Printed in the USA
LVHW031533061218
599502LV00019B/719/P